Guardian of the Great Lakes

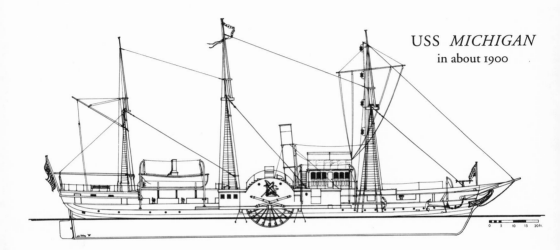

USS *MICHIGAN*
in about 1900

Guardian
of the Great Lakes

THE U.S. PADDLE FRIGATE *Michigan*

Bradley A. Rodgers

ANN ARBOR : *The University of Michigan Press*

Copyright © by the University of Michigan 1996
All rights reserved
Published in the United States of America by
The University of Michigan Press
Manufactured in the United States of America
⊚ Printed on acid-free paper

1999   4   3   2

No part of this publication may be reproduced, stored in a retrieval
system, or transmitted in any form or by any means, electronic,
mechanical, or otherwise without the written permission of the publisher.

A CIP catalog record for this book is available from the British Library.

Library of Congress Cataloging-in-Publication Data

Rodgers, Bradley A.
    Guardian of the Great Lakes : the U.S. paddle frigate Michigan /
  Bradley A. Rodgers.
        p.   cm.
    Includes bibliographical references (p.   ) and index.
    ISBN 0-472-09607-9 (hardcover : alk. paper). — ISBN 0-472-06607-2
  (pbk. : alk. paper)
      1. Michigan (Paddle steamer)   2. Paddle steamers—Great Lakes—
  History—19th century.   3. Ships, Iron and steel—United States—
  History—19th century.   4. United States.   Navy—Sea life—
  History—19th century.   5. Great Lakes—Navigation—History—19th
  century.   6. United States—History, Naval—To 1900.   I. Title.
  VA65.M553R64   1995
  359.3'25—dc20   95-48841
                                                             CIP

Frontispiece by John A. Tilley.

For my parents, Ronald and Shirley,
who demonstrated to me the values
of loyalty, honesty, and discipline;
and for my old friends who have gone on,
Bob Siebert and Rob Reed.

Preface

LATE IN 1989, while about halfway through the research for this book and after having published an article about it in a prominent northern journal, I was contacted by the chamber of commerce for a port town located on the shore of Lake Superior. The caller asked if I knew the present disposition of the USS *Michigan,* explaining that the city possibly had funds for restoration of the ship, as it had figured saliently in their local history. I sadly explained that they were forty years too late to save the steamer, that it had been destroyed in 1949. Upon hanging up the phone I went into reverie concerning the implication of this call, had it been made forty years earlier, the safeguarding of a tangible piece of our history. To walk the decks of the vessel that had imprinted so many lives would have been important to people and more easily understood than a history relegated to the dusty pages of dull texts. Nonetheless, the *Michigan* is gone and only an accurate, readable manuscript will allow people to touch, albeit through their imaginations, this once great ship. To this end I redoubled my efforts and present here the story of the USS *Michigan,* a modest, overdue epitaph, for the people, the times, and the ship.

Acknowledgments

IT CAN BE SAFELY SAID that if books depended entirely on the author to be written, few would ever be finished. Quite often scores of people support the book-writing effort by passing on research, maintaining archives and historical repositories, and proofing the endless drafts for which the author needs a critical review. This work was no exception. Therefore, I wish to thank the staffs of the various historical societies and museums on the lakes who supplied me with information and encouragement. I would also like to thank Dr. Andrew Lambert, Dr. Carl Swanson, Dr. Donny Hamilton, Dr. Jean Griffin, Dr. John Robertson, Dr. William Still and Dr. Pat Wolend-jack for their patience and fine technical assistance. Special contributions were also made for the illustrations of this book, particularly by Dr. John Tilley, who supplied a fine line drawing of the ship. Thanks also go in this area to Mr. Theodore J. Karle, Mr. C. W. Cowles, and Mr. Pat Labadie (of the Duluth Canal Park Museum) for many of the historical photographs. Finally, it is unlikely this work would have come to early fruition without the support of Pat, Leck, and Amy Mitchell.

Contents

Introduction

A BIOGRAPHICAL STUDY of the USS *Michigan* is significant for several distinct reasons. Most prominently, as the first iron-hulled war steamer in the U.S. Navy, the *Michigan* epitomized a marine technological advance that made obsolete several thousand years of wooden ship construction and improvement. The USS *Michigan* was the earliest and most important contribution of the United States to a class of vessel that served as the missing link between wooden battleships and fully armored iron and steel warships. Designed and conceived in 1842, this revolutionary iron steamer represented an astonishing naval breakthrough, coming less than thirty years after the end of the War of 1812, where sailing frigates reigned supreme.

In part, an examination of this ship's career cannot ignore the important private-sector economic and social trends that gave rise to iron hulls and steam power, particularly when these advances, newly arrived from Europe, promised to revolutionize naval architecture.. The mid-nineteenth-century United States found itself in a unique geographic and economic situation, isolated but with enormous resources. This isolation tended to slow U.S. adoption of iron in ship construction but also produced some astounding individual advancements, such as the USS *Michigan.*

The naval study of the USS *Michigan* also necessarily encompasses a significant segment of the formative years of the steam navy. It would be remiss to examine the mid-nineteenth-century naval technical revolution and not include the thoughts of Secretary of the Navy Abel Parker Upshur. Categorized as a political conservative, Upshur was nonetheless a farsighted visionary in the field of naval science and marine architecture. In his short tenure as secretary, he single-handedly established our modern concept of the navy and naval organization.

A third aspect of the naval history side of this work touches on the sociology of naval life on the Great Lakes, which is unique in U.S. naval

history. The *Michigan* was stationed at Erie, Pennsylvania, for such a long
time the town became known as the "mother-in-law of the navy" for the
many sailors and officers who married and maintained families there. A close
view of the shipboard life, therefore, not only sheds some much-needed light
on the life and times of all nineteenth-century navy men, but partially
illuminates the lives of freshwater merchant mariners who, on enlistment,
made up the greatest share of the crew.

Not merely a naval ship's history, this work is equally important for the
fact that the USS *Michigan* is one of the richest single sources of mid-
nineteenth- to early-twentieth-century Great Lakes history. Indeed, this
ship's narrative is so intricately woven into the chronological fabric of
nineteenth-century Great Lakes events, it would be impossible to write a
history of one without the other. The voluminous reports accumulated
during the vessel's seventy-nine years of service rival entire historical repositories in detail and scope, illuminating a historically dim, yet exciting, period in
the history of the lakes not traversed by Light House Service, Lifesaving
Service, Revenue Service, or Coast Guard records.

The inland seas of North America comprise 2,500 miles of American
coastline and contain nearly 100,000 square miles of fresh water. The *Michigan*'s specific patrolling domain was defined by the upper Great Lakes of Erie,
Huron, Michigan, and Superior. Only Lake Ontario was off-limits due to the
great cataract of the Niagara Falls.

Duty on the northern lakes was often punctuated by dangerous weather,
from sudden hurricanes and blizzards to white squalls. The *Michigan*'s crews
experienced nearly every sea condition imaginable, often pitting the vessel's
seaworthiness and powerful engines against the elements, indiscriminately
rescuing Canadian and U.S. ships. Ironically, though built as a powerful
maritime predator, the warship may be the record holder for the number of
other vessels rescued from storms and strandings. During these efforts, several of its sailors made the supreme sacrifice. By the twentieth century nearly
one hundred vessel crews and owners owed the *Michigan* a debt of gratitude.
The navy ship's humanitarian efforts won the respect of lake merchants on
both shores, evincing the additional irony of a warship turned peace
ambassador.

Finally, the *Michigan* served as the U.S. government's troubleshooter on
the Great Lakes. Therefore, its actions (and sometimes inactions) tend to
reflect the attitudes and beliefs in Washington. In this light the ship often
symbolized the altruism and indomitable energy of frontier America, while at

other times it reflected the darker side of prejudice, self-serving power politics, and military-industrial intrigue.

The *Michigan* appears superficially in primary period descriptions of the U.S. Navy. Nevertheless, the "Old Northwest" was frontier territory, and as such, the vessel's exploits were never greatly publicized. The *Michigan*'s account could, with some justification, be entitled, "The Lost Navy Cruiser of the Old Northwest," for the mail, newspapers, roads, railroads, and telegraphs were few and far between. Yet, officers' and Navy Department reports, log entries, government documents, letters, bureau records, and manuscripts reliably relate the incredible experiences that took place—adventures that, for the most part, occurred beyond the reliable reach of the frontier press and literate society.

The records of the *Michigan* not only bring new historical subjects to light but also serve as a counterbalance or focus to other historical sources, often highlighting their partiality. This perspective is clearly demonstrated in the warship's quashing of timber depredations on Lake Michigan, its role in the destruction of the Strangite colony on Beaver Island, the armed suppression of the mining strikes in Michigan's Upper Peninsula, and the blunting of the Fenian invasion of Canada. Until now studies of these episodes have not included naval sources. This has been an important historical oversight, for the records of the *Michigan* offer a refreshing, relatively unbiased, and oftentimes the only eyewitness vista of these events. For accuracy's sake, all quotes are as they appear in their original form.

Though the iron paddle frigate has been the focus of several short histories, the authors have not adequately described this ship's entire career and seem even less able to pierce through to its true historical significance. Like coats of paint over rust, these narratives tend to hide this ship's fascinating saga and importance. This manuscript is intended, for the first time, to grind to the bare metal and present a narrative of the iron-hulled warship in the unique historical context in which it sailed.

I The Infancy of Iron

THE INTRODUCTION OF THE IRON HULL to the U.S. Navy is inextricably linked to iron shipbuilding developments imported from Europe. This chapter will explore the economics driving the transition in the United States, as well as the thoughts of Naval Secretary Abel Parker Upshur, one of the greatest proponents of its use in warship fabrication. Finally, a political analysis of Anglo-American relations will explain why the first seagoing iron-hulled U.S. warship began service patrolling the freshwater seas of the upper Great Lakes.

The U.S. Navy's first experiment in iron ship construction was launched at 3:00 P.M. Tuesday afternoon, December 5, 1843. At this time a sleek black warship slid down the ways in Erie, Pennsylvania, virtually unnoticed. The warship's "perfect symmetry and clean lines" belied the fact that it had balked on the launching ramp for nearly a day, temporarily frustrating the shipbuilders. Casual spectators happening along the waterfront would no doubt have been surprised had they knowledge of the vessel's genuine significance.[1]

On this day U.S. Navy contractors had produced a revolutionary new ship—a ship that, when fitted out, would combine new-type weapons, propulsion, and hull material; a ship that could outrun the fastest sailing frigate or devastate wooden warships, with shells from new pivoting shell guns mounted on its centerline. The new warship was stronger yet lighter and far cheaper than the sturdiest wooden hulls. It could also absorb battle damage through a system of watertight compartments that were virtually impossible to duplicate in wood, due to its inherent flexibility. Though comparable in appearance and layout (but not actual configuration) to the newest wooden frigates, the USS *Michigan* was not a conventional ship any more than the first iron projectile points were conventional to the late Bronze Age. Both advancements signaled the end of one era and the beginning of another.

The *Michigan* represented a class of historically significant iron-hulled frigates and sloops developed by several navies in the 1840s. Later, more publicized armored ships, such as the French *La Gloire,* British *Warrior,* and USS *Monitor,* were largely developed from the successes and failures of these earlier nonarmored iron-hulled vessels. It is significant, however, that the early iron-hulled warships embodied as many successful design innovations as (or more than) the later more-famous vessels, all without the benefit of naval predecessors.

Created years too soon for the technical classification of cruiser, the USS *Michigan* was nonetheless designed to outgun most contemporary warships and outrun those it could not outgun. Rated a first-class paddle steamer, the *Michigan* is best described as a paddle frigate, paddle cruiser, or steam frigate. All these ship classes designate as fast, heavily armed support vessels, able to operate independently from the battle fleet.[2]

Though the *Michigan* was named for a state, as is customary for U.S. battleships, it was not constructed to fight in traditional line of battle. That is, the ship was not intended to fight another line-of-battle ship, or liner, side-by-side, exchanging broadsides. The vessel's paddle wheels prevented the mounting of an optimal number of broadside guns and may have been vulnerable to close-in fire from an enemy broadside. There is little doubt, however, that a *Michigan*-class paddle cruiser would have been a powerful opponent for any sailing frigate in the open sea, using its superior speed and heavy guns to attack at an advantage, raking enemy ships from medium to long range. In like manner, the *Michigan* could have harried larger warships or chased down merchantmen, for in the 1840s few ships in the world could match this vessel's fourteen-knot cruising speed, and no ship capable of catching the *Michigan* was powerful enough to harm it.[3]

To examine more closely the introduction of the iron warship to the U.S. Navy, the narrative is best broken into its economic and political components. Its technical innovation, its actual performance, and the slow acceptance of iron in naval architecture must, by necessity, be relegated to the next chapter.

THE ECONOMICS OF IRON

The first half of the nineteenth century saw both France and the United States faced with the unenviable and financially unattainable position of matching the British Royal Navy ship for ship. By 1840, France had fewer than seventeen fully operational sailing battleships, while the United States had fewer than ten. Great Britain, on the other hand, had nearly forty.[4] This great disparity in naval power persuaded these three nations and other naval powers to experiment with new designs in ordnance, iron ship construction, armor plating, and steam propulsion. France and the United States, in particular, experimented to find new ways to mitigate Britain's naval advantage, while the Royal Navy experimented to keep abreast of any new developments that might threaten its naval supremacy.[5]

Of the four areas of naval technological advancement, only iron construction and armor promised to offset economically the Royal Navy's numerical advantage. Ordnance advancements, particularly shell-firing guns, threatened wooden ship preeminence, popularizing the once all-powerful wooden, three-decked ship-of-the-line as "an egg shell armed with a hammer." Nevertheless, all navies soon had access to shell guns and continued to use unarmored wooden ships. Thus, the advantage still lay in numbers, and ordnance advancement did nothing to change the naval power status quo.[6]

Advancements in steam propulsion offered a great tactical advantage to maneuverable steam ships. Since wooden warships could be converted to steam power, the advantage again lay with Great Britain.[7] Iron construction and armor, however, promised to move all navies back to square one. It was impractical to hang armor plate on the sides of three-decked wooden battleships and proportionately more expensive for a navy heavily committed to wooden hulls, such as Great Britain's, to convert to iron hulls.[8] In this light, economics became a prime motivating force behind the launching of some experimental iron warships in the early 1840s.

Abel Parker Upshur, who became the U.S. secretary of the navy on October 11, 1841, was already familiar with new developments in naval technology.[9] A well-informed civilian, Upshur was unencumbered by the navy's bias toward tradition and convention. He surmised, quite correctly, that "The application of steam-power to vessels of war, and the improvements which have recently been made in artillery, are destined to change the whole system of maritime war."[10]

Only two months after taking office he petitioned the president for increased naval spending and government subsidy of private enterprise in the construction of steam-powered merchant ships.[11] Upshur knew the U.S. Navy was too small and underfunded to expend much effort building experimental vessels. One obvious solution to this problem was to boost private-sector experimentation through subsidy, which would allow the private sector to absorb the risks while letting the navy share in the rewards of experimentation.

Upshur also believed, however, that sufficient progress in steam engineering, artillery, and iron-hulled ship construction had been made for the Navy Department to build its own experimental vessel. In November, 1841, he initiated construction of an iron-hulled steam-powered warship.[12] In his justification to the president, Upshur stated:

> Steamships have been built in Europe altogether of iron. As far as the experiment has been made, it is understood to have been successful. I recommend that it be made here also, with at least one vessel of medium size, sufficiently large to afford a fair test, without exposing too much to the hazard of failure. The great abundance of that material found in all parts of our country affords us every facility which can be desired; and our workmen will soon acquire, if they do not now possess, the requisite skill in converting it into vessels. We may thus acquire a cheap and almost an imperishable naval force, while, at the same time, we afford encouragement to some of the most useful branches of our home industry.[13]

Iron advocates were very persuasive in their arguments propounding iron ship construction, making the promotion of "home industry" one of the most significant reasons that the navy considered the use of iron ships.[14] Even builders and owners of wooden ships saw the advantages of iron construction. According to one shipbuilder from Buffalo, New York, an iron ship was more cost effective than a wooden ship even if the initial costs of the ships were equivalent; "an iron boat is worth and would wear [longer than] two made of any other materials besides would draw less water as they only weigh as five is to fourteen—which is all important in running into our shallow harbors. . . ."[15] Iron warship construction thus brings to light an early military-industrial partnership. Iron industry advocates had a demonstrably good product to sell, and the navy was a potential buyer. Further exchanges between Congress, the navy secretary, and various U.S. iron-rolling mills demonstrate that this was a growing collaboration.

In the early 1840s iron ship construction was new to the United States but quite well developed in Great Britain. The process of converting rolled wrought iron plates into vessels originated in England about 1787 and was the direct result of two newly developed processes: the puddling process, for refining large quantities of wrought iron, and grooved rollers, for producing plate. Henry Cort developed and patented both procedures in 1784. Until then, plate iron was produced by placing small quantities of refined wrought iron under trip-hammers. Ordinary trip-hammer plates were not sufficiently uniform for conversion to watertight or pressure tight vessels, but Cort's plates were. By 1786 wrought iron boilers produced steam for Cornwall mining engines. It was quite obvious that if an iron vessel could be produced to contain pressure, it must also be watertight. This observation was not lost on canal boat producers. By the next summer canal barges and lighters of wrought iron plied canals near Birmingham.[16]

Within a quarter of a century the British experimented with small iron pleasure craft culminating in the steam-powered *Vulcan* constructed at Glasgow in 1818. By 1821 enough was known of iron construction for Charles Manby and Charles Napier to produce a commercial wrought iron steamer, the *Aaron Manby.* From that period, ironship building in Britain was carried on by naval architects, persons trained and skilled in marine vessel construction and theory.[17]

The development of iron ship construction in the United States, however, proceeded at a much slower pace and along quite different lines. The first iron steam vessel, and indeed the first iron vessel, produced in the United States was the *Codorus,* built in 1825 by nail cutter John Elgar of York, Pennsylvania. Elgar naturally used the only material (besides wood) available to him: the thin wrought iron sheets from which nails are cut. This small, ingenious side-wheeled vessel was reported to have worked well for river use. It used an upright high-pressure boiler for its lone steam cylinder.[18]

The *Codorus* proved to be an interesting experiment in marine architecture and was perhaps one of the few iron vessels ever built from nonconventional rolled plate. Serious usage of iron in vessel construction in the United States, however, awaited the arrival of plate rolling techniques that would produce a much stronger product. The first indication that U.S. rolling mills could produce plates suitable for vessel construction occurred with the fabrication and launching of a Lehigh Coal Company barge in 1829 near Philadelphia. Philadelphia boilermaker Jesse W. Starr fabricated this barge. From this period forward, mechanics and boilermakers carried out iron vessel construction and experimentation in the United States.[19]

The U.S. boilermakers and mechanics cared little about publishing experimental results on the vessels they fabricated. This seems natural since they were not naval architects and were disinterested in perfecting seagoing craft. They were generally content to construct canal barges, of which some one hundred were produced by 1840.[20]

Though U.S. rolling mills could produce plate of sufficient size and thickness for marine usage, few if any naval architects of the early to mid-1830s were willing to work with the new material. Iron ship construction required far more specialization than was involved in traditional wooden shipbuilding. Shipwrecked sailors had proven throughout history that with tools such as adzes, axes, and saws, a new ship was simply a matter of trees and time. Ironworking, on the other hand, required exact plans and specialized yards equipped with iron machining tools, cutters, punches, drills, and hoists. American shipyards and marine architects were simply not equipped to cope with the new material.

The reason for American backwardness in this area is obvious: there was no market for iron ships until their usefulness and low cost were proven. Even then the United States did not, and would not for some time, face the timber shortage that Europe was forced to cope with, so wooden vessels remained an attractive alternative. Nonetheless, there is some indication that wood and iron costs for ship fabrication were fairly equivalent in the United States by the early 1840s. In spite of this, the retooling of the shipyards and reeducation of shipbuilders greatly slowed U.S. adoption of iron.[21]

Early on some U.S. shipping owners, impressed by the reputed qualities of English wrought iron vessels, wished to experiment with these ships. As there were no American shipyards that could handle iron, the shipping magnates were forced to import prefabricated ships from yards in England. John Laird's yard in Birkenhead supplied no fewer than seven ships to U.S. owners in the 1830s, five of which worked out of Savannah, including the *John Randolf* that was shipped to that city in 1834. Delivered in pieces from England, these ships were generally supplied with U.S.-built engines.[22]

To protect and promote the infant U.S. iron industry, an import duty of three cents per pound was placed on imported iron plate and products. It appears doubtful that this measure had much effect, since imported wrought iron ships even began to turn up on the western rivers, where their imperviousness to snag damage was much admired.[23]

Finally in 1838, Charles W. Copeland of the West Point Foundry in New York, produced the 222-ton steamer *United States* from native iron. This unusual catamaran-type vessel was constructed for use on Lake Pontchartrain. The *United States,* however, did not signal the end of imported ships. British yards were no doubt more efficient than U.S. yards, and the cost of English iron, even with the import duty, was about the same as native iron. In 1839 another Laird-built iron ship, the *Robert Stockton,* distinguished itself by crossing the Atlantic, fully assembled, to become the U.S.-registered *New Jersey.*[24]

The second rolled-plate iron ship produced of native U.S. materials and facilities, the *Valley Forge,* heralded the growing iron centers in the Ohio River Valley. This ship was launched in 1839 at Pittsburgh, Pennsylvania. It was designed to ply the Mississippi and Ohio Rivers. Constructed entirely of native materials, this ship ably advertized the virtues of iron. To identify new markets, area shipbuilders brought the *Valley Forge* to the navy's attention. In the builder's estimation the ship compared favorably with wooden steamers, proving iron to be safer, more durable, and easier and less costly to repair. In addition, they concluded that wrought iron would far outlast wood for riverboat use as there was no danger from dry rot, and corrosion was minimal over a two-year test period. Robinson and Minis Company of Pittsburgh, the ship's builders and owners, inspected the vessel in 1841 and estimated that the ship would last another twenty-five to thirty years at present upkeep—five to six times the average life of a wooden steamer on western waters.[25]

Another economic factor tipped the scales in favor of iron ship construction in the United States. At about the same time that the reports of the *Valley Forge* arrived at the secretary of navy's office, U.S. iron manufacturers discovered that the abundant and readily available supplies of American anthracite coal could be used to smelt iron, which reduced the cost for wrought iron over the charcoal-refining technique previously in use. This cost reduction further promoted the manufacturing centers in the U.S. heartland. Cities such as Pittsburgh and Cincinnati were centrally located on river and canal transportation hubs in areas rich in anthracite, iron ore, and limestone. Iron prices plunged dramatically from thirty-five dollars to twenty-five dollars per gross ton in 1842.[26]

Information on iron ship construction also become increasingly available through private firms and from naval inquiries in Europe. In May 1840 Royal Navy architect Augustine Creuze published the first descriptions of the British East India Company's warship *Nemesis.* The *Nemesis* and its sister ship, *Phlegethon,* were constructed at Laird's yard and were intended for duty in the Far East.[27] These were the first iron-hulled fighting ships produced, and they received much attention from the U.S. Navy. Creuze's favorable report was carefully read by the Navy Department while naval constructor Samuel L. Hartt scrutinized the *Nemesis* in person, evaluating the vessel type for U.S. naval usage.[28]

As Laird's was interested in promoting iron ship construction and the ships were constructed on private contract, there seems to have been no military secrecy.

The private sector, therefore, in both Europe and the United States proved the advantages of iron ship construction, yet naval usage of iron lagged by several decades. Eventually some navies, including France, Great Britain, Mexico, and the United States, planned and purchased prototype iron warships.

In the United States, Secretary Upshur became familiar with and appreciative of the progress made in the design of iron ships. Though he grasped the overall advantages of free enterprise, he remained mindful of the dangers involved in public contractual bidding, particularly when an agency was forced to accept low bids regardless of quality. Upshur directed the Navy Board of Commissioners to research possible contractors in advance of the bidding process for his iron-hulled experiment to ascertain which manufacturer could produce the best product. Secretary Upshur explained the reasoning behind his unusual method of finding a builder by saying of his iron experiment:

> If successful, it would bring into much more extended use a metal abounding in all parts of our country, and forming the most important part of its mineral wealth; Hence an importance was attached to the undertaking, far beyond the mere value of the vessel itself.[29]

In the spring of 1842, the navy contacted a firm in Pittsburgh that it considered best qualified to build the iron steamer. The company of Samuel Stackhouse and Joseph Tomlinson consented to build the ship for thirteen and three quarters cents per pound.[30] This firm, formerly known as Michael Stackhouse and Joseph Tomlinson, had a fine reputation. It had been in existence since well before the War of 1812, when it helped fit out Oliver H. Perry's fleet on Lake Erie with anchors.[31] The concern was also reputed to have constructed more "boats" than anyone in the western country and was among Pittsburgh's earliest and most competent engine-manufacturing establishments.[32]

Though the various rolling mills and yards of the fledgling U.S. iron industry were united in their promotion of the use of iron in ship construction, they did not mask their fierce competitiveness. Predictably, the award of this unorthodox navy contract set off a firestorm of controversy. Infighting between the rolling mills inevitably spilled over into political free-for-alls between the cities and states that competed.[33]

As it turned out, the navy secretary's actions thoroughly ruffled the feathers of several members of Congress representing states in competition with Pennsylvania for ironworking contracts. Rep. Nathanial Greene Pendleton of Ohio argued strenuously that free enterprise had been thwarted because bidding on contracts to build the iron vessel was not made public. Pendleton, supported by Rep. Charles Hudson of Massachusetts and Senator Richard W. Thompson of Indiana, created enough debate over the issue that it went to the full House. On June 20, 1842, the House of Representatives passed a resolution demanding to know from the navy why bidding for the steamer was not made public. The resolution also questioned why the steamer was to be constructed of an (as yet) unproven material.[34]

Secretary Upshur's reply to the Congress remains the most informative written account of the navy's decision to experiment with iron warship construction. The secretary expressed his fear of the often shoddy work that accompanied low bids: "I should not have felt myself bound to accept the lowest bid, because my object was to procure the best workmanship and the best materials, and not merely to build an iron vessel at the least possible cost."[35] Upshur also explained that public bidding had heretofore not been the usual course followed by the navy in procuring ships. Concerning the use of iron, Upshur reiterated what he had told the president the previous December.

> I determined to build this vessel of iron instead of wood, for two reasons. In the first place, I was desirous to aid, as far as I could, in developing and applying to a new use the immense resources of our country in that most valuable metal; and, in the second place, it appeared to me to be an object of great public interest to ascertain the practicability and utility of building vessels, at least for harbor defense, of so cheap and indestructible a material. Experiments which had been already made, here and in Europe, although highly encouraging, were not perfectly satisfactory, nor had they been so numerous as to afford any certain rules or principles for conducting such work. . . . Hence an importance was attached to the undertaking far beyond the mere value of the vessel itself.[36]

Upshur went on to direct his explanation at his detractors in the House and Senate by detailing his reasoning for his choice of Pittsburgh and Stackhouse and Tomlinson. Pittsburgh, he explained, was chosen because it had the best material and facilities. In addition, the work quality there was comparable to the reputed fine work done in Cincinnati, Ohio. Stackhouse and Tomlinson was chosen because of its good reputation. Moreover, its proposals submitted for the construction costs were as low as those of the other companies asked to submit bids. Furthermore, it was the only company to submit a proposal for the engines within the required time limit.[37]

Secretary Upshur's explanations were apparently acceptable. On August 2, 1842, the House mildly censured the naval secretary by concluding that the Navy Department had erred in not making public the proposals to build the iron ship. Not surprisingly, the committee also concluded that the ship should have been built in Cincinnati, Ohio, and transported to Cleveland via the Pennsylvania and Ohio Canal.[38]

RELATIONS BETWEEN
THE UNITED STATES AND GREAT BRITAIN

The economic setting of the early 1840s was a prime motive in Secretary Upshur's decision to build an iron warship, but the political ingredient of this story remains important concerning the ship's deployment. Elucidating his choice of construction site, the secretary stated, "The seaboard country was out of the question; and I did not consider it wise, in the then condition of our relationship with England, to begin such work on the boarders of a lake commanded by her naval power."[39] The new iron-hulled man-of-war was to be placed into service on the Great Lakes and stationed at Commodore Perry's old base of Erie, Pennsylvania, "where a fleet could be built in safety in case of war."[40]

Events were occurring in the late 1830s that looked as though they would lead the United States and Great Britain to war. Britain built fortifications and a defensive canal system in Canada. In addition, the Royal Navy fortified its dockyards in Bermuda. Disputes concerning the Maine and Oregon boundaries and the ill-fated Canadian rebellions of 1837 continually aggravated relations between the United States and Great Britain, often pushing them to the brink of disaster.[41]

A fallacy has arisen that the border of the Great Lakes is peaceful and has been so since 1814. This misconception is perpetuated because the agreements made to limit arms and armament after the War of 1812 have been viewed out of the context of the times. As is often the case, arms agreements are marriages of convenience, upheld only when it is advantageous or cost-effective to do so.

Following the War of 1812, a naval arms agreement, the Rush-Bagot Agreement or the Agreement of 1817, limited for a time the burgeoning naval arms race on the Great Lakes. This limitation occurred because it was costly and unproductive for both sides to continue arming.[42] Neither side hesitated to ignore the agreement when it felt threatened.

In 1837, disgruntled residents of Upper Canada, supported by U.S. citizens, fomented a revolution in Canada similar to the American Revolution, hence their adoption of the term *Patriot* for identification. They seized Navy Island on the Niagara River and attempted to establish a revolutionary government. This action led to a British commando raid that destroyed the rebels' supply steamer and left one Patriot dead. Navy Island was subsequently abandoned, and the movement collapsed or went underground. Following this provocation, Britain understandably felt justified in arming and equipping military vessels on the lakes to protect Upper Canada. The Patriots for the most part operated out of unassailable positions in the United States. The United States also procured the services of steam transport vessels to ferry troops, in a belated effort to halt Patriot attempts to cross the border and foment trouble between the two countries.[43]

Late in 1838, after it was apparent to the United States that the rebellion had run its course with Patriot defeats at Windsor and Prescott, U.S. Secretary of State John Forsyth protested to British Minister Henry S. Fox about the continued British naval presence on the lakes in apparent disregard of the Agreement of 1817. Fox explained to Forsyth that it was necessary for the British to maintain a naval force that exceeded the Rush-Bagot Agreement, "in consequence of the unlawful and piratical acts of hostility to which these provinces are at present exposed." Fox placated Forsyth, for the moment, by explaining that this was only a temporary measure that would last only for the duration of the emergency.[44]

The following year, 1839, also proved peaceful on the Great Lakes. That autumn Fox explained to the secretary of state that he thought British naval forces would be laid up if one more winter passed without further disturbances. Continued British concern, however, over the poor strategic situation British forces faced on the lakes compelled them to continue their unilateral arms buildup.[45] The U.S. State Department naturally became increasingly concerned, particularly when British naval vessels openly patrolled the lakes. The renewed patrols were apparently initiated in reaction to a border incident in Maine and to the much-publicized arrest and trial in November, 1840, of a Canadian citizen on murder charges stemming from the Patriot rebellion.[46] In 1841 further issues added to the growing diplomatic tensions, including U.S. complaints that armed Royal Navy steamers explored the different harbors on the U.S. shore of the lakes.[47]

Finally, on September 9, 1841, influenced by the recent developments and the continued British naval presence on the lakes, Congress passed a bill entitled the Fortification Act, which earmarked appropriations for various fortifications and ordnance stores. Rep. John W. Allen of Ohio attached an amendment to this bill that called for: "the construction or armament of such armed steamers or other vessels for defense on the northwestern lakes, as the President may think most proper, and may be authorized by existing stipulation between this and the British Government, $100,000."[48]

By this time President John Tyler and Secretary of State Daniel Webster believed the British ministers were sandbagging the subject of naval armaments on the Great Lakes to stall U.S. counteractions. Tyler saw no alternative to authorizing the secretary of the navy to implement the statutes passed in September for the defense of the lakes. On November 27, 1841, Naval Secretary Upshur ordered members of the Board of Navy Commissioners to "take the necessary measures for construction of one steamer to defend Lake Erie."[49]

Although the board of commissioners began work on the iron steamer, construction was soon transferred to the various bureaus created by Secretary Upshur to replace the board. The board proved to be a great hindrance to the navy secretary's farsightedness. By 1841 the board of commissioners reportedly had been transformed from a fairly efficient organization to a bureaucracy of "old men who opposed the construction of steam warships, blocked radical changes in design, and frustrated the efforts of the more imaginative naval architects and shipbuilders."[50]

Fortunately, the United States and Great Britain resolved many of their differences the following year with the Webster-Ashburton Treaty. Royal Navy patrols on the lakes continued, however. British Minister Fox explained that Great Britain wished that the Agreement of 1817 remain in place but that active British naval force was necessary for a further unspecified length of time. This naval force eventually consisted of five patrol ships: the 500-ton steamer *Minos,* the 750-ton steamer *Cherokee,* the 174-ton steamer *Mohawk* (the first iron-hulled war vessel on the lakes), and the schooners *Montreal* and *Experiment.*[51]

By this time Secretary Webster considered Fox's yearly explanations for the continued British violation of the Rush-Bagot Agreement to be totally without basis. Work on the U.S. iron warship continued. Early in 1843, an additional six iron-hulled revenue cutters were ordered, two of which were ostensibly intended for the lakes.[52] In a national emergency these large patrol vessels could have joined the more powerful iron paddle frigate, to form the nucleus of a fleet.

CONSTRUCTION

U.S. Naval Constructor Samuel L. Hartt received the task of designing the new ship. Charles W. Copeland drafted the engine plans. These two men had previously collaborated on the design and construction of the fine wooden paddle frigate *Missouri,* built in 1841.[53] Though Hartt was familiar with wooden ship construction, he had little information and even less experience in the design of the new iron ship. His examination of the *Nemesis,* however, combined with a careful inspection of the freight steamer *Troubadour,* allowed him to estimate scantling and plate sizes for the new warship, while adhering to a largely conventional wooden ship internal design. Hartt's plans and a lofting model were completed by March 25, 1842, less than four months after receiving notice from the Board of Navy Commissioners to design the new ship.[54]

Hartt's duties as naval constructor included not only the design of the iron ship but also the supervision of its actual construction. In early summer 1842 the constructor arrived in Pittsburgh with his son and promptly hired eight men: three ship's carpenters and five apprentices (and additional laborers). These workers helped him complete the full-size wooden molds on which the hot wrought iron plates would be shaped using hammers and mallets. By July, Stackhouse and Tomlinson was ready to roll the plate for Hartt's crew to shape.[55]

Work on the iron vessel proceeded at a fast pace throughout the summer of 1842. Hartt completed the rolling and shaping of the plates by fall, and the hull was assembled in Pittsburgh to insure the vessel's proper fabrication before shipment to Erie. By early spring 1843 the ship was disassembled for shipment via the Erie-Beaver Extension Canal and the Pennsylvania and Ohio Cross-Cut Canal. The ship was reassembled at Erie in the summer and fall of 1843.[56]

On August 24, 1843, the first captain of the iron paddle frigate arrived to supervise the final preparations for the launching. Commander William Inman traveled to Erie from his home of Lawrenceville, New Jersey, to find himself "without any of the appliances, usual to our Naval Stations."[57] Erie, Pennsylvania, was truly a frontier town with very few of the facilities needed for a naval base. Inman even had difficulty finding a room in which he and his clerk could live and work while supervising the fitting out of the ship. The navy officer was nevertheless impressed by the warship taking shape on the waterfront. In one letter to the navy secretary he stated, "we shall have here one of the finest iron steamers of her size in the world."[58]

The attempted launch of the iron paddle frigate occurred at 4:00 P.M. Monday, December 4, 1843, and was announced to the surrounding countryside by the report of a cannon and the chiming of church bells. The previous Friday a practical joker had fired the cannon, bringing people in from far and near to witness nothing more than exasperated shipwrights explaining that there would be no launch that day.[59]

The Monday launching also proved to be an embarrassment for the navy. Though the people were dutifully summoned, "when the last block was split out from under her, she very majestically and gracefully ———— stood still."[60] The strongback on which the vessel rested was placed at a very superficial angle to the lake's surface due to the shallowness of the water into which the ship was to slide. The engineers calculated this would prevent a too-rapid entry and attendant damage caused to the ship if it grounded on entering the bay. By 3:00 P.M. the next day, this time without announcement, the engineers managed to coax the vessel into the water without injury. At launch the frigate displaced a mere three feet ten inches of water. Lines taken before and after launch indicated, to the accuracy of the instruments, that the vessel had not altered shape at all. Wooden ships generally alter shape slightly on launching, often spoiling the perfect hull lines that the builder counted on for maximum speed and efficiency under power.[61]

Two days after the actual launching President John Tyler christened the ship USS *Michigan* in honor of the recently proclaimed twenty-sixth state.[62] Praise for the beauty of the ship seemed universal. One jubilant journalist reported, "She is a beautiful model for a good sea boat and fast sailor ———— is much admired for her perfect symmetry and clean lines, and is supposed to be fully equal in strength to the largest frigate." Another reporter reminded readers about the reason for the ship's construction, stating, "Her model is beautiful, and, judging from the way she sets in the water now, if ever she gets after one of Queen Vic's craft, she will make them think she's 'old iron sides' in good ernest."[63]

There was much work to be done on the vessel during the winter, spring, and summer of 1844. First, the engines and boilers were installed. Then the wooden decking, cabin partitions, and rigging were fitted under contract with marine chandler Joseph Long.[64]

While his vessel was being fitted out, Commander Inman recruited men to serve on board. Finally, on August 19, 1844, Inman reported that the ship was officially transferred to the government by the contractors and was now ready for service.[65]

The entire cost of the *Michigan,* according to ship's purser William A. Bloodgoode, was $152,478.71. A similarly sized large wooden sloop of war constructed during this time period, such as the *Cumberland,* cost slightly over $320,000. Wooden frigates such as the *Raritan* or *Congress* were slightly more expensive at $353,000 to $355,000.[66]

The *Michigan*'s value as a warship would not be proven until extended cruises tested its durability, economy of use, and suitability of purpose. Its construction, however, demonstrated that U.S. industry, though slow to initiate, had by 1843 become equal to the task of fabricating a seagoing ship of iron. Indeed, iron construction displayed excellent cost-effectiveness over wooden construction, at least for warships.

Nevertheless, it is doubtful that a *Michigan*-class vessel would have been possible in the United States at this early date had it not been for three circumstances. First was the foresight and organization of Secretary Upshur and his willingness to experiment with new naval technology. Second was the new anthracite coal smelting technique that reduced costs to the point that iron could successfully compete with wood in expense. The third condition, though certainly not least in importance, was the importation of advanced nautical iron technology from the private sector in Britain, which allowed U.S. constructors to gain valuable naval engineering insights despite the fact there was virtually no iron shipbuilding experience to draw on in the United States.

Though several navies were willing to experiment with its use, universal acceptance of iron ship construction remained far from a fait accompli. The iron shipbuilding industry faced difficulties in acceptance for both naval and merchant use. As will be seen, the performance of the *Michigan* and other iron ships became critical in the trials that determined the suitability, safety, and economics of iron shipbuilding.

III Performance, Perceptions, and the Tests of Iron

COMMANDER INMAN'S STATEMENT concerning his future command proved prophetic. What the United States Navy bought for its $152,478.71 tested in fact to be a durable, fast, efficient, and powerful warship. Yet only a few years after the ship's launching, the perceived weaknesses of wrought iron in warship construction nearly ended its use and did limit naval consideration of more *Michigan*-class paddle frigates.

This chapter will outline how the weight of naval tradition, public opinion, and problems in testing combined to delay the adoption of other wrought iron warships before the American Civil War. To accomplish this, the USS *Michigan*'s construction detail and performance will be compared with other warships of the time, both iron and wood, to highlight the biases incorporated in mid-nineteenth-century naval presumptions—prejudices that even today carry weight in naval history analyses.

OVERALL DESIGN

The USS *Michigan* was a medium-size warship, for the time, with an overall length on deck of 167 feet, 6 inches and a hull beam of 27 feet.[1] These statistics figure in tons burthen (not displacement) to 582.[2] The ship's outward waterline appearance was similar to a wooden steam frigate, as was the internal arrangement. Steamers at this time were arranged, as far as was possible, on the internal layout of a sailing ship of war. Crew's quarters were forward on the berth deck, and the officers' quarters and wardroom were aft. On paddle steamships, however, officers' and crew's areas were separated by the centrally located engine room, which occupied nearly one-third of the belowdecks spaces.

It is difficult to ascertain whether Hartt set out to design the *Michigan* specifically as a copy of the *Nemesis,* but certainly the body plans are quite similar. As form follows function, however, this ship type is also specifically and uniquely suited to the lake environment. Seas encountered on the Great Lakes could at times be as massive as those found on the ocean, yet the waves, owing to the unique properties of fresh water, would be of greater frequency. The lakes also posed many problems due to their geographical setting, which includes shoals, shallow river ports, and an often constricted coastal environment. Hartt must have reasoned that for the northern lakes the navy needed a shallow-draft vessel that was also extremely seaworthy. Since these were the same design parameters and restrictions placed on the *Nemesis,* it is little wonder they were similar.

The answer to these environmental problems lay in the design of a wall-sided ship with a nearly rectangular amidships cross section, as compared to the nearly circular or elliptical body plans for most wooden warships of the day.[3] The rectangular body plan with its flat bottom and nearly ninety-degree turn of the bilge was a great contribution to naval architecture. This modern below-the-waterline configuration gave the *Michigan* three advantages over older-style warships. The first advantage, and indeed the main reason for this ship's configuration, was that a flat bottom reduced the draft of the ship. The flat bottom, combined with the fact that an iron hull weighed a little over one-third as much as a wooden hull of the same dimensions (one-half fully fitted out), produced an average draft for the *Michigan* of seven feet six inches, or about half that of an average oceangoing wooden frigate. A wooden ship would be nearly impossible to build on a similar body plan, as it would be inherently weak at the sharp turn of the bilge, due to wood's relatively feeble ability to resist compression.[4]

A second advantage to the flat bottom and rectangular cross section was that the iron ship was more stable in any sort of sea. The new hull shape eliminated much of the pronounced side-to-side rolling motion produced by round-bottomed wooden ships. This stability made the iron frigate a splendid gun platform. The *Michigan*'s gunlayers, unlike their wooden ship counterparts, did not have to compensate to as great an extent for the roll of the ship when training their guns on target. The *Michigan*'s gun crews were consistently and demonstrably more accurate than many of their navy brethren.[5]

A third, and possibly unintentional, attribute of the underwater configuration of the iron ship was that it allowed the vessel to be very fast. Because iron ships were much stronger than wooden vessels, they could be given a much higher length-to-beam ratio. An iron ship could be built with a length that was eight or nine times its beam. The ends of an iron ship could also be made much finer without risk of hogging or sagging. Hogging and sagging occur when the ends of a ship droop because they displace less water than the center of the ship, creating the same effect as would develop if a bridge span were supported only under its center, not its ends. To combat this phenomenon, wooden ships are generally stubby, their length being only four or five times their beam. Additionally, the ends of a wooden ship are usually very bluff, or rounded, in order to build in extra support and create maximum water displacement. Both a finer shape and a high length-to-beam ratio contribute greatly to a ship's speed.[6]

The *Michigan* had a better than six-to-one length-to-beam ratio, which was very high compared to most wooden ships. Additionally, the new frigate had a sharp entry or bow, much like later clipper-type bows. These factors, plus the ship's powerful engines, allowed the *Michigan* to become the fastest ship on the Great Lakes, as well as in the U.S. Navy, for some time.

SPEED UNDER STEAM

In a congressional report, the warship was listed as having achieved twelve knots per hour under steam.[7] This is an excellent speed for the time. However, in reality, the *Michigan* was much faster. After commissioning trials (from which the congressional report was evidently based) and subsequent improvements in the cruiser's paddle wheels, it was never allowed to run a speed trial with a full head of steam, due to restrictions on coal consumption set by the navy.[8] Routine times listed between ports, however, punctuated by captain's accounts, give a much better indication of what the *Michigan* was actually able to do. For instance, on May 18, 1846, the ship steamed from Buffalo to Erie in six hours and twenty-nine minutes. Though this averages to twelve knots, the time given in the report included fifteen to thirty minutes spent to build steam and recover ship's boats. Therefore, the ship's running speed can be estimated at over thirteen knots, "on a medium head of steam." Commander Stephen Champlin, the vessel's new captain, was the first of many commanders to report his pleasant surprise at the *Michigan's* speed. Of the Buffalo-to-Erie run he reported, "The quickest passage I believe, she or any other vessel has ever made."[9]

Between 1847 and 1848 the *Michigan* routinely logged thirteen knots between ports, though its boilers never carried more than one-half to two-thirds head of steam.[10] In the spring of 1848, with the ship fresh from a winter engine overhaul and dry dock in Buffalo, a new commander, James

McIntosh, reported a routine speed of fourteen knots on eighteen and one-half inches of steam. "I am so far much delighted with the *Michigan,*" McIntosh wrote. "Her engines work beautifully and she is easy and fast—she mite [*sic*] bear 30 inches [steam pressure] with safety."[11]

The *Michigan*'s battle speed can now only be estimated, and of course it depended entirely on the condition of the engines, boilers, hull, and weather. Yet the ship demonstrated a cruising speed of as much as thirteen to fourteen knots and never less than twelve knots on a medium head of steam. It is logical to assume, therefore, that the paddle frigate could have exceeded fourteen knots when in good condition, on thirty inches of steam. This was a phenomenal ship speed for the 1840s, clearly making the *Michigan* one of the fastest ships in the world at that time.[12]

Enhancing the advantage of sheer speed was the fact that, at speed, the vessel was easily handled and maneuverable. Commander James Jouette, a long-term naval veteran, offered his unabashed opinion that "she handles better than any vessel I have ever known."[13] This was high praise coming from a blue-water navy man and was echoed time and again in the correspondence of the *Michigan*'s commanders.

HULL DESIGN

The wrought iron hull of the USS *Michigan* was formed of plates five feet to ten feet six inches long and thirty inches wide at the amidships bend. These plates tapered to sixteen inches wide at the bow and stern. The iron was one-eighth of an inch thick on the upper edge of each plate, expanding to five-eighths of an inch thick on the lower edge. The *Michigan* was lapped, or clincher built, with the plates overlapping three inches at the midships bend and two and one-half inches at the bow. Adjacent plates were fastened together by a single row of rivets. Strakes were formed longitudinally by fastening the ten-foot plates to each other with an internal ribband, or butt.[14] Lap strake construction was preferred in early iron ships because it resisted rivet shearing and was easy to fasten and caulk.[15]

According to some shipbuilders, the *Michigan*'s average hull thickness of one-half inch was equivalent in strength to but much lighter than an oak-built hull with an unrealistic outer hull planking five inches thick. In reality, the tensile (compression) strength of oak varies to such a degree that generalizations and comparisons are hard to make.[16] The structures produced by these two materials, however, behave very differently. Wooden ships tend to flex and "work" under stress, which causes leakage and wear between parts. Iron ship hulls, on the other hand, tend to take stress as a solid, homogenous unit, referred to as a girder. Therefore, the actual strength of an iron hull is considerably greater than would be expected by comparing the simple ratios between the tensile strength of wood and iron.

Backing the tremendously strong outer shell of the *Michigan* was a skeleton created from 4-by-4½-inch, T-shaped (L-shaped at the ends of the ship), three-eighths-inch-thick wrought iron frames on two-foot centers. The frame spacing was similar to that on wooden ships but greater than the spacing of fifteen to eighteen inches recommended by some of the more well-known British naval architects.[17] The *Michigan's* frame spacing did not increase at the ends of the ship in order to save weight, as it did on English-built vessels. Deck beams were formed from the same T iron as the frames. The decking placed over these beams was pine planking three and one-half inches thick.[18]

Seven evenly spaced, box-shaped iron keelsons provided the paddle frigate's longitudinal strength. Five of these structures ran the length of the ship while two ended after the engineering spaces. The central keelson had a height of sixteen inches, and all were fastened internally with L iron and one-half-inch diagonal iron rods.[19] Supporting the longitudinal structure were the ship's iron-plated coal bunkers, which extended along the sides of the engine room for its entire length, from the turn of the bilge to above the waterline. As well as adding longitudinal strength, the coal bunkers gave the engine room added protection against shot and shell penetration, placing two layers of iron and five feet of hard coal between the engines and an enemy's guns.

As was the case in all early iron ships, the *Michigan* had an external keel of iron, which was seven inches wide and extended down four and five-eighths inches. The stem and stern posts were massive iron beams one and one-half inches thick. The stem was seven inches wide and extended for twenty-six feet, and the stern was six inches wide and extended for fifteen feet six inches. These posts carried the stresses of the bow and stern and were heavily secured to the hull by the outer hull plates.[20]

The *Michigan* was also supported internally with four watertight transverse bulkheads and a watertight iron berth deck. Watertight bulkheads were first attempted in the United States on the earlier wooden steam frigates *Mississippi* and *Missouri*.[21] Two of *Michigan's* bulkheads extended from the floors to the weather deck on either end of the engineering spaces, dividing the ship into thirds. Two other watertight athwartship bulkheads extended from the floors to the berth deck approximately twenty-five feet abaft the bow and twenty-five feet forward of the stern.

A unique feature of the *Michigan* was its watertight iron berth deck, which lay on the forward and aft transverse bulkheads and extended to the engineering space bulkhead. This effectively gave the *Michigan* a double bottom forward and aft of engineering and allowed the vessel to be compartmentalized not only longitudinally but also, for the first time in a U.S. Navy ship, vertically. The iron berth deck also gave the ship's girder tremendous longitudinal strength for resisting tension and compression, the two opposing forces which come into play as heavy seas alternately lift or leave a ship section unsupported. The bulkheads were of three-sixteenths-inch iron plating. Doors in the bulkheads could be closed off via specially designed sluice gates should the ship take on water.[22] Theoretically, the *Michigan* should have been able to stay afloat if two nonconsecutive compartments became flooded.

Not armored, the *Michigan* was nevertheless massively reinforced and very heavily plated for its size, especially by today's standards. There are several reasons for this overbuilding, not the least of which was that marine architects of this time period were not fully aware of how much stronger an integral iron structure was than a wooden one. By the 1860s enough practical experimentation had been accomplished to construct mathematical models. Calculations began accurately to predict the strengths of iron and steel structures. Insurance underwriters, especially Lloyd's of London, encouraged this scientific approach to ship construction. Lloyd's was particularly interested in ascertaining a ship's strength, through general uniform regulations, before it was insured.[23]

The stoutness of the *Michigan's* hull saved the ship from certain destruction on several occasions. One of the more spectacular of these near disasters occurred during the early morning hours of May 6, 1853, when the *Michigan*, while upbound on Lake Huron, was rammed squarely broadside adjacent to the mizzenmast by the 700-ton propeller-driven steamer *Buffalo*, racing downbound at its maximum speed of about eight knots.[24] It is unheard of for a wooden ship to survive being rammed in such a fashion. Although the side of the *Michigan* was considerably damaged internally and staved in, there was not a single leak below the waterline.[25]

DAMAGE CONTROL

Had the ship been cut below the waterline, high-capacity steam-driven pumps might have saved it. Though steam pumps were not new, those installed on the *Michigan* were a significant improvement, particularly over the hand-operated models used in sailing vessels. The *Michigan* was outfitted with two main bilge pumps, one operating off each of the main engines, and three independent steam auxiliary pumps. The auxiliary pumps could be operated while the engines lay idle and could serve multipurpose uses such as bilge, fire, sanitary, or boiler feeds. These pumps operated exceedingly well. On their first trial, water was shunted to the main-deck fire hydrants with such force that the pressurized water blew the brass couplings off the connecting pipes, damaging the ship and the auxiliary pumps.[26] This demonstration of water force is consistent with the characteristic strengths of piston pumps, an extremely reliable and powerful type of pump not normally prone to clogging. Each of *Michigan's* five steam pumps could easily ship many times the volume of water of hand-driven contemporaries. In addition, the vessel was outfitted with two high-volume hand pumps in case the steam from both boilers failed.[27]

Should the *Michigan's* hull sustain damage due to shell or shot fire, a special parasol or umbrella plug could be installed from inside the ship. This device was simply thrust through the hole and opened. Water pressure held the plug in place. Should the vessel need more permanent repairs but not have the opportunity to visit a repair facility, drills, plates, and bolts made a sturdy temporary patch. Repairs, therefore—emergency, temporary, or permanent—were all easier and cheaper to carry out in an iron hull than a wooden one.[28]

A ship's powder magazine is obviously a vulnerable target and is traditionally located on a deck below the waterline. The *Michigan's* powder magazine and shell room, however, were not only located below the waterline but could be flooded should fire or severe battle damage threaten that area of the ship. This safety feature was impossible on wooden ships as their flexible hulls precluded the installation of flood cocks and the necessary compartmentalization to contain the flooding.[29]

ARMAMENT

Another great advantage of an iron warship's hull strength lay in its ability to carry a large amount of heavy ordnance, both in individual gun caliber and overall number, in comparison with a wooden ship of comparable size.[30] The *Michigan* was pierced on the weather deck for fourteen guns, seven on a side, plus two gangway ports.[31] The vessel's largest, most powerful guns, however, were two eight-inch pivoting shell guns mounted on the centerline of the ship at the forecastle deck at the bow, and the quarterdeck at the stern, giving the ship a maximum of sixteen guns (eighteen including the gangway ports) with a nine- or ten-gun broadside. Extended pivot ports allowed the eight-inch guns an arch of fire on either side of the ship.[32] Before the advent of iron, and later steel vessels, the mounting of a ship's heaviest guns in the bow and stern exacerbated the problems of hogging and sagging and was not normally attempted on wooden sailing vessels. The longitudinal strength exhibited by the iron-hulled *Michigan* precluded any hogging and sagging.

Funding for the ordnance of the *Michigan* was provided by Congress in an act passed on August 4, 1842. This motion dispensed $59,097 for ordnance and stores on the Great Lakes. More than $12,000 previously had been procured by Congress on March 3, 1841, for the same purpose. This money was to be used to purchase thirty eight-inch shell guns and seventy-five thirty-two-pounder chambered guns to be stored at naval depots at Sackets Harbor, Buffalo, and Erie. The armament for the *Michigan* was to be furnished from the ordnance stores sent to Erie.[33]

The cannons to be supplied for use on the warship were two eight-inch 63 cwt shell guns of U.S. design on pivot mounts. These were to be complemented by fourteen thirty-two-pounder chambered guns of 41 cwt in broadside.[34] The U.S. smooth-bore eight-inch shell gun was a very powerful and successful heavy gun. It fired a fifty-one-and-one-half-pound shell or a sixty-three-and-three-quarters-pound solid shot.[35] The eight-inch gun had an extreme range of nearly two miles and an effective shipboard range of two thousand yards. The thirty-two-pounder solid-shot guns also had a two-thousand-yard effective range at five degrees of elevation. Both guns could fire red-hot shot, solid shot, or shells.[36]

The devastating effects of shell fire on wooden hulls were aptly demonstrated in French Navy tests on the old wooden liner *Pacificature* in 1824. At that time, exploding shells for naval ordnance were an innovation of the French inventor Henri Paixhans. His shells proved extremely dangerous to wooden ships because they lodged in the hull before exploding. The explosion created gaping holes, sprung planking, and the great possibility of the most dreaded calamity on a wooden ship: fire. Though early shells had problems with their fuses—some going off too soon, others not going off at all—a few hits could prove more devastating than hours of continuous pounding with solid-shot guns. Red-hot shot was another danger to wooden ships and was perhaps more effective than shell fire in destroying wooden warships.[37]

Armed to its potential, the USS *Michigan* would have been one of the most heavily armed steamers in the U.S. Navy, superseded only by the launching of the first *Merrimack*-class steam frigate in 1855.[38] The attempted procurement of guns for the iron warship, however, classically demonstrated

Secretary Upshur's wisdom in not always allowing the lowest bidder to gain navy contracts.

Congress's censure of the Navy Department in 1842, concerning public bidding procedures for the iron steamer, forced the navy to advertise publicly for the ordnance to be supplied on the lakes. Ordnance and Hydrography Bureau Chief William M. Crane in September advertised openly for bidders to supply guns to the Upper Great Lakes naval depots (and thereby also supply the weapons for the new iron warship). These advertisements were posted in New York, Buffalo, and Pittsburgh newspapers.[39] During the next two years, two different contractors, having submitted impossibly low bids, failed to deliver the guns and indeed produced only a few working models, a large percentage of which burst on test firing.[40]

Finally, in exasperation, and as an apparent expedient to procuring the thirty-two-pounder chambered guns for the *Michigan* from contractors, the navy sent guns from navy yards in the East. Although the ship received its main battery of two eight-inch pivot guns, it was forced to substitute a much smaller secondary battery of four thirty-two-pounder caronades for the thirty-two-pound chambered guns that were not delivered.[41] A caronade is a short-barreled, short-range weapon designed to cause a maximum of damage at a range of a few hundred yards.

In the long run, the artillery problems mattered little, for the public advertising for ordnance contracts, demanded by Congress, alerted the British to the *Michigan*'s completion and impending armament. This awareness, in turn, precipitated yet another international crisis. During the ensuing diplomatic melee, the ship was stripped of all great guns except its forward eight-inch shell gun.

The Agreement of 1817 basically called for a decrease in the number of naval ships to one per lake. It also placed a ban on warships larger than 100 tons. Any remaining vessels were to be armed with a single eighteen-pound gun.[42] Tensions in 1844 abated only when the United States agreed to remove all the *Michigan*'s guns but one, proving peaceful intent, if not exact compliance with the stipulations. The guns removed from the ship were stored close at hand in a warehouse in Erie.[43]

Shorn of weapons, the *Michigan* was still a powerful engineering marvel and naval deterrent. The steam frigate was sent on its first patrol in the late fall of 1844, mainly to show the flag and aid vessels in need of assistance. During its career the *Michigan* had many chances to prove the strength and durability endemic to its iron hull and the power and reliability built into the steam machinery.

ENGINES AND BOILERS

The engines that provided the *Michigan* with its powerful sea legs were one of the most remarkable aspects of the vessel, both for their efficiency and for their durability. As with the hull, the engines were designed to function in the Great Lakes environment. For an engine design, Charles Copeland chose the direct-action inclined condensing engine. This type of steam engine had a low center of gravity, making it preferable for oceangoing paddle ships likely to face severe weather conditions.[44] The two engine cylinders of the *Michigan* were placed side by side at an inclination of twenty and one-half degrees from the keel. Oak timbers supported the cylinders and attached to the keelsons. Two piston air pumps for reducing the pressure in the jet condenser were placed inboard of the engines at the same angle as the engines. The diameter of each steam cylinder was thirty-six inches, and the diameter of each air pump was twenty-nine and one-half inches. The stroke of the pistons was eight feet, and the pistons were directly connected to the paddle wheel shaft via twenty-four-foot connecting rods.[45]

The engines weighed more than eighty-eight tons, producing 333 horse-power at twelve knots, with a nominal horsepower of 110. The size and weight of the *Michigan's* engines were average for a paddle steamer of this time period. Low-pressure condensing engines of this sort were large but efficient in contrast to the much smaller high-pressure noncondensing sort used for propeller-driven ships.[46] The power and durability of these engines were demonstrated on numerous occasions during the ship's career. Commander Stephen Champlin mentioned that while driving through a November storm in 1847, "Carrying only our usual head of steam we passed several steamboats with the greatest ease." He added, "The ship has proved to be inferior to no boat which floats upon the lake."[47] Champlin's comment points out that during storms and heavy seas wooden steamers were often forced to slow or even idle their engines—"when needed most they work least"—because wooden ships flexed so much that the steam machinery could be damaged.[48] Iron-hulled ships, on the other hand, had no such restrictions placed on their engines during foul weather. When needed most, the *Michigan's* engines delivered time and again.

On another occasion, early in December, 1854, the *Michigan* attempted to aid the Central Railroad steamer *Mayflower*, which had gone ashore on Point Pelee in a dense fog the evening before. Point Pelee lay some 110 to 120 miles west of Erie. During this rescue attempt the *Michigan* nearly became a victim but for the strength of the ship's iron hull and steam engines. While racing across the lake to aid the grounded ship, the *Michigan* was overtaken by a storm from the southwest described by veteran Commander John S. Nicholas as a "fearful hurricane. . . . a gale and a sea, which after nearly 40 years of sea experience I never saw surpassed."[49] While seeking shelter in the lee of Pelee Island, the warship ran on a reef and stuck fast. The *Michigan* was soon in dire straits, with the hull grating and pounding on the reef. The ship was soon under such compression that the bottom of the hull was forced upward so that the engines became jammed on their connecting rods and the main crank. Fortunately, quick-thinking engineers idled the engines before they could damage themselves or the ship.

Meanwhile the crew worked frantically to off-load twenty-five tons of coal and chop away at an ever increasing deck load of ice. The wind continued to blow at hurricane force. To make matters worse, the temperature plunged to six degrees Fahrenheit. Miraculously, and only because the *Michigan* was a warship with a relatively large crew, the ship was lightened sufficiently to float free of the reef. If the engines did not come back to life, however, the ship faced wrecking someplace else. Its anchors had been buoyed off to save weight, and the sails were useless in the fierce wind.

Free from the tremendous compression of the reef, the bottom flexed back to its original shape and the ship's engines again rumbled to life, driving a much-shaken captain and crew back to Erie. Though he failed in his gallant attempt to aid the *Mayflower,* a relieved Commander Nicholas commented, "If I could respectfully recommend to the Department the Constructor C. W. Copeland, who built the Engines of the U.S. Steamer *Michigan,* I should unhesitatingly state that his work is perfect as the Engines rotate like clock work."[50]

Amazingly, and a compliment to both Copeland and Hartt, neither the engine nor the hull required repairs after the grounding.[51] Perhaps the greatest compliment to this ship's engines' durability is the fact that they operated almost continuously for seventy-nine years of service on the lakes before their first breakdown.

The warship's two iron boilers supplied steam for the engines and were positioned in the forward half of the engine room. They weighed 31.9 tons and carried 25.25 tons of water. The boilers were positioned side by side, with the fire doors facing aft, and were nineteen feet long, eight feet six inches wide, and nine feet three inches high, producing an average steam pressure of fifteen pounds per square inch. The boilers could act independently to power the engines or be used in tandem. Steam from the boilers could be shunted not only to the engines and pumps but also to vents on deck to scald and repel boarders in case of attack.

The *Michigan*'s first boilers were described as flue, leg, or lag boilers for their design. The strength of this type of boiler came from the inside of the boiler rather than the pressure shell due to the internal lag bolt fasteners. The term *flue* refers to the venting of the bituminous coal combustion products through brass tubes in the water jacket to increase the heating surface.[52] This seems an odd design since marine engineers knew that brass and iron placed in direct electrical contact produced a galvanic couple, which generally accelerated the corrosion of the iron. This process always held true unless there was a massive preponderance of iron to copper. Apparently, the boilers were just the right mass of iron compared to copper, because they lasted without replacement until 1860.

The *Michigan*'s coal bunkers accommodated 120 tons of coal. At an average consumption of 1,400 pounds per hour, this was enough for slightly over seven days' cruising at average speed. This capacity gave the ship a more than adequate two-thousand-mile cruising range at ten knots.[53] The *Michigan* could burn wood and anthracite (hard), but most often it burned bituminous (soft) coal. Special vents were later added to the boilers to allow forced-air venting in the firebox. The enhanced combustion efficiency allowed the *Michigan* to burn bituminous coal while producing only the amount of smoke normally produced while burning cleaner anthracite. The ship reportedly produced almost no smoke with anthracite.[54]

The power produced by the *Michigan*'s engines was converted to momentum by the two side radial paddle wheels, each with sixteen spokes. The sixteen paddle buckets were actually made up of four separate paddles in close proximity, equivalent to a paddle bucket seven feet six inches by twenty-six inches. The diameter of the paddle wheels was twenty-one feet ten inches, with a two-foot-eight-inch dip for each paddle. The side wheels were protected by semicircular paddle boxes of similar plating as the hull.[55]

Paddle wheels, despite their anachronistic visage, were actually a very efficient means of propelling ships, particularly if the vessels were equipped with low revolution-per-minute (rpm) engines. Paddle wheels and their attendant machinery were also highly reliable and not often prone to breakdown. The *Michigan*'s paddle crankshaft connecting the two side wheels was twelve inches in diameter and supported by pillow bearings mounted on a large A-frame structure of timber grounded on the keelsons. The paddle wheels rotated at a maximum of twenty-three revolutions per minute at twenty inches of steam pressure. At this rpm the pistons reciprocated only once in slightly less than three seconds, relegating engine-killing friction and attendant problems with lubrication to a minor concern. Propellers require relatively high-rpm engines, which are much more susceptible to component fatigue, wear, lubrication failure, and breakdown.[56]

There were, however, at least four potential drawbacks to the use of paddle-wheeled warships. First, although side-wheelers handled rough water much better than stern-wheelers did, neither type kept its paddle buckets totally submerged as it rolled. While quartering a sea (steering at a 45-degree angle to the waves), a side-wheeler had a tendency to lurch or corkscrew in the direction of the exposed wheel, which made for an uncomfortable ride. Paddle-wheelers, however, were less apt than propeller driven ships to sustain damage if the vessel ran aground. They were also less likely to lose efficiency through fouling by marine assemblages such as barnacles, a constant problem for iron and even brass propellers in the ocean.[57] If the *Michigan* had been a propeller driven ship, its story would have ended with the grounding on Pelee Island in 1854.

The second drawback to side paddle wheels was that they prevented the mounting of broadside guns. Mid-nineteenth-century naval tactics dictated that battleships carry as many broadside guns as possible. Thus, paddle-wheeled ships were not suitable as liners. When gun caliber and accuracy increased, however, and cruiser strategy was accepted and formalized, the value of steam frigates or cruisers increased. One physical disadvantage the *Michigan* did have compared to others in its class was that the paddle wheel shaft rose above main deck level. This position precluded the movement of guns fore and aft to replace damaged guns during battle.[58]

The third potential disadvantage of the paddle wheel was that it was more exposed to enemy fire than were propellers. Though obviously true at first glance, the exposure of the paddle wheels and crankshaft machinery to gunfire may not have been the Achilles' heel that it might seem. Historian D. K. Brown records one of the few instances in which a paddle-wheeled warship was put out of action at the battle of Eckenfjorde on April 5, 1849.[59] This incident was indeed an exception. In the many fierce naval actions of the Civil War, involving both paddle-wheelers and propellers, few ships were entirely disabled after receiving artillery hits to their paddle wheels. Ships were most often disabled after receiving damage to their steam machinery or boilers or taking hits below the waterline. The problem of vulnerability to attack lay not with the paddle wheel, but with the overly large low-pressure steam machinery used to power most side-wheelers.[60]

The last, and perhaps the most important, disadvantage of the paddle wheel was that, unlike propellers, paddle-wheeled ships did not operate well under sail alone. The inefficiency of the steam machinery of the day and the distance between coaling stations required oceangoing steam vessels to sail as much as possible while on foreign station to conserve coal. For a paddle steamer to sail efficiently, the paddle buckets below the waterline had to be removed. That was a time-consuming operation that left the paddle-wheeler vulnerable to emergencies. Propellers were more efficiently removed and refitted, usually by hoisting them through the fan tail with a sort of "window sash" arrangement.[61]

The sailing factor posed no problem for the *Michigan* on the Great Lakes because coal stores were never farther away than two days' steaming. A *Michigan*-class warship on foreign station, however, would have had tremendous problems. Should coal supplies be located more than seven days' distance, the ship would be forced to rely on sail. Its dubious sailing qualities, compounded by bottom fouling, practically insured that the ship would not have been able to keep up with the fleet on sail power alone.

A comparison of paddle wheels and propellers would not be complete without mention of the famous Royal Navy trials of the propeller *Rattler* and the paddle wheeler *Alecto*. This series of races and tugging contests seemed to prove that propellers were more efficient than paddle wheels.[62] Because the *Rattler* had more powerful engines and was sixty tons heavier than *Alecto,* however, the only thing proven was that a larger, more powerful ship can outrun and outpull a smaller, less powerful ship.[63]

RIGGING

The *Michigan* was primarily a steamer, not a sailing vessel equipped with steam auxiliary. The ship's sails were for training and emergencies. The warship was originally barkentine-rigged, carrying a combination sail pattern, square-rigged on foremast and fore-and-aft-rigged on the other masts.[64] For the ship to proceed under sail power alone, the below-the-waterline paddle buckets had to be removed and the wheel shaft locked in place.[65]

It is clear that the qualities that made the *Michigan* an efficient steam vessel likely insured that it would have been a poor sailing ship. The warship's shallow draft, not offset by a centerboard, virtually insured that it would be a poor windward sailor, too easily drifting to the lee. This drawback may have been partially obviated by the ship's lapstrake construction, with each stake joint acting as a keel.[66]

The *Michigan*'s sails could rarely be used in conjunction with the vessel's engines, as the sail pattern tended to heel the vessel, making it difficult to keep both paddle wheels in the water while under way. On rare occasions, if the wind was directly off the stern or stern quarter, sails could be used in conjunction with steam, adding perhaps a knot to the ship's speed. Commenting on the warship's sailing characteristics, Commander James Jouette stated, "Her powers of sailing are very limited owing to her rig and the small amount of canvas she spreads." The secretary of the navy concluded in his report to Congress in February, 1854, that "this vessel seldom carries sail, and never much."[67]

CAPABILITY

Despite the *Michigan's* poor sailing qualities, the design's overall success can hardly be debated. The warship was fast, durable, a potentially powerful and stable gun platform, and economical to build and operate. The *Michigan's* design innovations were a generation ahead of ships built even after the paddle cruiser had seen a decade of service. Perhaps a useful example of the *Michigan's* capabilities would be to pit it (fully armed) in a theoretical confrontation with a *Niagara*-class U.S. steam frigate launched in 1855.

The *Niagara*-class auxiliary steam frigates were extremely large, wooden, propeller-driven steamers weighing five thousand tons and armed with a battery of eleven-inch guns, seven in broadside. The *Niagara* had ten times the tonnage of the *Michigan,* seven times the crew compliment, and seven times the initial cost. Yet, the *Michigan* had several meaningful advantages over the new ships.

In speed, the *Michigan* was faster at fourteen knots or more to the eleven of the *Niagara* (unless there were strong winds blowing). This speed allowed the *Michigan's* commander to choose battle and firing ranges. The *Michigan* also represented a much smaller target than a *Niagara*-class vessel, which likely offset the greater exposure of the smaller ship's steam machinery.

The two ships' guns had approximately the same range. The *Michigan's* eight-inch cannons, however, could be worked nearly as fast as its thirty-two-pounders, and both had an immensely faster rate of fire than an eleven-inch gun. The *Michigan,* in fact, could fire at least two broadsides to each one the *Niagara* fired.[68] This ability made the amount of iron thrown per minute more nearly equal than might be supposed, at 768 pounds for the *Michigan* to 952 pounds for the *Niagara.* American Civil War naval engagements demonstrated that the eventual outcome of an action depended far more on the number of shots and hits than the size of individual shells fired.

In addition, though questions remain concerning the effects of shot and shell fire on iron hulls (as will be discussed), most authorities agree that shell fire is less destructive on iron hulls than wooden ones.[69] Therefore, though smaller, the *Michigan*'s guns would have an effect per hit as much as, or perhaps greater than, the *Niagara*'s larger guns.[70] The steadiness of the gun platform and easy access to ammunition would also likely tally in the *Michigan*'s favor. Finally, the *Michigan*'s damage control capabilities were superior because it was successfully compartmentalized.

Obviously, such theoretical comparisons cannot take into account the vagaries of naval combat: wind, weather, current, visibility, and training, among others. Yet, a fully armed *Michigan*-class paddle frigate with a high and accurate rate of fire, exceptional speed, and maneuverability would be a tough opponent for the newer, much larger steam frigates. Certainly, matched cost per cost and ton per ton, seven *Michigan*-class paddle frigates would overwhelm one *Niagara*-class steam frigate under any circumstance.[71]

THE TROUBLES WITH IRON

The *Michigan*'s cost and potential raise the question of why the U.S. Navy did not employ more iron vessels, paddle-wheelers or propellers, before the Civil War. The navy commissioned only four iron ships prior to 1860: the *Michigan, Allegheny, Waterwitch,* and *Scourge.* In the early 1840s, the navy also experimented with the floating armored Stevens' Battery, which was never completed or purchased, and a galvanized vessel at Washington, for which the navy lacked the funding to complete.[72] The other iron vessels under government employ were plagued with numerous design flaws. Though these flaws were not necessarily the fault of their iron hulls, nevertheless they combined to make the *Michigan* seem a freshwater technological fluke. Hunter wheels, for example, condemned iron hulls through "guilt by association" because of the spectacular failure of these vessels, most particularly the *Allegheny,* the second U.S. vessel constructed by Stackhouse and Tomlinson.[73] The resources squandered on the Hunter wheel concept set back U.S. naval architecture by a decade. Hunter wheels were underwater horizontal paddle wheels designed by Lt. William W. Hunter. Devised to address the perceived problems of paddle wheel vulnerability to gunfire, the masking of the broadside to cannon ports, and the incompatibility of sail and paddle wheels, the Hunter wheel was too inefficient to propel large ships.[74] The mechanism also did not address the real problems, the size and vulnerability of low pressure steam machinery.

Early on, several problems accompanied the introduction of wrought iron in merchant and warship construction. English marine engineer John

Grantham identified six of these in 1842: (1) compass deviation, (2) leewardness in steering, (3) prejudice against a new material, (4) high insurance premiums, (5) bottom fouling in sea water, and (6) stiffness of hull, which reduced speed. Of these obstacles, several had no tangible basis and only one was not resolved by 1845.

Steering and other sailing qualities were known to be entirely a matter of hull form, not hull material. Iron ships at this time were generally purchased as shoal draft vessels due to their lightness. Given flat bottoms and little draft, it is no secret why they were leeward sailers (pushed sideways in the wind). As an understanding of the properties of iron increased, the prejudices against it decreased. Insurance premiums were also reduced as the strength and safety of iron ships was proven in practice and iron construction techniques became standardized.[75]

By 1839 Royal Astronomer George Biddell Airy appeared to have solved the problem of the effects of an iron hull on ship's compasses. Airy determined that the placement of magnets and other various pieces of metal around the compass compensated for the attraction of the hull. The solution, however, remained a highly technical art that few people understood. His U.S. counterpart, Mr. Foye (no first name given), was called in on several occasions to adjust the compasses on the *Michigan*. This adjustment was achieved in a process known as "swing ship," in which the ship was manually swung by its crew, in a turning basin or river, to all points on the compass while the binnacle was adjusted.[76]

Shipping accidents, however, continued to be blamed on the compass, even after Airy's revelations. In nearly all of these cases, the cause for the faulty compass was readily apparent. In the loss of the *Iron Duke,* for instance, the iron tiller passed near the compass each time the ship turned, which naturally caused the compass to deviate. In the ship *Ironside* a cast-iron stove in the cabin directly beneath the binnacle caused the compass to deviate.[77]

Bottom fouling, on the other hand, was a problem without apparent solution. The fast and abundant growth of marine organisms, particularly coralline algae and barnacles, on the hulls of iron ships greatly reduced their speed and efficiency in the water. To combat this difficulty, early iron ships were shunted between salt water and fresh water between voyages. Fresh water killed the rapidly multiplying shellfish. This process was not always a practical solution, however, particularly on long voyages. In the early 1840s antifouling paints seemed a possible solution, and it was expected that a successful paint would soon be developed.[78] This expectation proved illusory, however.

Since the latter part of the eighteenth century, the usual method for inhibiting marine growth on wooden ship hulls was to cover the ship's bottom with copperplate. Copper ions given off by the plate are poisonous to organisms attempting to make a home on the ship. Placing copperplate on an iron ship, however, was a difficult proposition because of galvanic coupling, or the connection of metals with dissimilar corrosion potentials, and the ensuing rapid corrosion of iron in electrical contact with the copper.

By 1860, though hundreds of antifouling paints were tested, few showed much promise. Naval architects reconsidered copper sheeting as the only solution. The only practical way to do this was to first sheath iron ships in wood. The wood formed an electrical insulator between the copperplate and the iron hull. Obviously, it added both weight and expense to iron ships. Experiments also attempted to use electrically passive glue to hold the copper sheets to the iron hulls, but the results were disastrous.

The merchant service initiated the use of composite ships to alleviate hull to fouling. These vessels were built with iron frames and wooden hulls. Composite ships could be copper sheathed and were briefly seen as a possible solution to the problem of fouling. Unfortunately, corrosion problems with their hull fastenings created an insurance liability.[79]

Until the fouling problem was resolved, iron warships had to be hauled and cleaned every couple of months. The *Michigan* did not face this problem, as it was stationed in fresh water throughout its career. A few coats of red lead-based paint functioned sufficiently as a bottom coating.

Another major obstacle to iron warship construction cropped up shortly after the *Michigan* was launched. Gunfire tests conducted by the British, French, and U.S. navies in the mid-1840s easily rekindled the bias against iron-built warships. Though the results of the tests were often contradictory and always ambiguous, they gave opponents of iron the opportunity to create a negative perception. This perception held sway in public and naval circles despite the fact that it contradicted several of the tests and, most important, the practical experience gained by iron ships in combat.

The tests began at Gavres, France, in 1844. French Navy tests indicated that wrought iron stood up well to gunnery tests and as little as twelve millimeters thickness resisted shot penetration. Royal Navy gunnery tests at Woolwich Arsenal in 1845–46 on targets made to simulate iron ships were indecisive but indicated that without a wood backing, iron could splinter on the impact of shot.

It was the unofficial gunnery testing on the British steam launch *Ruby* that convinced opponents of iron construction that these ships were unfit for combat. They did not take into account that the *Ruby* was in very poor condition and was not heavily constructed to begin with. U.S. gunnery trials conducted in 1847 apparently failed to add substance to the English tests.

Between 1849 and 1851, the Royal Navy conducted additional tests on targets simulating the sides of the iron frigate *Simoon*. These tests indicated that solid shot and shell made small holes on entry but much larger, more jagged holes when passing through the disengaged side of the ship. Wooden backing and rubber interior sheathing known as Kamptulicon lessened the effects of splintering but did not stop it. In light of the perceived weakness of iron and the ambiguity of the different tests, the Royal Navy relegated its iron steam frigates to troop transports, hoping to keep them out of harm's way.[80]

The world of practical experience, however, had already thrown several iron warships into combat, and their ordeal by fire seemed to contradict completely the negative experimental results. On several occasions in the early 1840s, *Nemesis* came under fire from Chinese forts. At one point the vessel received fourteen hits in a single engagement. The vessel's commander, William Hutcheon Hall, reported that the effects of splinters were no worse, and perhaps better, than would be expected in a wooden ship.[81]

Reports from the Laird-built Mexican iron sloops *Guadeloupe* and *Montezuma* confirmed Hall's observations. In 1843, both ships fought on numerous occasions against both forts and other ships. In one battle, the *Guadeloupe* drove off the Texas twenty-gun corvette *Austin,* using its larger, but fewer, guns. Though the *Guadeloupe* received numerous hits, the warship's captain reported that the effect of shot was considerably less than would be expected of a wooden vessel. There were few, if any, dangerous splinters.[82] In 1847, the British iron gunboats *Harpy* and *Lizard* fought a close action with a shore battery on the Paraná River in South America. Though a fiercely contested battle at an impossibly close sixty yards range, there were only ten casualties on the ships (none mentioned from splinters), and a few glancing shots did not even penetrate the iron hulls. Preliminary, well-publicized accounts of exaggerated damage and casualties seemed to vindicate the negative bias against iron. The perception alone turned this indisputable credit to iron warship construction into a resounding condemnation in public opinion.[83]

By 1850 the perceived weakness of iron to battle damage swayed public and naval opinions against the use of this metal in warship construction. Yet, in this instance, as with many others, some of the experimental data swayed opinion but failed to reflect reality. The only objective data on this subject strongly suggested that unarmored iron ships, in genuine combat, were probably better off than wooden ships in the same situation. Furthermore, the resilience demonstrated by the *Michigan* in resisting a broadside ramming and severe grounding in frigid temperatures further questions the validity of the experimental data to reflect reality.[84]

There were undoubtedly more variables involved in calculating damage in complex structures, such as a real ship, than were compensated for in these early, simple tests. Of more importance historically is the ease with which these trials reinforced the already negative perceptions concerning the suitability of iron in warship construction. In any case, the introduction of armor protection muted these arguments.

In the United States the cause of iron construction was greatly impeded by the death of Abel P. Upshur and Thomas W. Gilmer in an experimental cannon explosion aboard the U.S. steamer *Princeton* on February 28, 1844. Gilmer had replaced Upshur as navy secretary but remained dedicated to carrying out the former secretary's experiments. The spectacular failure of some of these investigations, such as the Hunter wheel, permitted the new naval administration to discontinue iron hull experimentation into the 1850s.

The slow acceptance of iron as a suitable material for the fabrication of warships resulted from a combination of factors. In the end, bottom fouling was the major determinant, followed by wrought iron's perceived poor battle qualities.

The momentum of several thousand years of wooden ship building tradition should not be overlooked as a contributing factor in the slow acceptance of iron. This factor is particularly important in the United States, where wood supplies were still plentiful and an adze was easier to wield than a forge and rolling mill. Navies of the day continued to have a vested interest in wooden ship construction. Individual shipbuilders, apprentices, and sailors were unfamiliar with iron construction and likely distrusted a new and unproven technology. They had reason to be distrustful since their lives depended on their ships. All of these psychological factors contributed to the ease with which gunnery tests and exaggerated battle damage swayed public opinion against iron construction.

With these factors in mind, even the success of the USS *Michigan* did not, and could not, convince the navy to build an iron squadron before the Civil War. The knowledge and experience gained by the men who served on the *Michigan* and the other iron navy ships, plus similar information obtained through the private sector, were not lost, however.

Ironically, the Royal Navy was forced to lead the way back to iron in the late 1850s, in response to the armored French battleship *La Gloire*. Both continental navies realized the introduction of armor to iron ships virtually solved all the problems, except fouling, thought to be plaguing iron warship construction. The impressive armored iron battleship HMS *Warrior* underscored Britain's renewed appreciation of naval iron technology.[85] Certainly, U.S. sailors who served on board the *Michigan* during the early morning hours of May 6, 1853, and who survived the great storm of December, 1854, were not surprised by iron's resurrection and preeminence.

IIII *The Attack of the*
Lake Michigan Timber Pirates

THE RECORDS OF THE USS *Michigan* contain scattered valuable information on Great Lakes ice conditions, water levels, and general weather conditions. Most important to a historical study, however, are the accounts of the human travails occurring on the lakes during this important period. Westward migration continually created new markets for manufactured goods, while raw agricultural and mineralogical materials were shipped east in ever larger quantities for refining. Economics fueled the lakes trade but also generated most of the darker aspects of the region's history.

This section begins with an outline of the new warship's routine activities and yearly patrol route, but—just as the *Michigan* was—it is quickly drawn into the whirlwind illegal timber trade. Illicit timber cutting and smuggling were epidemic in the lakes region during the warship's early patrolling years. The parallels between running timber, alcohol, or drugs are quite stunning. Each activity brings to the fore greedy and vicious criminals and each was, and is, known for their particular brand of violence. In this category the timber smugglers are one up on the others, for it is doubtful that even Al Capone or a Colombian cartel would attempt to sink a U.S. Navy cruiser.

On October 1, 1844, the USS *Michigan* began its historic, nearly century-long patrol of the Great Lakes. The vessel's first port of destination was Detroit. From there, it proceeded to Cleveland, then doubled back to make its first passage to the upper lakes of Huron and Michigan, arriving in Chicago on October 19 for coaling. The ship proved to be a popular attraction at all of its ports of call, and visitation on board by average citizens was encouraged.[1]

A typical cruising season for the *Michigan* ran from the end of March or the beginning of April to nearly the end of December. Ice was frequently encountered if the seasonal envelope was pushed. Despite the supposed delicacy of its paddle wheels, the warship proved it could operate without damage in half-inch-thick ice.[2] A nine-month cruise generally included two voyages to the upper lakes of Huron and Michigan and the crisscrossing of Lake Erie from Detroit to Buffalo four to five times.

During these cruises, most sizable intermediary ports were visited as well as islands and strategic straits such as Mackinac and the Saint Clair River. Commander John Nicholas reported that during the cruising season of 1854, the vessel sailed 11,865 miles. While commenting on lake sailing, Nicholas explained to the navy secretary, "I think the service bids fair to be the most arduous of any that I have been engaged in since I have enlisted in the Navy . . . the number of miles sailed by this ship in performance of her duties, will compare favorably with that of any ship engaged on any foreign station except that of the East Indies and Pacific."[3]

During the short winter's layup, the *Michigan* stayed at Erie, where a houselike structure was built over the after section to protect the vessel and give the crew more comfortable winter quarters. The officers could generally afford homes in town to stay with their families, or they sometimes lodged at the privately owned U.S. Hotel just down the street from the wharf.[4]

Though the warship heightened morale at frontier U.S. lake ports, its actual duty, as ordered by the secretary of the navy, was to patrol the lakes and assist vessels in distress. To this end the warship was very handy indeed. After one decade of service the *Michigan* rescued or assisted at least thirty-eight different vessels (see appendix A), some of which were found in dire circumstances. Battling the elements on the great northern lakes was at times far from easy or safe duty. Fall and winter storms destroyed many ships. The unfortunate vessels sometimes fell victim to the numerous reefs and shoals in the lakes while others foundered in the deep, frigid waters. The *Michigan* suffered its first casualty only seven months after its first cruise. On April 21, 1845, seaman George H. List drowned when one of *Michigan*'s launches overturned after a successful attempt to free the steam packet *Buffalo* from the shore near Erie. His remains were never recovered.[5]

Other hazards such as sickness and accident were simply a part of life in the nineteenth century. Between 1849 and 1852 a cholera epidemic raged across the Great Lakes and hindered the cruises of the *Michigan*. The ship's surgeon, William Maxwell Woode, was surprisingly cognizant of how the disease was spread and immediately reported its effects in the lakes region to the Navy Department. This epidemic was apparently transmitted from the East Coast (likely through the Erie Canal), and though the *Michigan* was relatively safe at Erie because of untainted well water, the ship was unable to cruise below Green Bay and the Beaver Islands in Lake Michigan.[6]

Manmade sickness also visited the ship in the form of "painters disease," or lead poisoning. Painting the *Michigan* was a major operation that entailed moving the galley off the ship and housing the crew on shore for up to a month while the paint dried and the smell subsided. As the paint was lead based, the sailors were susceptible to its toxicity and were often discharged as a result.[7]

Accidents in small boats, on winter ice, and with gun misfirings also caused casualties. In one such case on August 27, 1849, while President Zachary Taylor and Pennsylvania Governor William Johnston looked on, the *Michigan* attempted to fire a salute for the arrival of Vice President Millard Fillmore, who was aboard the steamer *Fashion*. As the warship had only one gun mounted, it was loaded and quick-fired successively, as it had been on the previous Saturday with the arrival of the President. After the tenth discharge a spark was missed by the sponger, and the eleventh powder charge went off prematurely. Gun Captain Patrick Murphy was slightly injured as the vent stopper blew out. The boatswains' mates servicing the piece were not so lucky. Peter Gilbert died instantly, and John Robertson lived only three more hours after the accident.[8]

Other dangers encountered on the great northern lakes were not as obvious as storms, accidents, or sickness, having their roots instead in the political corruption and avarice engendered by the white migration westward and the scramble for the region's new, untapped resources.

The *Michigan*'s first test as a patrolling warship came in response to the timber depredations of federal land in the western Great Lake states of Wisconsin, Michigan, Illinois, and Minnesota during the early 1850s. Though historically obscure, this episode became an eerie harbinger of the gangland prohibition wars to come in the 1920s and 1930s and reveals much concerning the U.S. government's attempted ban on smuggled commodities.

Both the timber depredations and the gangland wars were centered in Chicago and Milwaukee, and both revolved around smuggled merchandise—timber in the 1850s and alcohol in the 1920s. Much less publicized than gangland Chicago, the timber depredation nonetheless proved to be nearly as vicious an episode as its twentieth-century counterpart. In both instances people were killed, property was destroyed, and fear and political corruption ran rampant. A further parallel saw federal authorities called in to control the illegal trafficking. Predictably, federal forces won some battles but lost the war. These analogous historical events demonstrate the government's inevitable helplessness in the face of greed.

The Attack of the Lake Michigan Timber Pirates is necessarily a maritime account, for transportation is the key to any smuggling operation. In the 1850s, timber transportation on the Great Lakes required floating the timber to local sawmills via rivers and loading the logs or cut lumber aboard lake schooners for more distant destinations. At this time the fledgling railroads were only just influencing the lake's maritime transportation system. Therefore, the attempted federal interdiction of the timber smuggling in 1853 was in many ways similar to a military operation using combined land and naval force.

In this instance federal authorities hoped to stop the illicit timber trade by using the paddle frigate *Michigan*. Reports meticulously kept by officers of the U.S. war steamer offer a great source of information concerning the timber depredations and greatly augment the sketchy Department of the Interior reports and biased newspaper articles of the time.

The framework for the timber struggles and the navy's involvement began in 1817. In that year and again in 1822, laws were enacted giving the navy jurisdiction over federal lands as timber preserves to safeguard the navy's supply of live oak and red cedar. An act passed March 2, 1831, was even more comprehensive, making the cutting of timber on federal lands a felony.[9] Responsibility for enforcement of the timber trespass laws was, at that time, passed from the navy to the solicitor of the Treasury Department.[10]

The large Great Lake timber reserves were composed mainly of white pine, a type of tree that originally fell outside the trespass laws. White pine became protected, however, after a landmark decision of the Supreme Court in the case of the *U.S. v. Briggs*. This ruling specified that timber besides oak and cedar was now protected under the act of 1831.[11]

As early as 1838 the solicitor began working with the state district attorney of Wisconsin to control the timber depredations that were fast becoming epidemic in the upper lake states. The first feeble attempt to control timber poaching was largely unsuccessful as it flew straight in the face of the American pioneer spirit: "The Lumberman is not conscious that he himself is a trespasser on the domain of Uncle Sam. Nor is he. Has he not the best title in the World? . . . He is earning by his strong right arm his title to the trees."[12]

The cutting and sale of timber from federal land was an extremely profitable business and well worth the small risk of being caught. Penalties reached a maximum of a few hundred dollars in fines or legal fees. On the other hand, an average logging crew of twelve to sixteen men in 1850 could make the extravagant sum of $4,000 for a winter's work.

Legally, timber could be acquired in only three ways: (1) previously cut logs could be purchased at a stipulated location; (2) stumpage, or the right to cut trees on certain land, could be purchased; or (3) the timberland could be bought outright, leaving the timber cutters with the problem of what to do with the land after it had been deforested.[13]

In 1851 the two-year-old Department of the Interior, and specifically the commissioner of the General Land Office, took over the responsibility for the timberlands from the solicitor of the treasury. Timber poachers soon found that the easy days were over. Department of the Interior agents were instructed to survey the timberlands and, with the help of U.S. marshals and district attorneys, bring timber trespassers to court.[14] If the agents won their court duels, they auctioned off the seized timber. As a financial inducement, and in accordance with the act of 1831, the agents were allowed to keep half of the money made by the sale of the illegally cut timber. The other half went to the Naval Pension Fund administered by the Fourth Naval Auditor.[15]

Entire forest cuttings were now confiscated and could not be bought back on a wink, handshake, and bribe under the table. The timber barons wasted little time fighting back, however, organizing to fix the federal auctions and buy back confiscated timber at a sham price. They also threatened and intimidated informers.[16]

Federal timber agents raised the stakes, selling the timber in distant markets where the lumbermen's organization had no influence. The poachers escalated the situation once again, however, stealing or burning the confiscated lots of timber before they could be transported. Compounding the federal agents' difficulties, the timber barons, who had grown rich from years of this illegal activity, used their wealth and influence to develop local political and judicial sympathy. On a national level the timber poachers generated political debate in Congress, purposely confusing the timber smugglers' cause with the just-land-use needs of settlers.[17]

By 1850 bootleg timber smuggling became widespread, and efforts to halt it only precipitated violence. In 1852 a deputy federal agent was murdered while trying to take possession of a raft of stolen logs near Dubuque, Iowa, on the Mississippi River. In Louisiana, only the cooperation of a U.S. Navy gunboat gave federal agents the muscle needed to confiscate cut timber on the Calcasieu River.[18]

At this time the timber and cut lumber trade on the Great Lakes centered on the burgeoning lake ports of Chicago and Milwaukee. The dredging of the bar on the Chicago River in 1835 and the completion of the canal to the Illinois River catapulted Chicago, in a decade, to the world's leading port for the export of dressed lumber.[19] Milwaukee was close behind. These boom-towns depended on their prominent citizens for economic success and supported them with the vitality of the frontier.

The Whig press in Milwaukee and Chicago added tinder to the growing fire by continually pointing out the perceived injustices wrought by the federal timber agents in the name of the newly elected Democratic President Franklin Pierce. The *Chicago Tribune* went so far as to advocate resistance by force and threatened, "if they [the agents] regard their personal welfare, they had better keep clear of all such transactions as that which they are about to engage in. If men cannot have a law protect their property, they will protect it themselves."[20]

Even Democratic papers such as the *Chicago Democratic Press* reported that there was a greater prospect of war in the Manistee River Valley than there was in Europe (a reference to the Crimea).[21] The Michigan Democratic press attempted to counter the Whig papers. After all, the lumbermen in question were, with few exceptions, citizens of Wisconsin and Illinois, yet they seemed bent on denuding Michigan of its forest resources. Of the stepped-up federal activity of 1853, the *Detroit Daily Free Press* commented,

> The object is simply to effectually break up the stupendous system of despoliation that has been practiced for three or four years past, to the utter ruin of the lands trespassed upon, and to the serious detriment of the interests of our state.[22]

The *Free Press* went on to attack the timber barons, "It is perfectly well understood that men occupying high positions in society and in office, in Illinois and Wisconsin, have been engaged in these depredations to an extent known to but few."[23] Quite naturally the money made in this illegal trade trickled down to all segments of frontier society, but nowhere was its influence greater than with the Great Lakes merchant marine. The timber pirates, as will be seen, held a great deal of influence over the lakes merchant fleet, particularly vessels operating out of Chicago.[24]

Into this cauldron jumped Isaac W. Willard, perhaps the toughest timber agent yet seen on the lakes. Interior Secretary Robert McClelland chose Willard to investigate both Michigan and Minnesota. The interior secretary was well aware of the problems facing the area, having just resigned the governorship of Michigan to become the secretary of the interior in Pierce's cabinet.[25]

Soon after his appointment in 1853, Willard witnessed logging gangs defy the law and intimidate agents and informants. He also observed government boats and property put to the torch, masqueraders reenact the Boston Tea Party with timber, and his own near assassination in a deliberate attempt to burn the inn where he and a fellow timber agent slept.[26] Willard, however, working with fellow timber agent for Michigan Harvey W. Henry and U.S. Marshal George W. Rice of Michigan, was not intimidated. These three chose to prosecute their jobs to the best of their abilities, and in the process they became the most unpopular people in the area.

The timber agent wasted little time gathering a survey party while consulting with Michigan District Attorney Ward, as to the area of greatest timber depredations. Since there were few roads and fewer railroads, transportation by land was extremely difficult. Willard thus requisitioned an open boat and proceeded in the early spring to survey the rivers from the Menominee bordering with Wisconsin to the Grand and Muskegon Rivers of Michigan's Lower Peninsula, a distance of five hundred to six hundred miles of coastline. As Willard surveyed, he gathered the evidence needed to prosecute the timber pirates and informed "any persons in possession [of unlawful timber] that it was claimed by the General Government . . ." Willard's biggest headache and expense was finding guards to watch the evidence while he prepared the arrest warrants. As he explained, "it is impossible to find a resident of the district who would not betray me."[27] Nevertheless, Willard confiscated huge quantities of cut logs, shingles, and shingle bolts, mainly in the Manistee River Valley.

In the early spring of 1853, Willard and his agents surprised at least one logging crew with their employer, Benjamin Bagnall, in the Manistee River Valley. The federal agents confiscated 260,000 board feet of lumber, including 3,000,000 shingles and 3,000 cords of shingle bolts. At one point the operation became quite confused, allowing many lumbermen to escape into the woods. Bagnall himself escaped "by jumping into a boat, crossing the river and taking to the woods." Nonetheless many men were indicted, including the masters of numerous lumber vessels.[28]

The unique setting of the Great Lakes permitted many lake men to work as lumberjacks in the winter and merchant jack-tars in the summer. It is therefore no surprise that the federal raids cemented the relationship between the lumberman and the lakes merchant mariner since in many cases they were one and the same person.

Shortly after the Manistee debacle, the timber pirates met at Grand Haven, Michigan, to organize armed resistance to the federal agents. Spurred on by the powerful lumber lords and merchant captains, the jack-tars and timberjacks demanded that the government return to the old ways or they would violently rebel. The laborers boasted that the timber revolt would be carried out on land and sea against *any* government service that got in their way. The rebellion was initiated with a formalized torching of federal boats and confiscated timber.[29]

Willard, of course, had no intention of giving in to the timber thieves and held a sale of the federally confiscated timber in Chicago. The wood was bought for half price provided it would be transported by the government at no charge. Willard valued the timber at $10,000. When the agent arrived in Chicago with the first shipment, however, scores of armed men drove him off by force.[30]

The unflappable Willard soon returned by himself to Chicago, where he picked up arrest warrants for the ringleaders of the revolt. The names on the warrants included the merchant captains Higgie of the *Whirlwind,* Clark of the *Irwin,* and Hammond of the *Barnum.* They were arrested in Grand Haven by a sympathetic marshal from Chicago with five to seven others. The "arrest" only served to warn the timber poachers that federal agents were looking for them. They were all released by the marshal on their own recognizance and naturally disappeared. Several of the merchant captains were rearrested by Michigan authorities but were forcibly released by their crews. Clark escaped to Chicago, where the local judge ruled that timber stealing was insufficient grounds for detaining a man in jail. Higgie and Hammond were caught once again by federal agents in Manistee and incarcerated on a chartered ship. The detention did not last long, however, as the two captains convinced the ship's crew to let them escape, probably by advising the men that they would never find work on the lakes again if they did not release them.[31]

Meanwhile, hundreds of miles from the timber revolt, the only U.S. Navy vessel on the lakes prepared for its first spring cruise and an unwitting encounter with the timber rebellion. The *Michigan's* captain, Commander Abraham Bigelow, had served on the lakes for over two years. In the winter and early spring, while his ship lay dormant and icebound at Erie, Bigelow lived with his wife and family in Chicago. He was not totally unfamiliar with the events unfolding in the upper lake states but knew nothing of the recent hornets' nest that Willard had stirred up.[32] That the timber revolt could be any danger to his ship likely never crossed his mind. No special precautions were made to mask the sailing date, and the Navy Department's orders were not made confidential, as they would have been had the navy known there was any danger. The sailing watches were not doubled, nor were the officers instructed that they might be sailing into a dangerous situation. Everything was routine on Lake Erie the spring of 1853 now that the cholera epidemic had subsided.

The powerful shipping interests of Chicago in league with the lumbermen were well acquainted with the *Michigan,* even though the ship had not visited Chicago for three years. It was obvious to everyone in Chicago and Milwaukee that the government vessel was a threat to the lucrative smuggling operations. Navy vessels had proven themselves to be far more effective than revenue cutters in the interdiction of smuggled timber, as was demonstrated in the recent, well-publicized actions in Louisiana.[33] Historical evidence suggests that the timber pirates apparently made their plans accordingly.

The only other vessel on the lakes that might have been used to stop the smugglers was the small sail-powered revenue cutter *Ingham,* which was conspicuously absent during nearly the entire timber revolt, arriving only after it could be protected under the heavy armament of the *Michigan.* The *Ingham* was described in one Detroit paper as a "burlesque," a "shabby affair, no more fit for the service she is than the veriest scow on the river. She cannot ordinarily find her way to the lakes without the aid of a steam tug."[34]

Obviously the *Ingham* was ill equipped to deal with the timber pirates, who held control and interest over the largest, most powerful merchant steamers. These steamers often served as consorts to the smaller timber schooners, towing several at a time. The cutter probably remained absent from the fray not solely because it was controlled by the Treasury Department and was not officially involved in controlling the timber depredations, but also to keep it from ending up as a ship loss statistic. Rammings were frequent on the lakes and often fatal for the ship being rammed. Unlike the navy, the timber pirates and the Revenue Cutter Service seemed well aware that an intentional ramming at night would be nearly impossible to prove.

In the later part of April, with the ice all but gone, the *Michigan* sailed to Buffalo to provision for the coming cruise. Afterward the ship naively steamed west across Lake Erie and in the late afternoon of Thursday, May 5, passed Detroit and stood out on the Saint Clair River with the sunset on the left and evening dead ahead on Lake Huron. The warship churned the calm lake water at its usual cruising speed. The running lights on the paddle boxes were carefully tended, though the brightness of the moon and clearness of the night precluded the need for lights, giving lookouts nearly unlimited visibility. As the *Michigan* steered northwest it was followed by a moderate breeze from the southeast. It was a beautiful, calm night, with the moon creating the illusion of a silvery road to the horizon.[35]

At 2:15 A.M. the deck watch noticed a light ahead, apparently emanating from an oncoming ship. The vessels were approximately twelve to fourteen miles apart and closing at about twenty miles per hour just off Point Aux Barques, Michigan. The officer on duty ordered the *Michigan* to steer north by northwest away from the light. At 2:40 A.M. the light was still seen to be approaching "close in upon us." The warship's helm was kept to port to steer well east of the oncoming ship. A port helm, or the act of turning the wheel to the left, in the nineteenth century caused the vessel to steer to the starboard, or the opposite direction to which the wheel was turned.[36]

The oncoming vessel, however, seemed mysteriously to mirror all the *Michigan*'s evasive maneuvers. At 3:00 A.M. the ships were only a few hundred yards apart and easily visible to each other in the moonlight. The approaching vessel was recognized as a large propeller, which continued to crowd the *Michigan,* though it had some forty miles of open water in which to pass.[37]

Converging closely, the vessels were not on collision course and looked as though they would pass port side to port side. Suddenly, however, the propeller swerved ninety degrees to the east and headed straight for the *Michigan*'s port bow. Lieutenant George M. Ransom, officer of the deck, could scarcely believe his eyes as he saw the propeller change course. He did not need the flicker of the propeller's green starboard running light to tell that the ship was coming straight at him and his comrades. Ransom immediately ordered the helm hard to port in a desperate attempt to pass the propeller port to port as law dictated. The officer also picked up his megaphone to shout at the propeller to turn its own helm hard to port, but no one answered his shouted warning.

The seconds must have ticked by like hours to Ransom and the men on watch. By putting the wheel hard to port, the broadside of the iron ship became fully exposed to the bow of the onrushing propeller. The *Michigan* slowly veered to starboard but was not moving fast enough to avoid the onrushing bulk. The marauder's bow loomed over the warship's port quarter-deck rail as the deck officer sounded the general quarters alarm to wake the 120 sleeping sailors, officers, and marines. The alarm had scarcely sounded when the rending shudder of hundreds of tons of wood and iron jolted everyone awake.[38]

Outwardly, the *Michigan* could hardly have been rammed in a more vulnerable spot, having its broadside exposed to the reinforced bow of the propeller-driven steamer. The propeller slammed into the *Michigan*'s port quarter abreast the ship's mizzenmast, having first reduced the warship's quarter boat to splinters. The propeller's bow proceeded to crush the port mizzen chain plates before it staved in the side of the *Michigan.* Commander Bigelow likely awoke to find himself buried under the ornate wooden paneling that once lined his cabin. Scrambling through the wardroom to get topside, the other officers had to climb over and around the remains of the intricate joiner work that now lay shattered everywhere.[39]

Passing the exterior wreckage, Bigelow could see that the force of the collision had not only severely dented the side of his ship, but also had made a veritable junkyard of the quarterdeck, with sprung iron deck beams, planking, railing, and rigging. Upon reaching the warship's bridge, his engineers informed him that although the ship was "much broken below," it had not sustained a fatal blow and indeed was not even leaking. This was fortuitous news since the ship's after most watertight bulkhead and berth deck had also been crushed and displaced by the force of the collision. Bigelow later explained to the secretary of the navy, "Had the *Michigan* been built of wood instead of iron, there is no doubt but that she would have been cut down below the water's edge and sunk."[40]

The other steamer apparently ricocheted off the *Michigan*'s port quarter and continued mysteriously down the lake unslowed, resuming its original southeasterly precollision course. When Commander Bigelow saw that the propeller was not stopping to offer assistance in case the *Michigan* was sinking, he became infuriated and ordered the warship to give chase. Though badly damaged, the ship's steaming efficiency was unimpaired. In a short chase the warship caught the propeller, though it was apparently doing its top speed, and ran under the vessel's stern to ask for identification. Ironically, Bigelow also asked if the steamer needed assistance. After several minutes a curt reply of no damage was received. The watch on board the propeller refused to identify the vessel, however.

The *Michigan* then ran up alongside the port side of the propeller to identify the ship from its nameboard. The propeller proved to be the *Buffalo,* the largest propeller-driven steamer on the lakes.[41] Predictably, for those familiar with the timber rebellion, the *Buffalo* was proceeding downbound from Chicago and the timber rebellion. Since Commander Bigelow had no idea why his ship had been the target of deliberate attack, he let the *Buffalo* go on its way, rationalizing that the ramming had been negligence.

The steamer *Buffalo* did not come away from the ramming unscathed, however, despite refusing help from the *Michigan.* Part of its stem had been knocked off, and the ship was leaking. The *Detroit Daily Free Press* stated, "The injury was not sufficient, however, to prevent her from leaving almost immediately for down the lake."[42] Today the idea of ramming an iron ship with a wooden ship seems preposterous, but the strength and advantages of iron were not well understood in 1853, and in any case the ramming ship, regardless of hull material, always has the physical advantage.

After reviewing the written reports and accounts of the deck watch and particularly the report of Lieutenant Ransom, who remained clearly suspicious that the ramming might have been deliberate, Commander Bigelow was still baffled, finding no motive for a deliberate attack on his ship. "As I cannot suppose that the Propeller was run into the *Michigan* intentionally, I am led to conclude that there was no lookout on board of her."[43]

Bigelow's subsequent interview with Lieutenant Ransom made him aware of several disturbing facts. Even if there was no lookout aboard the *Buffalo* that night, there was no reason for the ship suddenly to swerve off course after clearly going out of its way during the previous hour to get within easy identification distance of the warship. Also, if there was no lookout or helmsman, why did the vessel immediately resume its downbound course after the collision without offering assistance or identification?

Nonetheless, the commander filed an official protest at Mackinac Island and recommended that the Navy Department bring suit against the owner of the *Buffalo,* Mr. Walbridge, for the "careless, wanton, and culpable" manner in which the steamer was piloted. Ironically, the *Michigan* limped to Chicago, and the heart of the timber revolt, for the month-long $1,674.16 refit the attack necessitated.[44]

In Chicago, Commander Bigelow attempted to garner evidence concerning the collision, either to explain what had happened or to help in a suit against Walbridge. While his ship was repaired he discovered that the master of the propeller *Republic* was at the helm of his ship during the early morning hours of May 6, and he witnessed the *Buffalo* swerve off course to hit the *Michigan.* As the *Republic* was registered out of Cleveland, its master was either unaware of the possible plot of the timber pirates or was unintimidated by their actions. The *Republic*'s captain did not hesitate to place his testimony in writing.[45]

It is, of course, historical speculation that the ramming of the *Michigan* was intentional. The incident was never brought to trial, quite probably because the evidence is circumstantial. Several facts are clear, however. The officer on deck believed it was intentional. The *Buffalo* crowded the *Michigan* before the event and attempted to flee afterward. The episode occurred within days of the openly declared timber rebellion, and the *Buffalo* was downbound from Chicago. Additionally, the movements of the *Michigan* were easily predictable, observed, and transmitted via telegraph. In this light, it is interesting to note that from that time onward, Bigelow's orders concerning the timber rebellion and his ship's movements were transmitted via "Confidential Letters," the navy's nineteenth-century version of top secret.[46]

The collision put the *Michigan* out of action for nearly two months. A similar impact would have proven fatal to the revenue cutter *Ingham*, which nonetheless arrived in Chicago on June 15, under command of Captain Sands.[47] Safe near the bulk of repairing *Michigan*, the small ship could do little more than show the flag. The federal government was slow to react to the timber rebellion. Neither government vessel was prepared for hostilities, nor did they receive orders to do anything about the timber looting. This would soon change.

Unaware of the near tragedy that occurred on Lake Huron, timber agent Willard plodded gamely on in his attempts to save the public forests, hampered now by judicial and political corruption and the incessant intimidation of the timber lords and their men. The Whig press in Wisconsin and Illinois fully supported the lumbermen. The provocative articles helped enlist every poor timberjack and shingle cutter on the western lakes, turning the revolt into a sham patriotic revolution against federal tyranny. Letters of complaint against the federal agents for malice, violence, and blackmail flooded the Interior Department.[48]

In contrast, Willard seemed to have the backing of the press of Michigan. The *Free Press* countered the Whig papers with a volley of its own:

> We will undertake to predict that there is not money enough among the timber depredators to induce Mr. Willard, the timber Agent, to do any thing else than his plain, straight-forward duty; and if the timber-hooking friends of the [Chicago] *Tribune* think otherwise, they had better try him. And as for Col. Rice, the Marshal, he will do his duty no less promptly and faithfully.[49]

In mid-June Willard's team served several indictments on the masters of timber vessels in a Detroit court. Unfortunately, due to bureaucratic stalling, this blow to the timber pirates was not followed by indictments against the lumbermen operating on the coasts. The timber pirates used this opportunity to steal back the illegal timber while the evidence against them gathered dust. According to an exasperated Willard,

> he [Michigan D.A. Ward] expects me to attend to take charge of the arrests, collect the witnesses on a coast of six hundred miles which will have to be made in an open boat all to be done in three weeks while it takes him eight weeks to order such precepts made as would not take an ordinary man eight minutes.[50]

District Attorney Ward had promised the indictments in five days to Chicago

Judge McLean, Jr., in whom Willard had no faith anyway. To make matters worse for the agents, Ward left to vacation at the world's fair without delivering the papers. By the first part of August, having seen no progress on the indictments, Willard and Rice decided to bypass Ward's obvious stalling tactics by enlisting the help of a Michigan judge. Obtaining a search warrant, they inspected Ward's office and found the correct papers. These were then given to Michigan Judge Drummund (no first name given), who arranged for a trial the second week of September.[51]

It was also in the first part of August, after having circumvented Ward's stalling, that Willard and Rice indicted sixty mill owners for their part in the timber depredations.[52] It seems ironic that for all the screams of federal tyranny flowing from the rebellion, Willard obviously was not picking on the poor settlers, targeting instead the real depredators: the rich lumber barons, mill owners, and merchant vessel owners who were growing richer by the day on the public trust.

Willard and his agents were nevertheless still losing the battle for the forests. His enemies escaped by sea at will, and the vast quantities of seized timber were disappearing, restolen by the timber pirates at their leisure. Six hundred miles of coast was too much for a few agents to cover. Willard therefore decided to concentrate his efforts on the Manistee Valley, where only one-sixth of the shingles and one-third of the confiscated shingle bolts remained under his control.[53]

The situation, however, was about to turn around, for unknown to Willard, the secretaries of the interior and the navy had come to an agreement. True to the worst fears of the timber lords, the USS *Michigan* officially was thrown into the battle for the forests.[54]

Having returned to Erie after repairs from the first disastrous cruise up the lakes, Commander Abraham Bigelow received his first confidential orders from the navy secretary since he had taken command of the *Michigan*. On August 18, James C. Dobbin ordered Bigelow to proceed to Kalamazoo, Michigan, and cooperate with the U.S. marshal "in pursuing and arresting certain depredators upon the public lands." The commander was to "exercise strict economy in any expenditures as they were to be reimbursed by the Department of the Interior." This time the warship sailed unannounced up the lakes without mishap, picking up Marshal Rice on the way to Kalamazoo.[55]

Arriving at the mouth of the Manistee River on August 30, timber agent Willard was pleasantly surprised to see the *Michigan* hove into site. The federal agent and navy commander met and agreed that combined land and sea operations should commence immediately against the timber pirates. As Willard stayed to guard the Manistee River, Marshal Rice, on board the *Michigan,* raided the Herring River located twenty miles to the north. Backed by a platoon of marines in the ship's cutter, the marshal was able to capture another of the outlaw merchant captains, but the timberjacks escaped to the woods. Bigelow reported, "Two vessels which had come over for the purpose of taking away forcibly a quantity of shingle bolts, which had been seized by the Government Agent, got underway on our approach and left the coast."[56]

Keeping in mind the Navy Department's orders to economize whenever possible, Bigelow did not give chase to the two merchant ships. After the Herring River raid the *Michigan* dropped its prisoners off at New Buffalo, where the Michigan Central rail line whisked them off to Detroit and a speedy trial.

Arriving by sea unexpectedly, the marshal captured many more lumbermen in Chicago and spirited them to New Buffalo before the local courts could free them.[57] In only two weeks the presence of the cruiser, acting in cooperation with the federal agents, had knocked the wind out of the timber revolt. Faster than any other ship on the lakes, the *Michigan* seemed to be everywhere at once. There was, however, one outstanding fugitive who had eluded federal agents. Benjamin Bagnall, who had escaped in a small boat after being arrested in the first Manistee River raid, was at this time still at large, holed up in Milwaukee.

Commander Bigelow, apparently acting on a tip, ordered his ship to Milwaukee, arriving at 1:00 P.M. Friday, September 9. The federal agents quickly related to local authorities their intention to arrest Bagnall. Within hours, Bagnall was "arrested" by Wisconsin Deputy Marshal C. C. Cotton and "given parole."[58] The arrest and instant parole of these criminals was a common ploy used by sympathetic lawmen to warn the timber barons of their danger. Bagnall used Cotton's warning to disappear. The county law enforcers, not as influenced by Bagnall, were displeased by this turn of events. County Judge Welles immediately had County Sheriff Connover arrest Cotton on contempt-of-court charges. He also had Connover smoke out and rearrest Bagnall.[59]

A very complex jurisprudence then took place in the Wisconsin courts. The debate centered on whether the state, county, city, or federal law held sway in the case.[60] Bagnall's political power was obvious, and it was not at all clear that he would be brought to justice, particularly on his home ground. As the federal agents waited impatiently on board the *Michigan,* they received some unexpected support from on high. President Pierce, intently following the war on the timber depredators, sent a letter to the U.S. marshal of the District of Wisconsin ordering Bagnall's arrest. The marshal was to deliver him to the custody of the marshal of Michigan for "removing from lands of the United States with intent to dispose of the same for his own use and benefit, certain timber of the United States, contrary to provisions of the statute in such case made and provided."[61]

The trial naturally caused "a great deal of excitement" in Milwaukee and lasted the entire month. It was not every day that the government tackled the rich and powerful. Even the solicitor of the treasury added his weight to the court battle by sending another arrest warrant to the Wisconsin marshal. Finally, on September 30, the court ruled the trial "an absolute nullity" due to the fact that there was a law against states aiding or hindering federal courts.[62]

Bagnall was turned over to Wisconsin Marshal Ableman, who with the help of the federal agents and possibly marines from the *Michigan,* forcibly arrested the lumber baron for the third time. Bagnall was hustled on board the waiting steamer while his lawyers argued in vain at the dock. Suits were instigated against the marshal, and the Milwaukee press lamented, "there is no longer any security or safety for the liberty of the citizen" and labeled the arrest "A High Handed Outrage."[63]

Nonetheless, at great expense to the government, Bagnall was finally delivered up for trial in Detroit, where he was fined and the rest of the remaining timber in Manistee was officially confiscated and sold. The *Michigan* with Willard on board had not remained idle during the Bagnall trial but had patrolled Green Bay in search of more timber depredators. In mid-September Bigelow reported to Secretary Dobbin on their progress, stating,

> The marshal and timber agent find a favorable change in their position since this vessel has been ordered to cooperate—The tone of the marauders is changed, and they have ceased to abuse those employed by the government to protect the timber. Public opinion in this matter seems also to have undergone a change, and they no longer find advocates in the editors, of the public prints.[64]

The *Michigan* continued its patrols off the coast for several more weeks, capturing many prisoners and delivering them to New Buffalo for the train ride to Detroit.[65] Progress against the timber pirates went so well after the Bagnall case that by mid-October, Willard and Michigan Deputy Marshal William Moore decided the ship was no longer needed.

Before heading down the lakes, however, the *Michigan* was subject to one last parting shot, or bad joke, from the Chicago press. The Navy Department in Washington was shocked to read about the loss of the U.S. steamer *Michigan* in the October 6 edition of the *New York Herald*. The *Herald*, working on information supplied by the *Chicago Tribune*, reported the stranding of the *Michigan* during a storm on Lake Michigan.

Bigelow explained to the Navy Department,

> The employment of this vessel to aid the Marshal and his Deputies in executing the laws, has excited towards me the ill will and resentment of a class of men who have grown rich from the profits of this nefarious business and I have been subjected to abuse in a low paper, the *Chicago Tribune*, which is their organ. The reported loss of this vessel is from their malice.[66]

The government's victory over the timber depredators in 1853 was short-lived. In 1854 the timber barons, having been forced from the forest, employed a much more successful tactic than open rebellion. They turned their wealth and power into a tool to influence Congress. The new tactic paid off in spades.

By 1855 Congress disbanded the Timber Agencies under the guise of replacing them with a more economical system. The tough, dedicated, and uncorrupted agents such as Isaac Willard were let go. Responsibility for controlling the timber depredations was once again transferred to the local land offices because funding for enforcement had been eliminated. As one historian of the timber wars concluded, "Pushed by the routine business of their office, restricted by a lack of money for investigation, blocked on all sides by the stubborn frontier population, the local land offices did at best a haphazard job of law enforcement."[67]

It was soon business as usual for the timber pirates. The Treasury Department was also helpless to stop the transportation of smuggled timber on the lakes. By 1857 six new fifty-ton revenue cutters were nearing completion but were not in any case the swift steam-powered vessels that were really needed for the suppression of smuggling.[68] The navy in the special instance of the timber rebellion of 1853 was willing to let the Interior Department rent the services of the *Michigan* for a month or two, but the ship could not be transferred to the revenue service indefinitely.[69]

The May 6, 1853, ramming incident went no further with the Navy Department when it became apparent that it would have to prove in court that the collision was caused intentionally or by the negligence of the pilot of the *Buffalo*. Cases of negligence or conspiracy were extremely difficult to prove with only circumstantial evidence. Commander Bigelow, via his purser

Taylor, attempted to get the *Buffalo*'s owner, Walbridge, to reimburse the navy for damages, but to no avail.

Bigelow also continued to advocate for a lawsuit against Walbridge with his superiors in the Navy Department, apparently hoping to bring all the facts to light in a trial. Although there is no written evidence that Bigelow suspected a conspiracy, the vigor with which he pursued the case may indicate that he harbored deep suspicions. By the end of September, 1853, however, the commander was ordered to drop any proceedings against Walbridge. The navy explained in a terse telegraph message that it was "[n]ot expedient at this time to bring suit against owner of Buffalo will try and arrange matter without one."[70]

The federal victory in the timber rebellion of 1853 became a footnote in the Interior Department's ill-fated war to contain the timber depredations in the Old Northwest. Timber thieving and smuggling became too profitable and competitive a business to be controlled using any methods less than military force. Indeed, the *Michigan* proved to be an ideal tool for this task. Fast and powerful, its cruiser attributes were exceedingly useful. Though military force, in this case, proved it could stop the smuggling, the government eventually was unable to sustain this effort due to the powerful timber lobby.

In 1877 the government again unsuccessfully attempted to stop the timber trespassers. Yet the depredations continued virtually unabated until the turn of the century, when the timber thieves ran into the final penalty for their crime: there were no more woodlands.[71]

IV The Beaver/Mackinac War and the Assassination of King Strang

THE CREW AND OFFICERS SERVING ON BOARD the *Michigan* were like people anywhere: some were happy, some were argumentative, others seemed a bit deranged by their actions. In the latter case, for instance, the mischief created by Lieutenant William W. Pollock during and after cruises in the mid-1840s seems almost legendary. His final caper took place after he took offense at a newspaper article printed about his actions at the American Hotel in Buffalo. Apparently Pollock got into an altercation with a waiter at the hotel and created an immense commotion. The fracas attracted the attention of a newspaper reporter who printed an unflattering portrayal of Pollock in the next edition. Pollock, who did not seem to get along with anyone, least of all his shipmates, marched down to the *Buffalo Commercial Advertiser*'s office brandishing a pistol. Reporter William Jewett's instinct to turn and flee as Pollock opened fire saved his life. He was hit three times in the back pocket. His wallet caught two of the pistol balls and other sundries in his pocket caught the third. His pride was all that was injured. Pollock was tried, sentenced for attempted murder, and sent to Auburn Prison in Cayuga County, New York.[1]

Fortunately, Pollock's mental state was aberrant, and incidents like this were few and far between for the crew and officers of the warship. A close scrutiny of the accounts and incidents that concerned the ship over time reveals the overall professional conduct, the genuine selflessness and bravery of the crew and officers, and the reasonably objective or unbiased viewpoints (even with 20/20 hindsight) the commanding officers used to scrutinize many difficult problems, sometimes under tremendous pressure. The destruction of the Mormon colony on Beaver Island, however, points to circumstances in which the motives of the *Michigan*'s officers may have been decidedly less noble, judged by today's standards.

Religious history is difficult to analyze. The emotions involved tend to cloud, color, and psychologically influence the perceptions of participants, historians, and readers. The assassination of Mormon leader James Jesse Strang and the destruction of his sect on Beaver Island, Lake Michigan, in 1856, is no exception.

That the USS *Michigan* was involved in this tragedy may seem at first glance to be one of those inexplicable coincidences of history. On careful inspection, however, the relationship of the navy vessel to this calamity cannot be dismissed as pure chance. Historian Milo M. Quaife wrote of the connection, stating

> One hesitates, in the absence of specific evidence, to charge a responsible
> official with prostituting an agency- of the United States government to the
> furtherance of a private plot of assassination against one of its citizens; but the
> course of the commander of the *Michigan* before and after the assassination
> lends support to such a theory.[2]

Though Quaife's extensive study of James Strang and his Mormon sect reveals a possible relationship between the *Michigan,* or at least its commander, and the tragic circumstances that occurred on the island, he did not use the available naval records.

To better investigate Strang's assassination, this chapter will present a brief history of Strang and his church. There has been a prodigious amount of material written about James Strang and his people, seemingly from all points of view; thus it is not the intent here to constitute a comprehensive history of the church or the man.

Of perhaps greater importance is a study of the Beaver and Mackinac Island economic relationship and how it changed with Strang's attempted colonization of Beaver Island between the years of 1847 and 1856. This analysis may demonstrate that although religious bigotry certainly existed, to the detriment of the Strangites, it may have functioned as a facade for a deeper economic struggle—a dilemma that more easily explains the presence of a U.S. government naval vessel and is the reason this chapter is entitled "The Beaver/Mackinac War."

Finally, an examination of the *Michigan*'s archival documents will shed more light on the alleged conspiracy and the U.S. government's role in it. It seems possible that had this episode generated a court trial, some of the navy ship's officers might have gone to prison.

STRANG AND THE MORMONS

James J. Strang was a prolific writer and left in his wake many written sources of information, including two newspapers of which he was editor (numbering well over 100 volumes), many religious dictates, and a fragmentary diary and autobiography. Combining this information with eyewitness accounts, statements of surviving relatives, and non-Mormon newspaper reports creates a fairly complete, if not always accurate, record of his life and the tragedy that befell his followers.[3]

Jesse James Strang was born in Scipio, New York, on March 21, 1813. By 1816 the Strang family moved to Hanover, New York, where the boy grew to adulthood. Though apparently a sickly child, Strang later acquired a propensity for learning and great powers of oratory. His diary shows him to be a well-informed young person, perhaps overly conscious of the seeming hopelessness of the world's political situation. Young James saw himself as a "philosopher" who would devote his life "to the service of mankind."[4]

Beyond a healthy amount of ambition, Strang was fascinated with the idea of personal notoriety, chastising himself on several occasions, "Should I die now I have lived in vain. Oh the curse: to have done nothing for posterity." "I ought to have been a member of the Assembly or a Brigadier General before this time." "Fame, fame alone of all the productions of man's: folly may survive."[5]

Strang toyed with the idea of military service but, being from a relatively poor farming background, eventually got caught up in several more mundane pathways to procuring a livelihood. He taught school and edited a paper in Randolph and finally worked once again on a farm where he studied law and was subsequently admitted to the New York Bar by 1836. On October 20, 1835, a mill pond accident nearly ended Strang's brief and all-too-uneventful (for him) life. His survival placed him face-to-face with the nightmare and motivator of all young souls: "I would not live forever."[6]

In the early 1830s young Strang decided to transpose his name, eventually becoming James Jesse Strang. He worked as a lawyer at Silver Creek and Ellington, but since there was so little business and, as he put it, "Youth is not rich in its stores of time," therefore, he was easily swayed to move to Burlington, Wisconsin, to live near the Pearce family. Friends from his Hanover days, the Pearces had become relatives due to his marriage to Mary Pearce around 1836.[7] In Burlington, Strang formed a law partnership with C. P. Barnes.[8]

Mary's sister was the wife of Moses Smith, a Mormon since 1832. His brother-in-law apparently so influenced the now thirty-year-old James that he undertook a pilgrimage to Nauvoo, Illinois, early in 1844 to meet the founder of Mormonism, Joseph Smith. On February 25, 1844, Strang was baptized into the Mormon faith. The young, articulate convert apparently so impressed Smith that he was almost immediately made an elder and assigned the task of surveying the White River near Burlington for the possible location of a Mormon community.[9]

Though Strang threw himself into the task with his usual fervor and duly reported his findings, an untimely calamity overtook the Mormon Church. Joseph and Hyrum Smith, surrendering to a summons of the governor of Illinois, were lynched by a mob in Carthage on June 27, 1844. The Church, minus its prophet, was thrown into turmoil. Though Brigham Young and the Council of Twelve assumed leadership, Strang and Sidney Rigdom also claimed to be the appointed heirs of Smith. Strang produced a letter allegedly written by Joseph Smith on June 18 and received by Strang on July 9. In it, Smith, knowing of his coming fate, appointed Strang his heir and assigned him the task of continuing the Mormon Church at Voree, Wisconsin. Voree, meaning the Garden of Peace, was to be located near Burlington at present-day Spring Prairie on the White River, where Strang had just completed his survey.[10]

In the power struggle that ensued, Strang was excommunicated from the Church of Jesus Christ of Latter-day Saints, and he in turn excommunicated Young and the Twelve. Strang was not without support; a good many influential leaders rallied to Voree to further his cause. Brigham Young, however, prevailed with the greater number of Saints and within a few years moved the locus of the church to Utah. Strang was far from discouraged by Young's success. The Mormon church at Kirtland, Ohio, still recognized Strang as the new prophet, and the Strangites at Voree grew in number under Strang's leadership.[11]

On September 13, 1845, Strang uncovered several brass plates, working from an angelic vision. When deciphered by the new prophet, these plates implied that James J. Strang was holy vicegerent on earth. The discovery of the plates, Strang's initiation of the *Voree Herald,* the ruthlessness of Young and the Twelve, plus many Mormons' misgivings about heading west all insured that the Strangite congregation grew. By April 1846, the Strangite church was formally organized, with Strang as prophet and John C. Bennett as prime minister.[12]

Voree increased in population, but its organization, a theocratic communism, insured that the community would be plagued by crushing poverty since all property was jointly owned. People with money were quite naturally reluctant to join. In addition, those who worked hardest received no more benefit than the laziest, so community projects lagged. As will be seen, however, the grinding poverty of Strang's Saints at Voree insured that there would be little, if any, religious persecution by neighbors.[13]

In August, 1846, James Strang had a vision of a new land for his people, "a land amidst wide waters." Voree proved to have problems beyond the fledgling church's power to solve. First, the land in Voree was already owned and would not be donated to the penniless Mormon sect. It was obvious to all that under its current system the church was unlikely financially to pull itself up by its own bootstraps. Second, the Strangites were fractionalizing. Apparently, though the prophet was certainly not the crazed tyrant the gentile papers would later make him out to be, he was at best a dubious judge of character, or perhaps by his calling, he too easily overlooked obvious faults in people. In any case he was soon surrounded by an untrustworthy and factitious flock.[14]

The new land amid wide waters that Strang was referring to in his prophecy was the Beaver Island archipelago in northern Lake Michigan. The largest of these islands was Beaver Island, located some forty miles west-southwest of the vitally important Straits of Mackinac. The island contained nearly sixty square miles of arable land, lakes, streams, and forest. The Straits of Mackinac channeled all ship traffic going to or from the growing Lake Michigan ports past Beaver Island and its perfect deep-water harbor, Paradise Bay. Adding to these bounties was the fact that it was located in the middle of the best fishing grounds on Lake Michigan.

Twenty to thirty Native American families inhabited the island in 1847. It also had one trading post at Paradise Bay with some seasonally occupied fishing shanties. Knowing the land had been surveyed by the government and would soon be up for auction, Strang and a party of four studied the island firsthand in the spring of 1847. The proprietor of the North West Company's trading post, John Fisk of Rochester, New York, was also contacted. Thinking his post would do more business with the Strangites, Fisk welcomed the idea of a few families moving to the island. Strang initiated his congregation's move to the island by building a mission to convert the "Lamanites" (Native Americans). That winter four Strangite families lived on the island. By the next winter there were twelve.[15]

It was not until the next fall and winter, however, that Strang made the momentous decisions concerning the operation and direction of his church, which unwittingly planted the seeds of his own destruction. In the fall of 1849 Strang journeyed to the east to lobby for a reserve for his people on Beaver Island. Though he reportedly influenced several leading politicians, the government reported it did not own all the lands desired by the Saints. The islands were possibly considered state property. In any case the government recognized squatters' rights, so Strang committed his people to the large-scale migration from Voree to Beaver Island in the spring of 1850.[16]

The new colony on Beaver Island was to be a sort of theocratic commonwealth. Though they were expected to live in the communities set up for them on the island, each church family received 160 acres of farm and timberland in the interior. In return for the ownership of the land the Saints were expected to contribute one-tenth of their profits to the church. As might be expected, the economic about-face of the Strangites was dramatic. By the summer of 1850, fifty Strangite families lived on the island. The island's infrastructure made dramatic leaps forward. Before long a sawmill, a road, and a schooner were built.[17]

Strang's decision to embrace polygamy has been linked to his eventual downfall, damning him and his followers in the eyes of neighbors. Polygamy, however, was never a significant factor, either with the Strangites or with their neighbors, and seems not to have been practiced by more than twenty families. Strang himself took an additional wife that summer before his public announcement supporting polygamy.[18] Although polygamy probably hastened the onset of the religious bigotry, it was nonetheless a smoke screen issue.

Of far more consequence were the economic reforms instituted by Strang that automatically positioned Beaver Island as a powerful and growing rival of Mackinac Island, its neighbor to the northeast. Northern Lake Michigan, particularly Mackinac Island, was still reeling economically from the decline of the fur industry. The fledgling fishing industry on Mackinac was tenuous, even though it had no rivals. Historian Quaife explained the position of Mackinac before the settlement of Beaver by relating that Mackinac

> had the advantages of an entrenched position as center of trade. Considerable capital was invested in the business houses and other property of the place, all of which would be lost should trade go to another center. Consequently, as long as a rival was lacking, Mackinac continued to dominate the trade of the surrounding region.[19]

The abrupt introduction of a rival economic center on Beaver Island, staffed with organized, industrious people, insured that conflict akin to war would ensue with Mackinac Island. This war, sometimes hot but most often the cold war of propaganda and religious prejudice, commenced almost immediately and lasted for six years. The frontier governments, both local and state, were not only helpless to end the conflict but were generally in the forefront of the hostilities, fomenting trouble between the islands.

Before the arrival of the Beaver Island Strangites, Mackinac Island had no economic rivals. The tiny population meant that few counties near the straits had organized, thus the only traditional locus for state power in the area was Mackinac Island. Mackinac, with its fort and strategic location, had been hotly contested during the War of 1812 and was still the only regional seat of political and judicial power. Naturally, elected officials on Mackinac had no incentive to calm hostilities until their side gained the upper hand over their new rivals.

Despite Strang's overtures to the federal government for help and intervention, it remained common knowledge that the Strangites were critical of the U.S. system and considered their cause to supersede any national loyalty. In March, 1850, Strang's missionary in the east, George J. Adams, went so far as to publicly pray for the destruction of the United States. The adverse publicity engendered by such flagrant acts, plus Strang's public criticism of the government's actions in the recent war with Mexico, likely condemned him in the eyes of Washington's elite.[20]

With this in mind it is not surprising that the federal authorities were not only loath to get involved in the conflict to protect the Strangites but eventually put their only real power in the area, the USS *Michigan,* at the disposal of state authorities. These same state authorities had a vested interest in the destruction of Beaver Island as an economic center.

The fishermen of the area and traders of the North West Company were the first to perceive the threat from the Mormon sect and reacted accordingly. On July 4, 1850, the traders who lived on Beaver Island invited area fishermen, mostly from Mackinac Island, to join in their festivities, the culmination of which would be the expulsion by force of the Strangites. The first July 4 salute to be fired, however, came from the alert Saints, using a cannon procured for just such an emergency. The round shot from the gun skipped passed Whiskey Point, on which the trading post was located, and quickly deflated the revelry. A few more ranging shots, the sight of armed Saints on parade near their garrisoned tabernacle, and a schooner full of Saints anchored in the harbor ended the celebration and hurried the fishermen on their way.[21]

Spurred by victory in the Battle of Whiskey Point, James Strang consolidated his power. Four days after the Saints' bloodless triumph, the economic reforms instituted by Strang were symbolically formalized in his coronation as king of his church before some four hundred of his followers. The divine right of kingship was bestowed on Strang in the interpretation of yet another set of plates recovered by the Saints, called the Plates of Laban. Strang's translation of these plates was published in *The Book of the Law of the Lord* and contained minutely detailed instructions for forming the monarchical commonwealth with which the Strangites were now ruled.[22] The new king's powers were strictly limited to church members, and there is little indication that Strang abused his power. Although the church constitution contained a proviso for the implementation of capital punishment, the most stringent discipline ever doled out amounted to whippings.

The cold war between Mackinac and Beaver Islands now began in earnest, exacerbated by the defection of Strangite George Adams to Mackinac Island. Strang's efforts to counter the growing propaganda assault on his people can be seen in his initiation of the newspaper *Northern Islander*. Nevertheless, the counterpropaganda was doomed to failure before it started. The area fishermen and traders feared for their livelihood and were ready "to believe any accusation, however preposterous, that might be made against the Mormons."[23] The additional strain of a two-year cholera epidemic, which was particularly bad at Mackinac Island, added to the general tensions.[24]

Having failed in their direct assault at Whiskey Point, the Mackinac Islanders attacked Strang through the legal system. Working on accusations made by Adams, Mackinac County Sheriff Tully O'Malley arrested Strang on October 20, 1850, on charges that he threatened Adams's wife. The case was heard before Justice Charles O'Malley and thrown out on procedural problems.[25] It seems probable that Strang knew more about the legal system than did anyone on Mackinac Island.

It is interesting to note that the first call of the USS *Michigan* to Beaver Island occurred on October 9, 1850, during an attempt to aid the ill-fated steamer *A.D. Patchin* on the rocks off Killegalee Islands. For the first time the *Michigan* obtained cordwood from the island to sustain its dwindling coal reserves. The new dock in Paradise Bay and cut wood selling for fifty cents a cord demonstrate Beaver Island's newfound economic notoriety, especially for steamships.[26]

The spring of 1851 saw a renewal of the minor conflicts of the preceding year. In April one such occurrence engendered the first exchange of gunfire between Strangites and fishermen. The fusillade began when a Strangite constable confronted fishermen selling whiskey to Native Americans. Though no one was injured, the episode served as yet another pretext for Mackinac Island to launch legal proceedings against the Saints. Mackinac Sheriff Granger descended on Beaver Island with a posse of thirty Native Americans and eight to ten "drunken Irishmen."[27] Though thirty-eight Strangites were peaceably arrested, all were eventually acquitted.

While the Mackinac posse was still assembled, it made a raid on Hog Island, where Strang and a few men attempted to salvage a yawl lost in a steamer wreck. The posse destroyed both the yawl and the Strangite craft in their attempt to trap the Saints. Strang and his men, however, made a break in an old leaky fishing boat, leaving one man behind in their haste. After an adventurous two weeks, the Strangites were finally able to return, finding their comrade alive and unhurt.[28]

In May, 1851, the first blood was shed in the Beaver/Mackinac War. Two fishermen assaulted a Strangite who attempted to meet Sheriff Granger on Whiskey Point. Beaver Island Constable William Chambers, under orders of County Judge J. M. Greig (an elected Strangite) and Justice M. M. Aldrich, attempted to arrest the two fishermen who were holed up at the Bennett brothers' cabin on the island. The Bennett brothers were recalcitrant fishermen living on Beaver Island who apparently relished the possibility of harassing the Strangites whenever possible. As Chambers approached the house, he was fired on and wounded. The posse of thirty to forty men supporting Chambers quickly opened a fusillade of fire on the house, killing Thomas Bennett and wounding his brother, Samuel. Of the two remaining fishermen, one was captured and the other escaped. Though the posse's action was justified, the surrounding communities condemned the slaying as outright murder.[29]

The hysteria engendered by the Bennett slaying precipitated some of the most bizarre and highly questionable historic episodes involving the USS *Michigan*. On May 9, 1851, very soon after the Bennett incident, the navy ordered Commander Oscar Bullus to proceed to Lake Michigan under orders of U.S. District Attorney George C. Bates of Detroit. The chain of orders releasing the vessel for civil use was initiated by the U.S. commander in chief, Millard Fillmore. The president was visiting a brother in Detroit and no doubt became exposed to the inflammatory newspaper reports of the Bennett slaying.

Though Fillmore was a Whig, Michigan Democrats appealed to him to solve the Beaver Island problem. The Democrats in Michigan were naturally reticent to engender the anger of a large voting block such as Strang's Saints.

Their solution, therefore, was to pass the buck to the visiting president, knowing well that any move was likely to be the wrong one.[30]

Fillmore in turn looked to his secretary of state, who, under the advice of Democratic Senator Stephen Douglas, decided to begin legal proceedings to break up the Beaver Island sect. The attorney general was ordered to instruct the state district attorney of Michigan to begin proceedings against Strang with the full cooperation of the navy.[31]

Meanwhile the *Michigan* was at Dunkirk, New York, escorting the president and the secretary of the navy to the festivities marking the opening of the Erie Railroad's Road of the Hudson to the Lakes. The warship conducted Fillmore and William A. Graham from Detroit to the festivities and returned between May 15 and 17. Afterward the ship was dismissed from its duties as escort and took on supplies and coal in Erie, setting course for Lake Michigan on May 20.[32]

Before the *Michigan* reached Detroit, District Attorney Bates had time to acquire warrants for Strang and several others on charges of treason, robbery of the mails, counterfeiting, and trespassing on U.S. land. The embarkation of forty armed men under "General" Schwartz and Marshal William Knox, as backup to the warship's complement, gives some indication of the hysteria-generated action anticipated by the authorities. A U.S. commissioner also embarked on the expedition so that court could be held on board the *Michigan.*

The saga, according to Bates, began at 3:30 P.M., May 23, with the warship anchoring a "half musket" shot from the Mackinac County circuit courthouse. District Attorney Bates strode into the court and summarily arrested the presiding judge, J. M. Greig. Greig, a Strangite, was nevertheless the duly elected magistrate of the court and attempted to place Bates under arrest for contempt of court. Bates, however, gesturing toward the warship anchored nearby with its guns run out, stated that any hesitation or resistance on Greig's part would result in the destruction of the building and his own death. (There is no indication as to how Bates expected to escape the same fate if a broadside were fired into the building at that time.) Greig was forced to comply and was placed in irons belowdecks.

The *Michigan* weighed anchor and slowly steamed through the straits on course for Beaver Island. The reason for Greig's kidnapping soon became clear. The irate judge was hauled on deck and threatened with hanging from a yardarm if he did not inform Bates of the whereabouts of James Strang's house. Since Bates issued the threat, Greig did not take it seriously until

Commander Bullus informed him that the ship, officers, and crew were at the district attorney's complete disposal. The navy men would have no choice but to carry out Bates's orders, so Greig had no choice but comply.

At 2:00 A.M. the ship anchored off the coast of Beaver Island, having completed the leisurely five-knot journey. With cloth-muffled oars, a body of sailors pulled ashore, escorting Bates. The landing party, armed with cutlasses and pistols, made its way to Strang's house with the help of a shaded lantern and map supplied by Greig. Upon reaching their objective, a guard was placed at each door, and the main body of sailors entered the house, catching Strang and his family fast asleep.

By daylight Strang was a prisoner on board the *Michigan.* Threatened in the same manner as Greig, he was forced to issue a request that thirty other Saints board the ship, which by now had anchored in Paradise Bay near the new community of Saint James. The trial was to be held under the awning-shaded deck when the last of the defendants arrived. Since some of the witnesses lived near Detroit and were not present, the Strangites and their families—more than 100 people—were transported to Detroit on the *Michigan* for the trial.[33]

Strang's version of the episode, though much less colorful, is no less meaningful in its implications. Strang does not mention the early morning raid on his house, explaining instead that Judge Greig persuaded the authorities peaceably to arrest the Strangites and hold a commissioner's court on board the ship. Tensions were obviously heightened to the point that the forcible seizure of Strang and the other codefendants would have been the outcome of any resistance. It seems plausible that the plan for this action had been formulated and may have been the basis for the story related by Bates.[34]

In any case the prophet and thirty-eight followers were arrested, the commissioner's court was abandoned, and the prisoners were delivered to Detroit on board the *Michigan* for trial. The trial lasted from the end of May to July 9. Detroit newspapers quarreled over the possible outcome, with the Whig *Advertiser* attacking Strang and the Democratic *Free Press* defending him. During the trial the *Michigan* became an invaluable conveyance of witnesses and accused, leaving Detroit on June 17, picking up even more accused and witnesses at the various islands and settlements, and delivering them to Detroit by June 22.[35]

The first charge before the court concerned mail robbery. It is unclear why the trial lasted as long as it did. There was little or no corroborating evidence to support the allegations that Strang and his followers had held up a mail train, so the defendants were acquitted. As it soon became evident that the government's case for the other charges was just as flimsy as the first, U.S. District Court Judge Ross Wilkins dismissed all charges. James Strang conducted the defense with his usual fervor and inspired oratory, making it evident to even the unsympathetic Whig jury that the proceedings were inspired for simple harassment.[36]

The reasons for the Mackinac/Beaver War had by that time become obscured behind an impregnable wall of religious bigotry. Following Strang's courtroom victory in Detroit, Beaver Island became fairly secure, yet the unremitting propaganda war, if anything, worsened. Strang realized that the inhabitants of Beaver Island would remain at the mercy of the Mackinac County courts until it gained some political clout. He therefore resolved to run for the state legislature in 1852.

At this time Beaver Island was under the legislative jurisdiction of Newaygo County and the judicial jurisdiction of Mackinac County. On November 2, 1852, James Strang, carrying all 165 votes of his island, became a Michigan House representative from Newaygo County. Mackinac authorities, alarmed at this turnabout, attempted to arrest Strang on trumped-up charges before he could get to Lansing. This effort failed on the house floor; the legislators unanimously voted to seat Strang as the lawful representative despite the false charges.

Strang soon proved to be an able and just state representative. His first efforts, naturally, were to separate Beaver Island from Mackinac County's judicial jurisdiction. This separation was accomplished by 1853, with the formation of the county of Emmet, which included Beaver Island and a portion of the mainland adjacent to the island. As most of the newly formed county officials were Strangites or at least acceptable to Strangites, it appeared that Beaver Island had won a major victory in the Beaver/Mackinac War.

Had the Beaver/Mackinac conflict simply been religious prejudice, the legal separation of the two factions should have ended most of the squabbling. Far from ending, however, the war heated up due to the newfound political shielding the new county received and its vigorous enforcement of state alcoholic beverage laws. On election, the Strangite officials of Emmet County immediately began to enforce the liquor laws, in effect throwing the liquor dealers residing on Mackinac Island out of Emmet County. This action effectively cut Mackinac Island off from the $100,000 in fish caught by local Native Americans and sold to Mackinac traders in return for "fire water," a type of diluted whiskey spiked with tobacco and cayenne pepper. Traders produced this "Indian whiskey" for five cents a gallon and sold or traded it to the Native Americans for fifty cents to one dollar per gallon.[37]

Officials, merchants, and fishermen met on Mackinac Island on May 17, 1853, for what amounted to a formal declaration of war on Strang's Saints. The declaration, printed in a Detroit paper, listed the reasons for the meeting as excitement over alleged robberies, burglaries of boats and fish, denial of access to fishing grounds, and the destruction of six to eight fishing houses on Birch Point, all reputedly perpetrated by the "Mormons of Beaver Island." The declaration also asserted that the "Mormons" intended to "monopolize" the fishing grounds. The document concluded that if the law was not enforced by the state, local residents would take the matter into their own hands.[38] No evidence was ever substantiated in court that these accusations were true.

The Beaver Islanders were caught unaware of this declaration of war. On July 12, Sheriff George Miller of Beaver Island trekked to the mainland of Emmet County in the company of thirteen other islanders in search of jurors for the circuit court at Saint James. They landed at the small fishing community of Pine River. Here he and his party were attacked by a considerable body of armed men. At least some of these men had attended the Mackinac town meeting in May and decided that this was the time to press forward the open hostilities against the Beaverites. Six Strangites were wounded in the opening fusillade but fled in their boat, with three fishing boats from the village in hot pursuit. The chase covered a good portion of the twenty-five-mile distance to the island when the Pine River party overtook the Beaver Islanders. Just as it looked bleakest for the beleaguered islanders, the bark *Morgan,* under Captain Stone, responded to the frantic signals of Miller and his group and interceded on their behalf. If not for luck, the Battle of Pine River might well have been the Pine River Massacre.

The Pine River inhabitants fled after the incident, no doubt fearing reprisal from Beaver Island, which left the area open for colonization from the island the following year.[39] The *Michigan* made another appearance on the scene within weeks of the battle, while cooperating with federal timber agents in their war on the timber depredators (see chapter 3).

While in Chicago, Commander Abraham Bigelow received a petition from a Mr. Smith. The contents of this petition gave the commander pause to contemplate another military intervention on Beaver Island. Smith, purporting to be an old settler from the island, asked Bigelow to rescue his family from the island as he "had been driven away, as many others had been, by the persecutions and outrages of the Mormons."[40] Smith apparently intimated that his family might be held accountable for his transgressions against the Strangites.

On the voyage to Beaver, however, Bigelow found that Smith was an apostate of Strang's church, causing him to reconsider and abort his mission. Bigelow's statement concerning the incident was significant for the navy's future dealings with Beaver Islanders: "I did not consider it consistent with my duty, or proper, that I should interfere in the quarrels or dissensions of the Mormons, or any other sect."[41] Bigelow's actions in the case demonstrated that although he would not interfere in the internal affairs of the Strangite Church, he was not averse to helping an outsider confront the Saints.

For several years after the Battle of Pine River, Beaver Island acquired the upper hand in the economic struggle with Mackinac Island. According to Quaife, approximately 2,600 people lived on the island by 1856. This figure is based primarily on the census of 1854.[42] Strang's opponents on the island, however, claimed that the census was falsely quadrupled "to encompass sinister objects of his [Strang's] own, one of which is to derive from the state a larger proportion of the school fund." In written testimony presented to the *Michigan*'s commander and subsequently sent to Michigan Governor Kinsley S. Bingham, Christopher Scott and Franklin Johnson claimed that there were only ninety-four families on Beaver Island and eight on Gull Island, for a total population of some 515 people.[43]

In any case, though the Strangites were sufficiently powerful to be left alone, their reputation continued to slide. By 1856 the *Michigan*'s new commander, Charles H. McBlair, reported to the governor of Michigan, "I have every reason to believe that the greater part of the community has been for a long time engaged in a system of plunder upon the property of fishermen and others who may arrive at the island, and such as may be within reach of boat expeditions to the Michigan and Wisconsin shores."[44]

In contrast, James Strang summarized his opinion of his followers' predicament: "[T]here is something very rotten in the institutions of this country, when men of respectability and of peaceful and industrious habits must live with the assurance that whoever pleases may murder them, and never be called to account for it."[45]

Strang's assessment of his kingdom's precarious circumstances was essentially correct, but he apparently had no idea why this was the case. Apparently it never occurred to him that Beaver Island represented an economic challenge to Mackinac Island that placed him and his followers in the aggressive position of threatening their neighbors' livelihood.

The statements of federal and state officials also suggest that they considered Strang's sect a semiautonomous state within the United States. This situation was only tolerated because Strang was intelligent enough to legalize his authority by forming the county of Emmet. Governor Bingham commented to the *Michigan's* Commander McBlair, "Whence Strang was shrewd enough to form the islands into a county it has been difficult to regulate his activities."[46]

Strang was therefore incorrect to blame his predicament on the federal institutions, because it was only these institutions that protected him. His delicate political situation was actually a product of his ignorance of the economic basis behind the Beaver/Mackinac War. The prophet's poor understanding of how government functions to protect established economic order can be seen in his statement:

> The old governments have a kind of heart; a body of people, generally among the most intelligent, who have a permanent interest in the integrity and respectability of the administration; men whose standing, property and even their personal safety depend on a respectable share of justice in the administration; and who at the same time, control its affairs. In the United States there is no such class.[47]

Strang obviously did not understand that the economic elite of the new nation were in fact its heart, even down to the county level. He also did not understand that he and his followers were shaking the established order by their sudden economic success.

King Strang's murder seems to have been simply a matter of time. He was, after all, the strongest and the weakest link in the chain of command at Beaver Island. Though he was aware from 1850 onward that he was in danger, he took few steps to protect himself.

At 1:00 P.M. June 16, 1856, the *Michigan* entered the harbor at Saint James and docked at the wharf of Franklin Johnson and Dr. Hezekiah D. McCulloch. At about 7:00 P.M. Commander McBlair sent his civilian pilot, Alexander Saint Bernard, to request Strang's presence for a conference. As McBlair explained in a preliminary report,

> I had occasion to send for him [Strang] on business and he was on his way to the steamer in company with our pilot, when he was attacked and shot down with pistols by two of his former followers Alexander Wentworth and Thomas Bedford. He received 3 balls in his body and severe contusions, and when I left, though still alive and in possession of his senses he was thought to be in an extremely critical state.[48]

McBlair went on to state that the attackers fled on board the steamer for protection, at which time he secured them belowdecks. The commander accompanied the ship's surgeon, James McClelland, to the Prindle brothers' house, where McClelland dressed Strang's wounds and remained in attendance on the prophet until the ship left the next day. Strang was shot once each in the back of the head, the face, and the back; his prognosis was very poor.[49]

The attack occurred on the ramp leading to the dock in front of Mc-Culloch and Johnsons' store in plain view of the warship's deck watch and several bystanders on shore. That there was a conspiracy in the assassination has never been in question. As historian Quaife put it, "Never was an assassination plot gone about more publicly."[50]

Assassins Bedford and Wentworth were pawns in the plot. Bedford was apparently motivated by revenge in response to a church-sanctioned whipping he received for adultery. Wentworth was married to the daughter of Frank Johnson, one of the kingpins of a small group of mercantile plotters that had earlier been removed from the Strangite Church for various offenses. Other plotters included such disreputable characters as "Dr. Atkyn," an itinerant embezzler, and apostate church member Christopher Scott.[51]

The *Michigan's* arrival on the sixteenth and the unusual circumstances surrounding McBlair's request to see Strang immediately preceding the attack have fueled speculation that the warship was somehow linked to the assassination. Quaife speculated that Dr. McCulloch somehow persuaded McBlair to visit Saint James. Quaife, however, was not sure: "what arrangement McCulloch made with this federal official or what justification the latter had for his course, is far from clear."[52] Fortunately the navy records in this case are very detailed and clearly support Quaife's speculation.

On June 5, 1856, eleven days before the assassination attempt, the *Michigan* arrived in Chicago, having just left Beaver Island, where Commander McBlair received his first appraisal of "some circumstances arising from the secession of members of the community from mormonism and the malpractice of James Strang the leader and prophet."[53]

Obviously McBlair referred to the McCulloch faction. The *Michigan* either transported some of the dissidents to Chicago or met them there. Nevertheless, a significant meeting took place between the would-be assassins and the navy commander on June 5 or 6. The information McBlair received at the meeting caused him to become very concerned, so he took Franklin Johnson's and Christopher Scott's written depositions. These men, of course, were two of the ringleaders of the assassination plot. Along with these depositions and two copies of *The Book of the Law of the Lord,* McBlair sent his personal report of the situation to the governor of Michigan. McBlair's report observed:

> Among the population are from 10 to 12 persons who have more or less
> openly seceded from the church and are exposed to all the consequences of

Strang's resentment. It is said that there are a number of others who at heart are opposed to Strang but suppress their feelings from fear. . . . The firm of F. Johnson and Co., consisting of Franklin Johnson and Hezekiah McCulloch from Baltimore, together with their families are at open variance with Strang, owing to their secession from the faith and the desire of the firm to wind up their affairs and quit the island. They have in consequence incurred the odium and ill will of the sect to a degree which they think threatens not only their property but their lives, and are deeply solicitous that some prompt and vigorous measures of protection be rendered to them by the state.[54]

Commander McBlair then reported to the navy that "I propose leaving here in a few days for Erie touching at Beaver Island . . . and render such assistance to those citizens threatened by the hostility of Strang."[55] It is interesting to note that Johnson and McCulloch were from Baltimore, McBlair's hometown before he received command the *Michigan.*[56]

Instead of proceeding immediately to Beaver Island, the *Michigan* first touched at Milwaukee. This stop gave Scott and Johnson (and possibly McCulloch) time to return to Beaver Island carrying the pistols that were to bring so much calamity to the island. Bedford and Wentworth reportedly practiced openly with these pistols several days before the attack. The plot and entanglement of the *Michigan*'s officers is further brought out by the fact that McCulloch somehow "made over" his property to one of the officers of the vessel, to keep the Strangite Church from making any legal claims against it. McCulloch's communications with the *Michigan*'s officers quite probably linked him to the Johnson and Scott, meeting on board the *Michigan* in Chicago.[57]

Following the assassination attempt, the steamer stayed in port until the following day. During this time McBlair reported to the Emmet County sheriff that he had Bedford and Wentworth in custody and if the sheriff agreed, he should meet with the commander on board the ship after 10:00 A.M. on the seventeenth. Sheriff Miller wrote back on the seventeenth requesting a conference at McBlair's convenience. This conference apparently never took place. Clearly McBlair never intended to turn the men over to the Beaver Island civil authorities:

> It would have been the last act of inhumanity to have surrendered the prisoners into the hands of the authorities at such time. I would have been giving them up to the rage and fury of a rabble of religious fanatics whose revenge would not have stopped short of their immediate destruction.[58]

At 12:50 P.M. June 17, the warship cast off its moorings and steamed for Mackinac Island to deliver its prisoners and "about 7 families including those of the prisoners and numbering about 30 persons who thought their lives in jeopardy from the Mormons."[59] The prisoners were surrendered to Sheriff Granger at Mackinac, released in minutes, and treated like heroes.[60]

James Strang survived the assassination attempt and lived another twenty-three days. During this time he was evacuated to his parents' house in Voree for fear of additional assassination attempts from Mackinac Island. The prophet succumbed to his wounds on July 9, and though lucid during most of this time, he died without leaving a successor for his church.[61]

The Mackinac Islanders hastened to use this opportunity to utterly destroy their rivals on Beaver Island. On July 3, the Mackinac sheriff returned intent to arrest any remaining Strangite leaders. Bands of "drunken ruffians" arrived in his wake, ordering the disorganized Strangites from their homes and packing them off on any visiting steamers that had room to hold them. Three hundred people were reportedly forced to flee aboard the steamer *Iowa* a short time after Strang was evacuated to Voree. Apparently all the Strangite leaders had left for Voree, because the Beaver Islanders offered no armed resistance. The refugees left with no more than they had when they arrived. Their existence, paid for by sweat and blood, disappeared over a watery horizon. The conquering invaders summarily commandeered the possessions and homes left behind.[62]

The absence of the *Michigan* during this horrific miscarriage of justice speaks almost as loudly, in a sense, as if the warship had been there firing broadsides into the vandals. The ship's commander simply commented that upon return from their recent first visit to Lake Superior in July, "We found on our arrival at Beaver Island that the settlement of Mormons has been dispersed by an armed expedition fitted out at Mackinac and composed to some extent of persons who had suffered by their depredations." In typical fashion the wolves fought among themselves for the spoils. McBlair commented, "Disturbances had afterward arisen among the new settlers but quiet prevailed at the time of our visit."[63]

As an interesting epilogue to this sad affair, one of the Strangite leaders, George Miller, wrote a letter of accusation to Senator Lewis Cass, insinuating that the *Michigan* had been involved in the assassination. A remote navy inquiry into the episode ensued, quite probably the only official acknowledgment that the outrageous destruction of the community on Beaver Island had occurred at all. On September 15, Commander McBlair was ordered by Secretary Dobbin to submit a full report on the subject, which he did by September 24. The report was quite naturally unsympathetic to the Strangite cause and included a character assassination of George Miller.

What the report does show, however, is that McBlair was quite familiar with the Strangite organization, from the church's leaders to its judicial organization. He was also well aware of all the old charges brought against Strang, though he did not mention that these charges were proven false in a court of law. McBlair quite obviously believed the church at worst to be a treasonous organization and at best a simple band of "thieves and pirates." In discussing the actual reason why he summoned Strang to his vessel, McBlair wrote:

> I was satisfied of the truth of their [the McCulloch faction] statements and thought it my duty to bring to their protection all the moral influence of my official position. I accordingly sent for Strang with the hope of being able to advise him to abandon his schemes against them. It was unfortunately while he was on his way to the vessel under this invitation that he was waylaid and shot down.[64]

So ended the Beaver/Mackinac War. The navy inquiry was laid to rest with McBlair's written statement.[65] The local and federal governments were thoroughly unsympathetic to the Strangite cause, mainly due to economic factors. Religious prejudice against Mormonism also remained strong. The atrocities committed by both sides in Utah's Mormon War of 1847 had not been forgotten.

That Commander McBlair or other officers of the *Michigan* were in on the assassination conspiracy is still in question. The following factors, however, would not have been overlooked had the case gone to court. Commander McBlair was at best thoroughly unsympathetic with Strang's cause; this gave him a motive. McBlair met with the chief conspirators just days before the assassination and was officially very sympathetic to their public cause of escaping the island; this allowed him to participate in the plot. In addition, if the commander was as eager to protect the dissidents as he professed in his June 6 report to the governor of Michigan, why did he dally for ten days, even visiting Milwaukee before going to Saint James? This delay clearly gave the assassins time to arrive at Beaver and even to practice with the murder weapons before the vessel's arrival. Finally, McBlair had to know that the turmoil surrounding the assassination attempt would undoubtedly lead to more violence. Therefore, it made little sense for him to take his ship, the most effective means of quelling violence in the area, into the remoteness of Lake Superior, an action that made the *Michigan* unavailable to any authority that might ask him to prevent the invasion and forcible ejection of the Beaver Islanders.[66]

It is unknown whether McBlair knew of the plot or not. In either case he performed in the exact manner the assassins would have diagrammed. It also mattered little to the state and federal governments whether the navy commander was duped by clever conspirators or had acted in conjunction with them. The assassination, invasion, and eviction were condoned by their thunderous silence.

V
The Iron Diplomat and
the Civil War on the Great Lakes

LIFE FOR A SAILOR on the inland seas, both shore and sea duty, was unique. The annals of the *Michigan* surprisingly offer many clues concerning the lives of mid-nineteenth-century freshwater merchant mariners that are difficult to find elsewhere. This chapter will begin with a short exploration of the men who served on board the ship before describing the steamer's primary duty, the rescue of ships in distress.

The *Michigan* protected shipping on the Great Lakes before the Lighthouse and Life-Saving Services were introduced on the Great Lakes, a role now occupied by the Coast Guard. The warship was well suited in this capacity. Its iron hull and powerful engines allowed it to navigate storms and ice that would have incapacitated most wooden ships.

The *Michigan*'s efforts in safeguarding lakes shipping won the respect of merchants and sailors on both shores, giving Canadians an easy excuse to ignore the rescue ship's ominous gun ports. The Civil War, however, threatened the tenuous diplomacy won by the iron steamer. Confederate operatives from Canada attacked lake steamers and menaced Union cities and waterways. This chapter concludes with a description of these attacks and the efforts put forth by the captain and crew of the *Michigan* to thwart them.

GREAT LAKES JACK-TARS

Great Lakes merchant mariners made up much of the crew of the *Michigan*. Since their work was seasonal, they worked as farmers and timberjacks during the nonnavigation season.[1] These other occupations were relatively high-wage jobs, so the U.S. Navy made unusual concessions to compete successfully for these workers on a year-round basis. Inducements to serve in the navy on the lakes included a yearly enlistment period, at times an enlistment bonus, and year-round pay.

The term of enlistment for a crew member on the *Michigan* typically lasted twelve months even though the blue-water navy normally offered a multiyear enlistment.[2] The concession was made because lake workers simply refused to sign for longer periods. Signing on an annual basis meant that deckhands could take advantage of the frequent economic booms that accompanied large harvests, the opening of new canals and locks, and navigational improvements to ports and rivers. These economic growth spurts brought with them premium seasonal pay. Often it became necessary for the commanders of the *Michigan* to induce sailors with bonuses, such as three months' advance pay or an advance for uniforms.[3] During slack navigation season, which lasted from June 20 to August 1, and the winter months of January through March, it was easy for the *Michigan* to ship a full complement.[4]

The navy was unable, however, to compete outright with the merchant service in pay. A merchant deckhand in 1846 on the Great Lakes could make twenty to twenty-two dollars per month (this figure declined slightly to eighteen to twenty dollars in 1851), but he was paid only during the working season. Navy sailors, on the other hand, made about two-thirds this amount—but they were paid each month for the term of the enlistment, slack season or not. Merchant sailors suffered high unemployment during slack or sluggish seasons, which inevitably created a problem for the navy on the lakes: men joined the navy during the off-season and deserted during the navigation season.[5]

The navy also had difficulty recruiting for skilled positions. For example, the *Michigan*'s civilian pilots made sixty dollars per month, while merchant pilots made one hundred dollars per month and stayed on the merchant vessels for nine months of the year.[6] Nationwide economic booms compounded recruitment problems. The California gold rush nearly disabled the *Michigan*. Sea traffic to California increased at an incredible rate by 1849, creating a great demand for ships and sailors. Once in California, entire crews deserted to look for gold, stranding many ships. The Pacific Mail and Steam Company offered exorbitant salaries to induce sailors to their service and keep them from deserting. Deckhands could receive seventy dollars per month plus a five-hundred-dollar bonus for signing. Engineers made the incredible sum of fifteen hundred dollars per month with a thousand-dollar bonus.[7]

Aside from filling its own crew complement, the *Michigan* recruited mariners for the blue-water navy, having taken over this job from the rendezvous ship *Monroe* stationed in Buffalo until 1842. Cleveland, Detroit, Milwaukee, Chicago, and Buffalo became the *Michigan*'s most lucrative recruitment stations. In these cities the navy representatives distributed handbills advertising the benefits of a naval career, and members of the public were encouraged to tour the ship. At times, recruitment for sea service was relatively easy, particularly before and during the war with Mexico in 1848.[8]

WRECKS, RESCUES, AND IRON DIPLOMACY

The assisting of ships in distress, however, remained the *Michigan*'s primary mission. From 1854 until 1860 the warship assisted at least thirty-five more ships in need. The *Michigan* rescued several vessels on more than one occasion. The 1,700-ton paddle steamer *Mayflower*, for instance, was pulled off shoals in 1850 and again in 1852 before the *Michigan* was nearly destroyed trying to rescue it for the third time on December 4, 1854.

Breakdowns and strandings seemed to plague steam vessels on the lakes, while collisions, founderings, and crew exhaustion from leaky hulls plagued the smaller sailing craft (see appendix A). The *Michigan*'s power and invulnerability to damage made it an ideal ice rescue ship, often ferrying provisions to ice-stranded vessels. The steam frigate could also pull ships off bars and flats that men using kedges, winches, capstans, horse teams, and tugboats could not budge.[9] On several occasions the navy ship found sloops and schooners in sinking or waterlogged condition, with crews exhausted at the pumps. At these times a skeleton crew from the ship relieved the fatigued sailors while the warship towed the vessel to port.

The *Michigan* became so productive at rescuing stranded ships that it drew the onerous reputation around naval circles as a tug. This image did not sit well with the warship's officers and became a point of contention on at least one occasion.[10] The *Michigan*'s rescue operations also drew the ire of some lakes tug owners despite the fact that these smaller vessels often lacked the power to rescue their clients.[11]

The *Michigan*'s cutters, launches, and barges also conducted rescue operations. For instance, at 11:00 A.M. December 1, 1856, while a storm of rain, fine snow, and hail pelted down in a moderate gale from the northeast, the steamer *Golden State* ran aground on the bar off Erie harbor. The ship began to take on water and received a severe pounding in the rising surf. It looked to bystanders as though the ship would go to pieces.

Merchant sailors from the harbor quickly scrambled into a surfboat, which they carried over the breakwater. The surf proved too great, however, and the boat was driven to the lee beach on the mainland. Meanwhile, Lieutenant Magaw of the *Michigan* readied the ship's barge. Magaw, with a handpicked crew, attempted to take this vessel out of the harbor entrance. The force of the surf immediately drove them back. Magaw then attempted a new tactic. The sailors beached the craft inside the harbor and carried it over the breakwater, succeeding—with great effort—in reaching the stranded ship.

The small boat could not closely approach the ship for fear of being crushed against it in the surf, so passengers were forced to leap into the water, trusting the flotation ability of their life preservers. Magaw's crew picked them up when they surfaced. Eventually the lighter surfboat, commanded by George Berry of the schooner *Post Boy,* arrived at the shipwreck to pick up survivors. The two boats removed all the passengers from the stricken ship and delivered them to the propeller *Detroit* in the harbor for treatment for exposure.[12]

In several tragic cases the *Michigan* did not arrive in time to prevent disaster. When the bark *Sunshine* capsized off Long Point on July 18, 1859, the *Michigan*'s crew rescued six men on the overturned hull and found the bodies of two drowned children. On these occasions the ship incurred the sad duty of delivering the bodies to Buffalo for burial.[13] On other occasions the *Michigan* reported large debris fields, apparently from foundered vessels, but no signs of the ships or survivors.

In 1857 the navy began an inquiry into removing the *Michigan* from the Great Lakes. The investigation was instigated by renewed British protests concerning the vessel's violation of the Rush-Bagot Agreement. Not surprisingly, lakes merchant captains, shipowners, and insurance underwriters raised a storm of protest over the proposed move. Lake Captain E. M. Ward commented, "Her services are as free to the suffering Canadian Vessel as to the American, She is no longer regarded as an instrument of war but as an important auxiliary in the cause of peace."[14] Canadian merchants joined the fray, writing letters of protest to British Lord Napier, explaining in no uncertain terms that it was not in anyone's interest to hurt commerce on the lakes, and removing the iron steamer would definitely hurt commerce.[15]

The *Michigan*'s commanders received letters of commendation for rescue operations on several occasions. These included commendations for bravery and assistance from the U.S. Board of Lake Underwriters, the Aetna Insurance Company, the Northwest Insurance Company, the American Transportation Company, the Canadian government, and numerous shipmasters who had no insurance, their ships being their entire life and livelihood.[16]

These protests proved successful. The navy immediately dropped plans to remove the ship from the lakes. As a gesture of goodwill, the *Michigan* helped the Canadian government tow the Point Pelee light caisson into Lake Erie, since it was too large a burden for any Canadian tug to manage. While on this mission, the warship saved the propeller *Action* from certain destruction on a nearby shoal. The *Michigan*'s accomplishments helped cement the growing international ties with Canada and extinguished further British complaints for the time being.[17]

By the end of the navigation season of 1859, the *Michigan* had put in fifteen years of service. Though the ship was hauled frequently, the engines adjusted, and the woodwork replaced in 1848, its boilers were worn out and needed replacing. The crew was detached on December 20, 1859. A skeleton naval crew and private contractors took over in the spring of 1860 to effect repairs. The boiler replacement, with new vertical water-tube models, occupied much of the spring and summer.[18]

Late in the fall of 1860, before the ship was put back into commission, the navy acknowledged the *Michigan*'s superior reliability and steam efficiency by sending the Navy Board of Engineers to study it. This board included chief engineer Benjamin Franklin Isherwood, engineers Robert Long and Allan Stimers, and the *Michigan*'s chief engineer, Theodore Zeller. The findings of the board eventually made Isherwood famous in engineering circles.[19]

Isherwood conducted specific experiments to ascertain how much efficiency could be gained by steam expansion in common low-pressure, noninsulated engines. The engineers conducted these experiments on the ship's port side engine with the paddle buckets removed. During the investigation, Isherwood adjusted the engine's Sickel's valves to cut off the steam partway into the piston stroke. It was discovered that the engines were most efficient when the steam cut off 70 percent of the way into the stroke, or when the piston had traveled five and one-half feet of the eight-foot stroke. The previous cutoff for the steam was three and one-half feet into the stroke, allowing expansion to push the piston the remaining distance.[20]

Isherwood concluded that steam expansion in these simple low-pressure engines did not substantially contribute to an engine's power or efficiency.[21] Technically superior practices such as superheating, insulation, high-pressure steam, and compound engines had not yet made a great impact on U.S. naval steam engineering. Isherwood's simplistic yet reliable steam plants saw the

U.S. Navy through the nation's most troubling and bloody conflict, the Civil War.

THE CIVIL WAR ON THE GREAT LAKES

Few people are aware of how dramatically the Civil War affected the supposed noncombatant areas of the country. One of the most significant of these areas was the Great Lakes region. Back in commission early in 1861, the *Michigan* remained the only U.S. Navy warship on the lakes, where it played a vital role in the Union war effort.

The effects of the Civil War were slow in coming to the northern lakes. Indeed, the entire country seemed without a clue regarding the seriousness of the conflict and the immense sacrifice that would be involved. Only the calamity of the first battle of Bull Run hinted at the war's gruesome nature. Nevertheless, in March, 1861, the *Michigan* prepared to resume its annual routine patrol to various ports on the lakes. The vessel's new captain, John C. Carter, remained unaware that the clouds of war gathering to the south would eventually reach his vessel and disrupt the calm of the Great Lakes.[22]

On May 9, 1861, Commander Carter was instructed to proceed to various large city ports on the lakes for the purpose of enlisting men into the United States Navy.[23] During the course of the Civil War, the *Michigan* recruited more than four thousand men from the Great Lakes region to serve in the Union Navy. The first of these recruits, about nine hundred men, were sent to the Atlantic blockading squadron. In November, 1861, the officers of the *Michigan* were ordered to send their new recruits to Capt. S. H. Foote of the Mississippi squadron commanded by Admiral David D. Porter. Carter commented that it was easier to recruit men for the Atlantic, but he still managed to send about 70 percent of the new recruits to Cairo, Illinois, for service on the Mississippi. The remaining 30 percent continued to rendezvous at New York for service in the Atlantic.[24]

The merchant service and Revenue Cutter Service of the lakes began to feel the manpower shortage caused by the war. Wages increased accordingly. By the end of the 1861 navigation season, merchant service deckhands could make as much as three dollars per day or ninety dollars per month. Yet, navy recruitment did not suffer, while the Revenue Service under the Treasury Department was forced to offer hundred-dollar bounties for new recruits.[25]

The *Michigan* itself nearly became a recruit for the Atlantic blockading squadron, but it was too large to negotiate the Welland Canal.[26] President Lincoln's embargo on southern ports caught the Union Navy woefully short of ships for the task, particularly the fast cruiser types needed to capture blockade runners.

The *Michigan*'s wartime recruitment roll continued throughout 1862. In 1863, however, the *Michigan* began to help municipal authorities cope with the civil disorder brought about by the war. By this time the federal government realized that the war was becoming unpopular but was likely to continue for quite some time. Congress passed federal mandatory conscription laws on March 3, 1863. Before this time, state and local conscription had been used to fill in the gaps in the army left by casualties and falling numbers of volunteers. Unfair clauses in these laws, which seemed to cater to the rich, caused much anxiety and consternation in the North. For those that did not want to serve in the army, fear, anger, and civil unrest were the consequences of the draft.

On July 28, 1863, *Michigan* Commander John C. Carter reported,

> The visit of this ship to Detroit, Michigan, at this time was opportune. I found the people suffering under serious apprehensions of a riot in consequence of excitement in reference to the draft, probably brought about by unscrupulous sensational newspapers predicting such riots. The presence of the ship perhaps did something toward overawing the refractory, and certainly did much to allay the apprehensions of an excited, doubting people. All fears in reference to the riot had subsided before I left.[27]

By the end of August, the *Michigan* was ordered to help suppress riots in Buffalo and Milwaukee.[28] Reporting on the *Michigan*'s actions in Buffalo, Commander Carter related:

> I was called to Buffalo, New York, by urgent information that great danger was apprehended when the draft was to take place; that there was an organization of some 7000 ruffians determined to fire and destroy all the elevators, containing millions of bushels of grain, in the vicinity of the creek. I proceeded immediate[ly] to that place and put my ship in the best possible position to act in case of necessity.[29]

Four days after Carter's report, the navy increased the *Michigan*'s armament in the form of two twelve-pounder howitzers plus shrapnel and grapeshot ammunition. These howitzers were equipped with boat carriages and field carriages. Carter had these guns mounted on the forecastle and promenade decks in order to be as visible as possible.[30]

On October 22, 1863, the *Michigan* was ordered to proceed to Sandusky, Ohio.[31] A federal prisoner of war camp had been established on Johnson's Island in Sandusky Bay. The *Michigan* was ordered to cooperate with the army in guarding the Confederate prisoners incarcerated there. While the

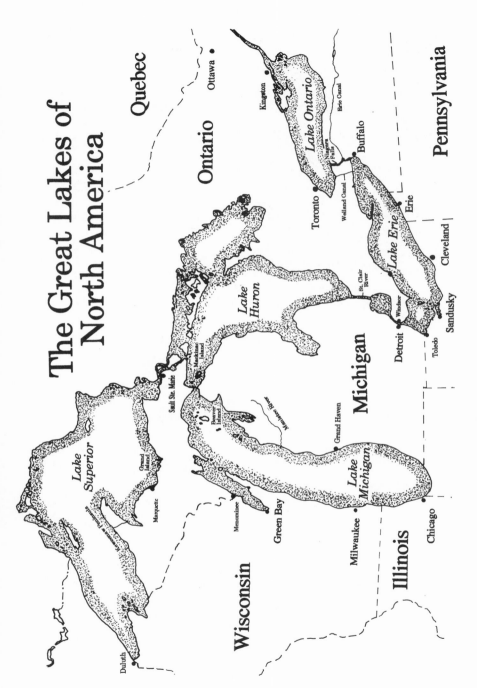

The Great Lakes of North America

U.S. Naval Secretary Abel Parker Upshur 1841. (Courtesy of the U.S. Naval Historical Center, Washington, D.C.)

The Michigan's *first commander, William Inman, September 1844, through November, 1845. (Courtesy of the U.S. Naval Historical Center, Washington, D.C.)*

This is the earliest known photograph of the USS Michigan, *reported to have been taken on September 17, 1868. However, it is a good likeness of the ship as it appeared any time after the addition of a pilothouse in 1848. (Courtesy of Theodore J. Karle, Mentor, Ohio.)*

USS Michigan
Cutaway View - August 1844

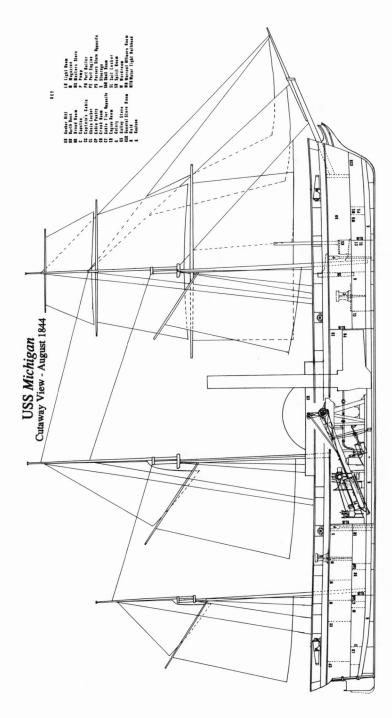

KEY

AB Anchor Bitt
BR Berth Deck
C Brod Room
CC Capstan
CC Captain's Cabin
CL Chain Locker
CP Chain Pantry
CR Crank Room
CT Cable Tier Opposite
E Engine Room
G Galley
GS Galley Stove
GSR General Store Room
H Hold
H Hoohom

LR Light Room
M Magazine
MB Masters Store
P Pump
PE Port Boiler
PE Port Engine
PS Posters Store Opposite
S Storage
SB Sail Cloth
SC Sail Locker
SP Spirit Room
W Wardroom
WR Warrant Officers Room
WR Warrant Officers Room
WTB Water Tight Bulkhead

Sheer and sailplans of the paddle frigate Michigan. Note the lack of a pilothouse. Watertight bulkheads extend to the maindeck fore and aft of the engine room and to the iron berth deck near the fore and mizzen mast steps. This view was made possible by combining Samuel Hartt's sheer and sailplans with an engine schematic from Weber and Isaacs, "Old Time War Vessel on the Great Lakes."

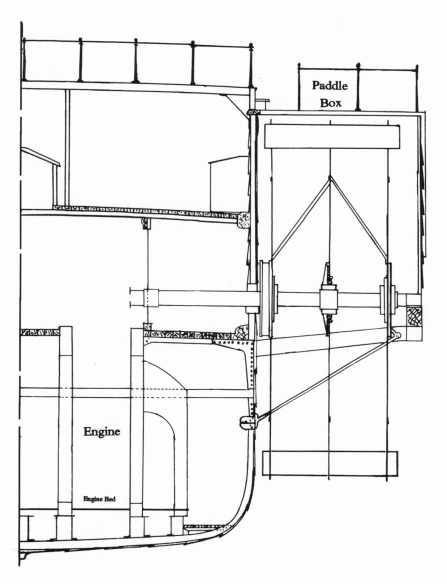

Half hull cross section, port side paddle box, view aft at frame no. 41. (Adapted from H.R. Spencer, "The Iron Ship" 1943.)

Contrasting Body Plans

USS Michigan
Steamer 1843

USS Congress
Frigate 1841

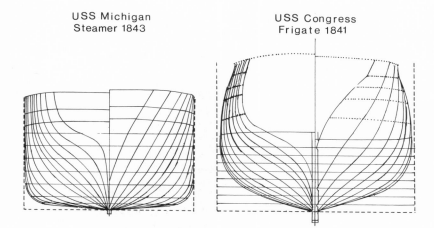

Contrasting body plans, USS Michigan *and USS* Congress. *Note the sharper bow and more angular curves possible with the iron hulled* Michigan, *allowing greater speed, stability, and a shallower draft.*

Though this photo was taken after 1905, it gives a good representation of the winter quarters look of the vessel, with both the forward and aft ends of the ship housed over. (Courtesy of Theodore J. Karle, Mentor, Ohio.)

James Jesse Strang. (Harpers Monthly 64 [December 1881– May 1881]: 553.)

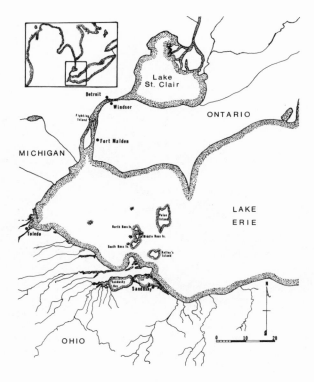

Western Lake Erie, a theater of operations for Confederate fifth column activities during the Civil War

The crew of the Michigan *at ease on the foredeck at about the time of the Civil War. Note that the ship is not yet fully armed. (Courtesy of the Reeder Collection, Mariner's Museum, Newport News, Virginia.)*

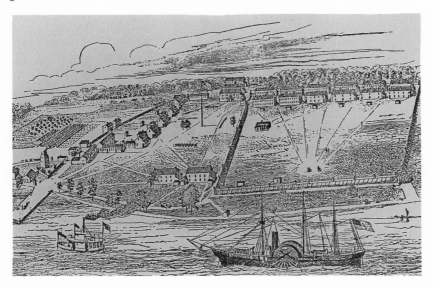

Depot of Confederate prisoners on Johnson's Island, Sandusky Bay, Lake Erie. (A Memorial to Johnson's Island, Courtesy of the Dossin Great Lakes Museum, Belle Isle, Michigan.)

U.S. Navy Chief Engineer Benjamin F. Isherwood. (Courtesy of the U.S. Naval Historical Center, Washington, D.C.)

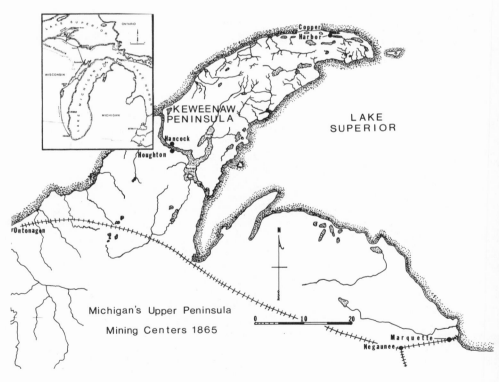

Michgan's Upper Peninsula Mining Centers, 1865

sailors of the *Michigan* drilled with the new guns, the marines performed guard duty on the island itself.[32]

In November of the same year, with winter closing in, Secretary of War Edwin M. Stanton gave an ominous warning to the mayors of the cities located on the Great Lakes. Stanton declared that the Confederacy intended to carry the war to the heart of the North in the form of shipborne raids from the provinces of Canada. At almost the same time the Navy Department informed Commander Carter that, "Reliable information is furnished this Department that a project is on foot in Canada to fit out steamers and attempt a rescue of the prisoners confined on Johnson's Island rifled guns will be sent to you."[33] These guns arrived only eleven days later. In total the *Michigan* received a dozen naval cannon to augment the two Howitzers and one eight-inch pivot already carried on the vessel.[34]

The oracular warnings by Stanton and the Navy Department concerned a plan formulated in the Confederacy that, if successful, would have grave consequences for the *Michigan* and the Union. By fall 1863, with no end to the war in sight and the defeat at Gettysburg still fresh in memory, the Confederate high command desperately searched for a way to weaken the Union. Some Confederate leaders believed that a blow struck directly at the relatively unassailable cities in the North by raiders operating out of Canada might be the key to the collapse of Union morale.[35]

Excitement over incidents such as the Trent affair and the blockade of Southern ports had strained relations between Britain and the United States to the breaking point. The Confederates therefore had been looking for a way to foment trouble between the two countries. War between Britain and the United States would certainly relieve some of the military pressure being placed on the South.

Earlier in 1863 Lieutenant William H. Murdaugh of the Confederate States Navy (CSN) submitted a plan that the Confederate high command believed had promise for success at that time. Central to the plan was the capture or destruction of the USS *Michigan* by Confederate-manned steamers operating out of unspecified ports in Canada. According to the plan, if the *Michigan* could be captured, it would be used to release the thousands of Confederate prisoners confined on Johnson's Island near Sandusky, Ohio, would serve as a Confederate raider to disrupt shipping on the lakes, and finally would shell lake port cities into submission.[36] Since the *Michigan* was the only warship on the upper Great Lakes, the successful execution of the plan would have devastating effects on the North.[37]

Confederate Secretary of the Navy Stephen R. Mallory approved the plan, and $25,000 was allocated, along with a makeshift crew of sailors and officers from the scuttled and burned CSS *Virginia,* formerly the USS *Merrimack.* Before the raiders could leave for Canada, however, Confederate President Jefferson Davis vetoed the plan. Davis postulated that the creation of an unfortunate political atmosphere between Britain and the Confederacy might result in the discontinuation of work on a Confederate armored cruiser then being built in Britain.

By the fall of 1863, however, the deteriorating strategic situation faced by the South caused the reexamination and grudging acceptance of desperate measures to help win the war. Confederate Secretary of War James A. Seddon and Naval Secretary Mallory called in CSN Lieutenant Robert D. Minor to review the Murdaugh plan. Minor carefully documented this plan and gave the details to the secretaries.

The Murdaugh plan was approved for the second time in September 1863, and appropriations were made for the operation. At this stage of the war the plan was considerably more expensive than the first attempt would have been. Funding amounted to $35,000 in gold, supplemented by the profits from a cargo of cotton that the Confederate agents sold in Britain for $76,000. The expedition of twenty-two men under command of Lieutenant John Wilkinson left Smithville, North Carolina, on October 7, 1863. They traveled to Nova Scotia aboard the blockade runner Robert E. Lee and from there split up to make their way individually to Montreal to meet at an agreed-upon date of October 21.

In Montreal the Confederate agents were able to purchase Colt revolvers and two nine-pound cannons. In a seemingly naive attempt to allay the suspicion of the local authorities, the would-be raiders bought dumbbells as ammunition for the cannon rather than shot. Volunteers were sought among approximately 180 Confederate escapees contacted in Montreal but only 32 agreed to participate in the risky expedition. The entire Confederate force amounted to 54 men.

While the Confederate rescue force in Canada was arming and organizing, the prisoners on Johnson's Island were notified of the rescue attempt in advance. The Confederate agents in Montreal had a contact in Baltimore who put their messages in the *New York Herald* personal columns. The prisoners on Johnson's Island apparently had access to the newspaper and were aware of the coded messages.

The next step in the plan involved commandeering a steamer bound for Chicago from Saint Catharines, Canada. The steamer would then be taken into Sandusky Bay at dawn and made to "accidentally" run into the *Michi-*

gan. The warship would be boarded and as a signal to the prisoners on the island that the vessel was in Confederate hands, a cannon shot was to be fired through the Union officers' quarters on the island.[38]

By November, 1863, the Confederate plans had advanced to the stage of buying passage on a steamer bound for Chicago, when Canadian Governor General Lord Monck warned the United States government of the plot. Apparently the Confederate agents were not as unobtrusive in Montreal as they had hoped to be. The Canadian government, concerned about the threat to its neutrality, felt obligated to report the Confederate activity. With the plan revealed and the *Michigan* alerted by the Navy Department, the Confederate raiders abandoned the rescue attempt and made their way back to the Southern states.[39]

The possibility of Confederate intrigue set an ominous tone for the 1864 cruising season on the lakes, but the *Michigan's* spring and summer cruises were routine. The only danger the crew of the ship seemingly faced was the dilapidated condition of their own vessel. Except for the boiler replacement in 1861 the *Michigan* had sailed since 1848 without major repairs or a complete overhaul and was beginning to show its age. Lieutenant Commander F. A. Roe, who relieved Carter as commander of the vessel toward the end of 1864, reported, "Every bit of wood-work in her was rotten, and it was not known when the vibrations of the steam engines would shake yards and masts all together in a mass on deck. . . . Her decks leaked like a sieve." The *Michigan,* however, would not be overhauled for another year.[40] During war, details like keeping nonessentials replaced and the comfort of the crew became secondary to the maintenance of the guns and steam machinery.

Despite the *Michigan's* respite from possible attack during the spring and summer of 1864, the ghost of the Murdaugh plan would not die. Jacob Thompson, former secretary of the interior, became a Confederate agent operating out of Canada. Thompson had funded several projects to demoralize the Union, including public peace rallies in Peoria, Chicago, and Springfield, Illinois.

The Confederacy donated money to the Sons of Liberty (an organization of Northerners opposed to the war) to continue the peace marches. Thompson, however, was not entirely satisfied with funding peace rallies, and he remained alert for a more direct approach to undermine the morale of the Northern cities. To this effect, he persuaded Confederate Captain Charles H. Cole, who had recently escaped from a Union prisoner of war camp, to examine the possibility of capturing or destroying the *Michigan* in Sandusky Bay.

Cole, evidently familiar with the Murdaugh plan, presented a similar proposal. However, unlike the previous Murdaugh plan, Cole's plot called for participation in the takeover by an insider. Cole was to go to Sandusky and assume the role of a businessman. He would then attempt to ingratiate himself with the officers of the *Michigan.* According to the Confederate timetable, the takeover attempt would occur on September 19, 1864. On that date Cole would go on board the vessel and attempt to incapacitate the ship's officers by getting them drunk or drugging them.

In the meantime a party of Confederates under the command of Acting Master John Y. Beall, having commandeered a steam vessel out of Detroit and having received a go-ahead for the plan via a messenger sent by Cole, would board the *Michigan* and subdue the crew. As with the Murdaugh plan, a cannon shot fired through the Union officers' quarters would signal the Confederate prisoners that the warship was in Confederate hands.

After the capture of the *Michigan* the waterfront of Sandusky was targeted. The Confederates would commandeer all available boats and ships. These vessels, convoyed by the *Michigan,* would transport the released prisoners to Cleveland. At Cleveland the Confederates were to disembark and proceed overland to Wheeling, West Virginia, and then to Virginia and safety. Though Cole's plan was risky, the chance to free thousands of potential soldiers for the South appealed to Thompson, so he agreed to fund the operation.

Cole arrived in Sandusky sometime in August, 1864. He proceeded to carry out his part of the plan and soon introduced himself to the *Michigan's* officers. Cole naively planned to try to buy the vessel outright by offering the *Michigan's* officers $2,000 apiece. He soon realized that the bribery attempt was impractical due to the strong Union attitudes among the ship's officers.[41]

Meanwhile Beall was proceeding with his side of the plan. On September 18, he secured passage on board the steamer *Philo-Parsons* out of Detroit. Beall's party of twenty-five Confederates boarded the vessel at various stops so they wouldn't draw undue attention to themselves. On the nineteenth, the *Philo-Parsons* left Detroit with Beall on board. At the next stop, Sandwich Island, four of his men boarded the vessel and at Malden, Ontario, twenty more clambered on board carrying a large chest. Early that afternoon Beall's men, using revolvers, hatchets, and knives contained in the chest, took control of the ship.[42]

The seizure of the vessel was bloodless. Beall ordered the crew to proceed to Kelley's Island, which was only five miles from Johnson's Island and the *Michigan*. Four more men got on board the vessel at Kelley's Island, though none of these was the expected messenger sent by Cole to inform Beall about how the plan was proceeding.

By that afternoon the *Philo-Parsons* was running low on fuel, so Beall ordered that it be sailed to Middle Bass Island to pick up more wood. At 4:00 P.M. the steamer *Island Queen* made the mistake of pulling alongside the *Philo-Parsons* to acquire firewood.[43] Beall and his men were shocked to see blue-coated soldiers on board the *Island Queen* but attacked the vessel nonetheless. The fight was short, with a dozen shots fired and one person hit. Another had been bludgeoned with an axe. Amazingly no one was seriously injured. The engineer of the *Island Queen*, Henry Haines, testified, "I heard someone exclaim, 'Shoot the son of a bitch,' and was immediately shot, the ball passing my nose and through my left cheek."[44]

The Union soldiers were off-duty troopers from the Toledo 130th Infantry Regiment. After years of war in the South, Confederates were the last thing these men expected to see on the Great Lakes, hence they offered little resistance.[45]

After taking the second ship, Beall realized that he could not afford to use any of his small band of men to guard prisoners. He therefore decided to strand the passengers on Middle Bass Island by scuttling the *Island Queen*. Beall had no idea if Cole's side of the plan was still proceeding because the messenger from Cole had not been at the agreed-upon location. At 8:00 or 9:00 P.M. the *Philo-Parsons* again approached Sandusky Bay. From their vantage point the Confederates could undoubtedly see the *Michigan*'s silhouette in Sandusky Bay.[46] It was probably still possible at this point that a light signal from Cole on board the *Michigan* could have brought Beall's men in to attempt to board the ship, but no signal was given.

Without Cole's inside help, the attack of twenty-nine lightly armed men on an alert, heavily armed warship had almost no chance of success. Beall reluctantly turned his commandeered vessel around and headed back toward Canada. The Confederates passed Fort Malden on the Canadian side of the Detroit River at approximately 4:00 A.M. Tuesday morning and marooned the remaining crew members of the *Philo-Parsons* on Fighting Island, between Detroit and Windsor. Beall and his crew then proceeded up the Detroit River to Sandwich, Ontario, part of present-day Windsor.[47]

At Sandwich, Beall's crew took their frustrations out on the *Philo-Parsons* by looting the vessel and then scuttling it while at the wharf. Most of the

Confederate party then escaped, but British authorities arrived in time to arrest two of Beall's men who were slow to leave the scene. One of these men was Beall's second in command, Bennett G. Burley.[48]

Beall and his companions were fortunate they did not attack the *Michigan* on September 19. Just as with the previous year's Murdaugh plan, federal officials had been tipped off in advance. The officers of the *Michigan* had prepared a trap for the Confederates.

On September 17, Lieutenant Colonel B. H. Hill, acting assistant provost marshall general of Michigan, was contacted by unidentified Canadian informants and told that there would be an attempted hijacking of the USS *Michigan.* Commander Carter was immediately informed of the plot.[49] Hill, however, felt that the attempt was too weak to succeed and ordered that it be allowed to continue to effect the capture of the Confederate agents involved.[50] Commander Carter would not take action until he was issued a second warning at midnight the next day.

Two hours after the midnight warning, at 2:00 A.M. on September 19, Carter sent Ensign James Hunter to arrest Cole. Hunter reported a short while later that the "barge returned with Cole a prisoner." In the meantime Commander Carter prepared his ship for battle.[51]

The trap set by Hill and Carter might well have worked if Cole had had time to send his messenger to Kelley's Island before he was arrested. As it turned out, Carter realized after midnight on the twentieth that the Confederates had fled. He was, however, unable to give any immediate pursuit of the *Philo-Parsons* because of an early morning Navy Department dispatch that ordered his vessel to remain and guard Johnson's Island.[52]

Within hours of this dispatch Carter did receive permission to pursue the Confederates and got his ship under way. On a hunch, Carter steamed westward, passing Middle Bass Island, where he found and picked up several of the stranded passengers from the *Island Queen* and the *Philo-Parsons.* On the basis of information given by these individuals, the *Michigan* raced to the mouth of the Detroit River, arriving by 10:00 A.M., only two hours after the *Philo-Parsons* had been scuttled at Sandwich a short way up the river. Not wanting to encroach on Canadian territorial waters, Commander Carter had his ship reverse course back to Middle Bass Island, where more refugees were picked up. The officer of the watch noted that he "saw *Island Queen* ashore on Check-a-Beona Reef but the water is too shallow to get at her."[53]

At 1:40 P.M. the *Michigan* returned to Sandusky. Commander Carter ordered a detachment of marines ashore to arrest John Robinson, who was implicated in the plot by Cole. Within an hour Robinson was in irons along with Cole on board the ship.[54] More than likely, Robinson was the messenger who was to contact Beall at Kelly's Island on the nineteenth.

On September 21, the *Michigan* was again out patrolling Lake Erie, this time looking for the *Philo-Parsons*. Commander Carter was now aware that the steamer had been hijacked by Confederates, but he didn't know that it had been abandoned by the raiders early the previous day. When the lookout suddenly shouted that he spotted the *Philo-Parsons,* the *Michigan* went to general quarters, and three twenty-four-pound Dalgren howitzers were loaded. A shot fired over the bow of the small side-wheeler brought it to a halt. A party of sailors and marines boarded the steamer and were surprised not to find any Confederate agents. The *Philo-Parsons* owner, having discovered the vessel scuttled in the Detroit River, had pumped it out and gotten it seaworthy in less than a day.[55]

On September 22, with the *Philo-Parsons* incident apparently over, Commander Carter requested that his prisoners, Cole and Robinson, be turned over to the area provost marshal. While the transfer of prisoners was taking place, a locally destructive storm hit the island. Carter commented, "this point was visited by a Severe Hurricane, sweeping in its violence the roofs of the long prison buildings, leveling picket fences on each side of the prison yard and felling over a hundred trees yet inflicting no severe injury to anyone." The warship received minor damage. The island prisoners, thinking that the destruction had been caused by the *Michigan*'s guns, in the hands of fellow Confederates, attempted unsuccessfully to escape.[56]

After the *Philo-Parsons* incident, the possibility of further Confederate raids out of Canada had to be taken more seriously by the U.S. military. The patrols of the *Michigan* became more active and less predictable. The warship stopped suspicious-looking ships with shots across their bows or blank cartridges.[57] Toward the end of the 1864 navigation season, the *Michigan* began searching vessels in various lake ports for gunpowder, arms, and ammunition in an effort to thwart threats of violence from the draft resistance.[58]

On November 9, Commander Carter received another warning from the Navy Department, stating that the Canadian propeller ship *Georgian* was rumored to have been purchased by Confederate agents in Canada and was being armed for an attack on lake cities.[59] Carter had sent a report two days earlier stating that he did not believe that the rumors originating out of Buffalo about the armed Confederate raider were true.[60]

Carter knew that even had the rumors been true, Lieutenant Colonel Hill had armed two tugboats and was watching every move that the *Georgian* made from Detroit. However, just to be safe, Carter assigned two of his men to infiltrate Canada and attempt to sign on as crew members of the *Georgian*. Apparently the men were successful, for they later reported that they "were on board the *Georgian* from day to day, swearing that they would like nothing so well as to have a fight with the Yanks, and they would release every prisoner at Johnson's Island."[61]

Despite Carter's assurances that the *Georgian* was harmless, the Navy Department ordered him to detain and search the vessel if it was found in United States waters.[62] This seizure was accomplished on November 20, 1864, when Hill's tugboats spotted the *Georgian* on Lake Saint Clair and boarded it. Although the *Georgian* was thoroughly searched, nothing out of the ordinary was found, so the vessel was allowed to pass.[63]

The *Georgian* spent the winter at Collingwood, Ontario, where, true to rumors, it was fitted out with a ram bow. The *Michigan's* two crew members were still on the *Georgian* and informed the *Michigan's* new commander, Francis A. Roe, of the ram. Roe immediately informed the State Department. An incensed Secretary of State Seward wrote to British authorities, who in turn confiscated the vessel and delivered it to U.S. officials.[64] Interestingly, the *Georgian* episode was yet another plot underwritten and planned by Jacob Thompson and John Y. Beall.[65]

As the Civil War wound to a close in the spring of 1865, the threat of Confederate action on the Great Lakes never subsided. Indeed, the fears and social tumult carried on well after the war on the battlefields was over.

The services rendered by the *Michigan* during the Civil War proved invaluable to the Union. The warship acted as a mobile garrison, stationed to contain urban hot spots or shipborne raiders. No other active navy ship could boast of enlisting half a legion of men to its country's service.

The rending of the North's social and economic fabric created the backdrop of the USS *Michigan's* next five years of challenge. The warship's greatest service, to remain a diplomat of peace, would shortly be put to its most severe tests.

VI   *Michigan's "Peninsula War"*

BY THE END OF THE CIVIL WAR the USS *Michigan* fulfilled more diverse tasks than its commanders ever conceived. Built to serve in the simple roles of fighting and patrolling, the ship had become a rescue vessel, an ambassador of goodwill, a recruitment rendezvous, a prison guard ship, and the strong arm of a government determined to keep civil order in its northern cities. The following episode falls into the latter category but exhibits a new twist: the willingness of the Union to use martial law to quell labor strife, a necessary measure to prevent the collapse of its war industry, and a necessary evil, some may argue, to preserve the Union.

There is a popular historical misconception that the first serious labor strife in Michigan's Upper Peninsula was the copper mining strike of 1913. However, forty-eight years previous to these copper country upheavals, a violent walkout was staged by both the copper and iron miners of the region, which resulted in the brief formation of the earliest labor union in the area. The subsequent destruction of this union via combined military operations, of first U.S. Navy and then U.S. Army contingents, demonstrate the importance placed on the region's mining industry by the country's political and industrial elite.

Michigan's mining strike may also demonstrate how the terrible conditions created by the Civil War promoted the spontaneous use of U.S. military force against labor organizations supported by political and industrial interests. The use of gunboat mediation in this case constituted an early and significant example of what one historian describes as "the readiness of the American political elite to support the economic elite in the quick and efficient repression of radical labor organizations."[1]

In order to better understand the mining strikes, and the role of the USS *Michigan* in them, it is necessary to briefly mention the historical setting and significant events that brought the major characters into conflict.

The spring of 1865 brought with it hopes of peace for the war-weary inhabitants of the United States. The Confederacy clearly teetered toward collapse but still managed to continue the Civil War on nearly a worldwide scale. By this time Confederate naval raiders had nearly decimated the Union merchant marine and had even attempted to attack the inaccessible northern Great Lakes. Only the USS *Michigan* patrolled this frontier region. Far from most of the fighting, the navy ship nonetheless seemed to attract its share of trouble. Before the war ended, the ship was responsible for capturing Confederate Naval operatives and foiling hijacking attempts (see chapter 5).

The warship's more mundane duties included recruiting thousands of lakes sailors for the U.S. Navy, guarding against Confederate infiltration from neutral Canada, guarding Confederate prisoners on Johnson's Island, and helping civilian authorities cope with the growing dissension of a war-weary population.[2]

The paddle frigate's newly appointed captain, Lieutenant Commander Francis A. Roe, had seen much of the naval war firsthand. This experience included a bloody engagement on May 5, 1864, when Roe had boldly attempted to chain his ship, the USS *Sassacus,* to the powerful Confederate ironclad ram CSS *Albemarle.* The battle resulted in a tactical victory for the Union (the *Albemarle* retreated), but Roe's vessel was badly mauled in the encounter, with many casualties. The combat nonetheless proved Roe to be an aggressive and tactically fearless naval officer. He received several commendations for meritorious conduct. Nevertheless, he was forced from battle due to bad health and received orders to captain the *Michigan* on the Great Lakes.[3]

With a change in commander the *Michigan*'s summer patrol also changed. The Navy Department instructed Roe to use the port city of Detroit as summer station instead of Erie, Pennsylvania, where the cruiser had been stationed since its launch. From Detroit, the ship could more quickly run to the upper lakes of Michigan, Huron, and Superior as the need arose.[4]

While the Civil War fighting had ended for the most part with the surrender of Lee's army in April, the struggle had all the appearances of continuing on a smaller scale through guerrilla warfare and subversive activity. These phantom threats caused as much disorder, fear, and apprehension as the war itself, due to the tremendous strain the struggle had inflicted on the fabric of the Union. Draft riots, labor strikes, war protests, and banditry forced authorities to declare martial law in several instances. On the

Great Lakes these disturbances centered in the larger towns plus the strate-
gically important iron mining center of Marquette, Michigan.[5]

Moreover, in the spring and summer of 1865, there appeared rumors of
Confederate plots to inflict attacks of retribution on Northern cities as
payback for the destruction of Southern cities. While in Detroit on June 22,
1865, Lieutenant Commander Roe reported "[h]earing that rebel emissaries
were going to some points on Lake Superior for the purpose of organizing a
piratical raid down all the lakes." Roe could ill afford to ignore this threat, as
Confederate Fifth Columnists had three times before attempted expeditions
in 1863 and 1864.[6]

Roe wasted little time navigating his vessel across Lake Huron but paused
at Sault Sainte Marie. The Sault Locks constituted a strategic bottleneck of
Lake Superior and a good place to intercept any Confederate raiders who
might have attempted to invade the lower lakes. After a week of vigilance and
no sign of the expected raiders, Roe decided to take his ship into Superior to
patrol the American south shore.[7]

The wilderness serenity between the Pictured Rocks lakeshore and Grand
Island constituted a second bottleneck of Superior's shipping lanes. As the
navy veterans basked in the isolation afforded by Grand Island, Lieutenant
Commander Roe reflected his war weariness:

> Here at anchor for a few days, in the solemn silence, the darkness of the
> enormous forest, the absence of all human life, strife, and activity, it was hard
> to conceive that in a far-away state . . . the roar and noise of war were going
> on. It was an almost unearthly relief to find one's self cut off utterly from the
> railway, the telegraph, the mails and the haunts of men.[8]

After four days of solitude Roe reluctantly gave the order to raise the ship's
anchor while a course was plotted for the iron mining center of Marquette.
Steam raised, the ship sliced the summer-calmed freshwater sea toward the
frontier town, arriving in the early afternoon on a sunny Monday, July 3,
1865.[9]

The commotion brewing in the hamlet of Marquette came in stark and
unwelcome contrast to the beauty and silence of Grand Island and the
shoreline of the Pictured Rocks. As the ship hove into sight, lookouts were
puzzled to notice the townspeople crowding the loading wharfs, shouting,
firing guns, and waving sheets, pillowcases, and anything else that could be
construed as a signal flag, in an apparent effort to attract the frigate's
attention.

On docking his ship, Roe learned that an "insurrection" was under way at the nearby iron mines. Using his navy vernacular, Roe described the mining trouble as a "mutiny," though the turmoil actually stemmed from a labor dispute turned violent.[10]

The well-timed arrival of the navy ship brought great relief to the towns-folk of Marquette, who for the most part were made up of mining company agents, officials, and their families. Apparently trained in the manual of arms, company agents and officers were nonetheless vastly outnumbered and out-gunned by the rioting miners.[11] Marquette did have a telegraph and a rail line, but help by land would have taken days; by then the town might lay in ruin.

Strike agitation undoubtedly preceded the mine closings by days or weeks, yet the actual strike seems to have been precipitated after the mining companies announced a wage cut on Saturday, July 1. The next day, Sunday, being the miners' traditional day of heavy drinking and fighting, became an ideal time for labor proponents to exhort the miners to action.[12] It seems no surprise that the spirit (and hangovers) generated on Sunday erupted into the potentially deadly situation that the crew of the *Michigan* faced on Monday. In all probability the ship arrived only hours after the village began to panic under the miners' threats.

It should be noted that at this time the Upper Peninsula mining towns suffered what may be described as typical boomtown conditions.[13] There was no police force and no sheriff. The mining agents policed both the mines and the town.[14] By the time Lieutenant Commander Roe and his men entered the fray, he could only relate that the miners "had stopped work, were rioting, and were making ready to march into town in force from their camp some four to six miles distant, and in a general raid to loot the groceries, the taverns, the stores, and the women and children." The miners also threatened to burn the town.[15] Fire was an extremely frightening specter to a frontier town enveloped by forest.

The underlying reasons for the miners' disaffection and "mutiny" can be deduced from the economic and social history of the Upper Peninsula. A nationwide economic depression followed closely on the heels of the Civil War. The mine companies and workers of the Upper Peninsula, both iron and copper, were not immune to the privations caused by this economic slump. The curtailing of war material production by the federal government added to mining industry woes and greatly diminished the demand for metals.[16] Consequently mines were closed, workers were laid off, and—most important in this case—wages were reduced.[17]

To add to the miners' plight, wartime inflation between 1861 and 1865 doubled prices while wages for area copper and iron miners increased by only 50 to 70 percent.[18] It is not surprising that the iron miners, under these increasingly stressful conditions, took a dim view of company justifications for wage cutting, mine closings, and workforce cutbacks. For the free-spirited frontier miner, who hardly needed an excuse to kick up his heels, these bleak economic prospects, coupled with the July 1 reduction in wages from $2.00 per day to $1.75 per day, became the last straw.

The laborers began their walkout by demanding a reinstatement of the $2.00-per-day wage and an eight-hour workday on Saturdays. The reaction of the Marquette townsfolk, however, demonstrated that what may have started as a labor dispute spontaneously erupted into a violent uprising. Thus the 1865 "Peninsula War," as it was dubbed in one tabloid, did not initially begin as an organized labor strike. Complicating the situation was the increasing fear in this remote area that a "broken and disseevered Union would ultimately become a fact."[19] News not only traveled slowly at this time but also was sporadically intermixed with rumors. The morbidity of these rumors gives some indication of what the Civil War had done to the psyche of the North. It is quite clear that nobody this far north seemed to know that the Union had prevailed. There were no victory parades or speeches, and the newsreel had yet to be invented.

The great discomfiture of the citizens of Marquette during this insurrection was exacerbated by the fact that, like most mining boomtowns, Marquette was virtually owned by the mining companies. In this light, it is not surprising that the town became the focus of the miners' attention and bitterness, as it had the previous year when strikers marched down the main avenue to shut down the loading quays, putting a stop to all mining activity in the area, even for the mines not on strike.[20]

In 1865 threats to plunder or burn the town as retribution against the mining companies' recalcitrant attitude demonstrated an escalation of strike agitation over the previous year. Undoubtedly laid-off laborers, who still lived in the area, joined the fray as the workforce had been cut back by 50 percent over the previous year.[21] This atmosphere set the stage for calamitous civil disorder and destruction.

Emboldened by the notion that federal authority had collapsed, the unhappy laborers began looting, burning, and destroying mining company equipment and property. The miners also began to tear up railroad lines and destroy railroad company equipment, linking the railroads with the mining companies as the cause of their problems.[22] The iron miners were apparently well aware that the mine and railroad owners might unite to suppress collective bargaining and union formation.

The officers and crew of the *Michigan* faced the situation with a sort of militant weariness born of the war. Though the mining insurrection was far from a routine problem, the sailors were experienced in dealing with civil unrest, and the vessel itself was in no danger due to its battery of powerful naval guns.

However, in defining the attitudes that would likely come into conflict during this crisis, it should be taken into account that many of the navy men were veterans of the war and had little sympathy for the miners, who, for the most part, had managed to stay out of it. In fact, most of the miners were recent immigrants who had arrived in the United States before the war, or were enticed into the country, ofttimes by the mining companies themselves, to fill the labor shortage created by the war. Compounding the potential animosity was the fact that an ordinary seaman made only sixteen dollars per month, as compared to the miners, who earned three times that amount.[23]

While fairly new to his ship and conditions on the Great Lakes, Lieutenant Commander Roe was not a stranger to battle or the threat of violence, and his acquaintance with it went back much further than his Civil War experience. Battles in China with "pirate" junks, in the Gulf of Mexico in support of the U.S. Army during the war with Mexico, and finally against the Confederate States Navy all predisposed Roe to think in military terms and to seek military solutions to problems.[24] Roe never mentioned the miners' side of the conflict in his reports, indicating his lack of sympathy for the workers. His knee-jerk reaction was to insure the safety of the town at all costs. The immediate question for the commander became one of how best to fully apply the warship and crew tactically before the violence turned to bloodshed and, if the situation did turn to bloodshed, how best to be certain his crew, the town, and the mining companies prevailed.

It seems obvious that Roe's responsibility as a government agent was to save the town and civilian property if possible. His subsequent actions and reported dialogue, however, suggest there were more than spontaneous protective motives behind the navy officer's decisions.

The necessities brought on by the Civil War almost immediately changed the government's traditional laissez-faire attitude toward work stoppages.[25] The very survival of the country depended on the steady flow of war material; therefore, the federal government became increasingly intolerant of labor disputes, particularly in strategic industries. In this case the *Michigan*'s commanding officer received no specific written orders to suppress the mining strike. He was, however, fully aware of the federal government's wartime attitude on the subject. His career depended on implementing decisions that ran parallel to those of his superiors. With this in mind, it is not surprising that Lieutenant Commander Roe decided not only to bring his ship and crew to combat readiness to protect the town, but also to mount an armed expedition to the mining camps to force the laborers back to work.

Roe immediately brought his ship and crew to readiness, arming his sailors and marines with pistols and Sharp's breach-loading rifles, supplemented by the usual naval hand-to-hand weapons. Though armed to the teeth, Roe's entire force of fewer than 130 sailors, officers, and marines were overwhelmingly outnumbered by the estimated 1,500 to 2,000 miners.[26] The paddle frigate's crew, however, enjoyed several advantages should any actual confrontation arise with the laborers. The ship's crew were well organized, with more than a few of them battle-hardened veterans like Roe. The sailors had artillery that could be mounted on field carriages. They also had the element of surprise, and regardless of the situation, they could fall back on the safety and security of their ship.

With the help of the local townsfolk, the ship's crew loaded two mobile twelve-pounder howitzers onto a railroad platform car. The guns, still on their naval carriages, were placed "one on each bow" of the car, and an armored casemate of boiler iron was built around them to protect the gun crews from small-arms fire. Ports were left in the casemate, from which the cannon muzzles protruded. When the artillery transfer was complete, the *Michigan*'s landing party, under Roe's direct command, boarded this gunboat on rails.

The steam locomotive likely pushed the train toward the mining camps so as not to overly expose the vulnerable steam engine. As the naval company approached the camps, the train halted and the leaders of the striking miners were called forth, according to Lieutenant Commander Roe, "to negotiate." However, it does not appear that any sort of bargaining dialogue took place. Roe simply issued an ultimatum to the miners. "They were told that twenty-four hours, and no more, would be allowed them, and if by that time they were not at work, and the ore loaded in the idle cars, that encampment would be stormed by shot and shell, and no questions would be asked or answered. There must be no more rioting, no more idleness, and no more threats."[27]

There is no evidence to suggest that this was a mere threat. As has been stated, Roe and some of his crew were veterans of the bloodiest war in

American history. The miners, as well as being totally surprised to see federal troops and artillery arrive out of the blue, were made fully aware of their danger. Armed sailors and marines paraded near the armored train, the first car of which prominently displayed the gaping muzzles of the two naval guns.

Fortunately for all concerned, the miners realized that in this case discretion seemed the better part of valor. Twenty-five cents per day lost much of its luster in the stark reality presented by Roe and the crew of the *Michigan*.

Though the workers were no doubt still angry, the rioting and threatened march on Marquette disintegrated. The laborers went back to work, and the pits began operating at normal capacity by the following day, delivering ore to the fleet of cargo vessels that had backed up since the mine shutdown. For the time being, the threat to Marquette and the mines was averted.

Roe kept a close watch on the situation for several more days to insure no further trouble erupted from the mines. Tempers smoldered, but no acts of violence seemed forthcoming. The warship's landing party with its howitzers reboarded the *Michigan* and the vessel churned off to the west, in the direction of the towns of Houghton and Hancock, and further troubles on Lake Superior.[28]

Houghton and Hancock were copper mining centers located in the heavily forested and mountainous Keweenaw Peninsula. A narrow, inundated cut, called Lake Portage, separated the two towns and traversed the entire peninsula. Though perhaps the largest ship yet to negotiate the portage, the *Michigan* had no trouble with the water depth due to its shallow draft. The warship's beam at the paddle boxes, however, was nearly fifty feet and must have made the waterway appear like a snake swallowing an egg. The vessel nonetheless squeezed down the channel to reach an anchorage off the town of Houghton by Saturday, July 8.

Commenting on the navigation of the large war steamer down the narrow, forest-lined waterway, Roe remarked: "The branches of the overlapping trees swept the hurricane deck as she steamed through. To a sailor reared and bred on the ocean it was a novel experience."[29]

The *Michigan* arrived at Houghton and Hancock to find the towns enveloped in much the same scenario as had occurred at Marquette. The copper mines were in upheaval, with the "Welsh" miners striking and in a "condition of revolt."[30] Roe's specific mention of Welsh miners may indicate that immigrant fractionalizing had played a part in the copper mining disorders. However, as with the iron mining industry, the plummeting postwar demand for copper created similar economic conditions in the Keweenaw as had existed in Marquette.

Determined to put a stop to the disruptive violence at the copper mines, the officers of the *Michigan* faced one great obstacle: the topography of the peninsula was too rugged to allow the vessel's artillery to support armed intervention by the warship's landing party. The use of force seemed particularly out of the question at the far-flung mines in the mountains surrounding the "little lake" where reportedly the "mutiny" was at its worst. Even the field howitzers needed relatively flat country or a rail line in order to be transported, and the Keweenaw had neither.[31]

From his experience at Marquette, Lieutenant Commander Roe concluded that the copper miners, like the iron miners of Marquette, probably lacked any real cohesion, had no union, and were largely made up of immigrant workers of various nationalities. On the basis of these observations Roe decided that rather than risk a confrontation with the miners in a place where his superior firepower would be of limited value, he would use psychological pressure to get the laborers back to the mines.

Roe issued an order to allow visitors on board ship. His aim was to impress the locals with the *Michigan*'s military hardware and crew preparedness in order to allay the townsfolk's fears while at the same time impressing the disaffected mine laborers with the fact that civil authority in the North was alive and well. Presumably the citizens, as at Marquette, were mostly mining company officials and their families. Many people availed themselves of this opportunity to board the federal warship. The local newspaper reported, "The boats of the steamer were kept continually running back and forth with loads of inquisitive visitors."[32]

In addition to allowing visitors to view the military hardware, the ship's crew made a show of setting up target ranges for small-arms and the big naval guns. A few days of visitations by townsfolk and miners, small-arms fire from shore, and an occasional thunderous cannonade from the vessel echoing throughout the mountains convinced the disaffected miners that, as Lieutenant Commander Roe put it, "the Union and civil authority," contrary to rumors, "had not collapsed." "A messenger to the mines, commanding them to resume work, was promptly obeyed, and this show of force alone was sufficient to restore peace and order."[33]

The U.S. Navy had a vested interest in preventing copper mining strikes had they occurred at any time during the war. Navy copper contracts were at stake, and the continued flow of this strategic material was essential to the Union war effort. Michigan's copper resources constituted the only considerable source of copper in the Union during the first part of the war and the chief source of the nation's supply after the war tariff decreased imported ore from Chile.[34] Regardless of the motivations behind the navy's interests in the

Keweenaw, it seems doubtful that these copper mining disorders were as potentially destructive as the Marquette strike. In Houghton and Hancock only a portion of the mining force was involved, and these workers were isolated far from urban areas.

Shortly after Houghton's miners had gone back to work, the *Michigan* sailed back to Marquette, arriving there on Thursday, July 13. The iron miners, emboldened by the absence of the warship, had renewed their strike for higher pay and fewer working hours on Monday, July 10.[35] To insure that they would not be surprised by a trainload of armed sailors and marines, they blockaded rail communication to and from Marquette. This blockade was particularly effective, according to the *Chicago Tribune,* because the miners "forcibly" enlisted the laborers of the Peninsula and Marquette Railroads to their cause. Only passenger trains were allowed through the blockade to Marquette.[36]

Once again the *Michigan's* landing party of sailors and marines armed with the two field pieces boarded their gunboat on rails. This time, however, the naval force could not approach the mining camp with their artillery due to the blockaded rail line. Oddly, although the miners had disrupted rail service to Marquette, they failed to cut the telegraph wire from town. Roe wired the army for reinforcements and on Saturday, July 15, a segment of the Eighth Veteran Reserve Corps infantry company arrived at Negaunee from Chicago via the Chicago and Northwestern Railroad.

The veteran Camp Douglas unit of sixty troopers commanded by Captain Munch and Lieutenant Stewart passed the smoldering remains of the Marquette Railroad's water station near Negaunee on their way to Marquette. Strikers reportedly had burned the station earlier that same day.[37] Though the laborers' rail blockade prevented the army from linking with the navy at Marquette, the soldiers' arrival placed the miners in a difficult tactical situation, locked between two forces.

Details concerning exactly who instigated the strike are sketchy owing to the lack of a united labor organization in a position to promote the laborers' side of the conflict. Indeed, a balanced history of the Upper Peninsula mining strikes is a difficult undertaking because the only extant accounts of the conflict come from military officers, mining company officials, and some generally unsympathetic newspaper reporters.

The "Peninsula War," however, seems to substantiate historian Gerald Friedman's assertion that "large scale immigration may have contributed to the remarkable unity of the elite in the United States." The mining and railroad company owners presented a nearly united front against the predominantly immigrant strikers. Although the *Chicago Tribune* chided the mining companies for not conferring among themselves to determine "a rate of compensation just and equitable to both parties," most of the contemporaneous press seems to side with the mining and railroad company owners, deriding the strikers as "unreasoning, turbulent masses" led by a few agitators.[38]

The railroad companies involved seem more disorganized than the mining companies, perhaps believing that a mining strike would affect them only indirectly. The Mining and Marquette Railroads, crippled by the violence and shutdowns owing to their local orientation, acceded to the strikers' demands to join forces in the rail blockade. The Peninsula Railroad refused to yield to the strikers and the Chicago and Northwestern Railroad, whose terminus was located at Negaunee, went virtually unscathed by the disruptions.[39]

After several weeks of dwindling ore production and threats of violence, most of the mining company supervisors were willing to raise wages back to two dollars per day; however, they still refused to consider the eight-hour work day on Saturday, apparently fearing the precedent set by reduced work hours. Only the Lake Angeline Mine Company acceded to both of the laborers' demands. Other mines, such as the Marquette, Superior, Cleveland, and Jackson, had few contracts to fill due to the economy and were not compelled to give in to the strikers.[40]

In desperation the miners held a meeting on the evening of Saturday, July 15. In this meeting they attempted to form a "Mutual Aid Association" to see them through the strike and insure future leverage in negotiations with the mining companies. However, despite their new union and the effectiveness of the work shutdown, their position became untenable. They were caught between the army, the navy, and—most important—the economy. After the army's arrival, the strikers held out for one more week. On July 23, the army was able to push through to Marquette, signaling the total collapse of the strike.

While the army unit stayed to quell any future disturbances, Lieutenant Commander Roe entertained visiting Prussian Minister Baron Gerolt on board ship. The baron apparently had witnessed the entire mining episode and wished to compare notes with Roe. He also knew something of the "Billious Fever" from which Roe suffered. Shortly thereafter, the *Michigan* returned to summer headquarters at Detroit.[41]

This post–Civil War mining strike has received little historical notice but nevertheless carries important historical implications. In total, the disruptions of 1865, in both the iron and copper mines of Michigan's Upper Peninsula, lasted sporadically for three weeks. Though there were no reported casualties, much property was damaged or destroyed, and the situation undoubtedly would have been much worse had the USS *Michigan* not arrived when it did.

The use of force, however, to compel laborers back to the mines demonstrates the value placed on the region by the financial and political elite and the cooperation shown by government and industry in 1865. The circumstantial evidence in this case strongly hints that the use of military power to end the strike may not have been merely a product of violent, desperate times or Lieutenant Commander Roe's personal disposition. Financial and governmental powers clearly acted in concert.

Business and political partnerships were reported on by area newspapers so matter-of-factly that in most instances, they were seen as one entity. For example, the *Chicago Tribune* reports the "railroad company have sent to Detroit, both for laborers to supply their places [the strikers] and for troops [U.S. Army troops] to regain possession of their road."[42]

Shortly after the Upper Peninsula strikes ended, the *Green Bay Advocate* reported that a "Military Expedition" was sent to Lake Superior for three reasons. The first explanation was to block the "miners' outbreaks." The second rationalization was that a U.S. Army presence would stabilize the region so that mining investors would be encouraged to speculate money after the recent upheavals. The third reason given was to protect the area from Great Britain should hostilities once again break out.[43]

As an adjunct to the mining disturbances, and as a result of the military expedition's recognizance, the government regarrisoned nearby Fort Wilkins at Copper Harbor located on the tip of the Keweenaw Peninsula. After military intervention in both 1864 and 1865, the army reoccupied Fort Wilkins in 1867 to have a more permanent base from which to insure the peace and maintain both civil and national protection for the mines.[44]

By the fall of 1865, the labor unrest in Michigan's Upper Peninsula became a thing of the past quelled not only by the army and navy but by prevailing economic conditions. With the disbanding of the Union and Confederate armies, the job market became flooded with workers. Mining companies found that labor could be had at a "discount," and no strike or insurrection was possible so long as there was a surplus of eager miners.[45]

Michigan's mining strike did not occur in a vacuum, but was part of the much larger picture of labor history in the Civil War. Other strikes took place in the Union during and shortly after the war, some of which were successful and some of which failed, also under military pressure.[46]

The true importance of the Upper Peninsula mining strike, and others like it, lies in its demonstration that the extraordinary attitudes and practices put into play during the war, such as military intervention and martial law, were not immediately revoked at its conclusion. Indeed, with communications as they were, there was no definite conclusion to the war on the Great Lakes. Fear and apprehension continued long after the last battles were fought. Perhaps the bellicose attitude instilled during this harsh time contributed to the bonding of the political and industrial elite, while it lubricated public acceptance of martial violence to settle economic disputes.

After the mining disturbances were over, the *Michigan's* officers entertained one more notable from the war. On August 4, General Ulysses S. Grant and his army staff visited the *Michigan.* Roe conducted the general some twenty miles into Lake Erie on what was called a "recognizance" mission. It seems likely that this voyage was the result of renewed tensions between the United States and Great Britain that were stirred by the war.

That fall, with his ship still in need of a complete overhaul, Lieutenant Commander Roe was finally able to cruise freely on the lakes. Unhindered by guard duty or the need to remain at station, Roe chose this opportunity to sail and make some observations concerning his command. Roe stated, the *Michigan* is the "[m]ost economical ship I ever knew in fuel; she is a good steady ship and has cost the government less money than any other gunboat in its service."[47]

During this cruise a new device was placed in the boiler firebox, which reduced the amount of smoke produced while burning soft coal to the equivalent of burning hard coal. The "smoke consumer" was the invention of Third Engineer Peter Smith. The newly patented device cut smoke emissions by 20 percent, saved boiler heating time by 40 minutes, and improved the general cleanliness and upkeep of the ship. The device apparently improved the ventilation in the boiler, making the combustion process more efficient.[48]

Before dry-docking for the winter at Mason and Bidwell's in Buffalo, the *Michigan* cruised 2,492 miles on 165 tons of soft coal. Ship's carpenter G. W. Elliot reported at this time that despite the generally run-down condition of the ship, its bottom looked very good, with no corrosion and few rivets missing. That winter the *Michigan* was internally reconstructed and put back into top condition.[49] This overhaul was fortunate. The spring of 1866 brought more trouble to the Great Lakes as a result of the political turmoil produced in the Civil War.

VIII *"The Fenian Ghost Is Walking Again"*

FROM THE END OF THE CIVIL WAR to the early part of the 1870s a political movement that profoundly affected the activities of the USS *Michigan* was afoot in the Great Lakes region. The resultant tragic invasion of Canada by a group of Irish-Americans calling themselves Fenians left at least a score of brave men dead, drew the United States and Great Britain once again to the brink of disastrous confrontation, and created a good deal of impetus toward Canadian public acceptance of confederation. As is the case with many historical events, this episode graphically demonstrates the passionate follies, individual gallantry, and inevitable humor of the human condition.

The Fenian movement and particularly the Canadian invasion attempts have been scrutinized in a dozen books and innumerable articles. The movement even became the backdrop for a romantic novel.[1] Yet the role of the USS *Michigan,* crucial as it was, has received scant attention or understanding. While most sources agree that the vessel was instrumental in halting the invasion, some admonish the navy ship for arriving too late to stop it, while others mistakenly refer to the ship as a revenue cutter. This chapter is an account of the USS *Michigan's* involvement in, and interdiction of, the Fenian raid into Canada June 1 through June 3, 1866.

It is as difficult today as it was in 1866 to conceive of a privately sponsored invasion attempt from one nonbelligerent country to another. The preposterous nature of such a venture belies the fact that it was attempted at all. Underlying this surface layer of absurdity, however, was the fact that the conflict was actually an extension of the political difficulties haunting United States and British relations following the American Civil War. Therefore, in order to understand the Fenian raids, it is necessary to outline briefly the roots and goals of the Fenian cause and dovetail them with the political machinations of U.S.-British relations.

Irish immigration into the United States and Canada was substantial in the first part of the nineteenth century. During the 1840s famines and British political persecution in Ireland increased this tide of immigration to a flood. Riding the crest were political agitators fleeing deportation from Ireland to Australia. Two such figures were John O'Mahoney and James Stephens. By 1857 these two had organized what they called the Irish Revolutionary Brotherhood, with O'Mahoney residing in the United States and Stephens in France. This organization, dedicated to the overthrow of British rule in Ireland, claimed 200,000 members, with a growing membership in the United States. To pursue their political agenda, Stephens moved back to Ireland within a year of the formation of the Irish Revolutionary Brotherhood. He was to head the organization, while O'Mahoney funded it from the United States.[2]

In 1859 O'Mahoney christened the U.S. branch of the Irish Revolutionary Brotherhood the Fenian Brotherhood, after the Fianna Eirionn, an ancient militia of pre-Norman Ireland.[3] By 1860 there were 1.6 million Irish people living in the United States, forming a substantial membership and monetary foundation for the brotherhood. The Civil War increased this figure substantially, with over 150,000 Irishmen joining the Union army.

The outbreak of the war not only increased immigration from Ireland but also initiated the disastrous political opportunism that grew between Fenian and Union politicians. Union recruiters went to Ireland offering vague support for Irish independence in return for enlistment in the U.S. Army. The Fenian leadership in turn encouraged Irishmen to join the Northern army to gain military training.[4]

The Fenian Brotherhood had by this time formed a government in exile at the Moffat Mansion in New York City, its itinerary still being the armed overthrow of British rule in Ireland. Increasingly, however, the brotherhood's leaders began to see that this goal could be more easily accomplished if trouble broke out between England and the Union.

To this end, anti-British rhetoric was extremely effective on both Irish and non-Irish Americans. This was particularly the case following episodes such as the Trent Affair, the Saint Albans raid, the attempted hijacking of the *Michigan,* the *Georgian* affair, and the disastrous depredations inflicted on Union shipping by the Confederate raider *Alabama.* The *Alabama* was built in Britain and manned largely with English seamen. By the end of the Civil War, Union frustration with England over these episodes and the supply of the Confederacy with weapons and ammunition was officially recognized with the Abrogation of the Reciprocity Treaty with Britain over Canada and a notification for abrogation of the Rush-Bagot Agreement.[5]

Meanwhile, though tensions between Britain and the United States soured, the brotherhood's chances to foment insurrection in Ireland were dashed. On September 14, 1865, the Irish Revolutionary Brotherhood's headquarters in Ireland were raided and *Erin's Hope,* a vessel loaded with arms from the O'Mahoney faction, was seized by the Royal Navy before it could off-load in Ireland.[6]

At Fenian Brotherhood conventions held that fall in the United States, it was conceded that prospects for a successful armed rebellion in Ireland were hopeless. A new, more radical approach was given its first serious consideration. This plan, put forward by new leaders of the movement, William R. Roberts and "Fighting Tom" Sweeney, called for invasion and entrenchment on Canadian soil to win over Irish-Canadians to their cause. A fleet of privateers would then commence operations out of "New Ireland" to harass British shipping. If all else failed, this plan was to create enough additional friction between the United States and Great Britain that war would ensue. According to the scheme, while Britain was occupied fighting the United States, Ireland would have its opportunity to revolt.[7]

During the early months of 1866, the leadership of the brotherhood passed back to the moderate O'Mahoney. *Harpers Weekly* predicted, however, "If the leaders pass round the hat to pay for a scrimmage, a scrimmage of some kind there must be or their own heads are in danger."[8] It was not surprising, therefore, that an initial invasion of Canada was attempted in April of that year. The attempted capture of Campobello Island in Passamaquoddy Bay, New Brunswick, was feeble and disorganized. Units of the Royal and U.S. Navies thwarted it easily and bloodlessly before it got off the ground.[9]

Most people in the United States became convinced that Fenianism could not be taken seriously due to the clumsy nature of this attempt. Secretary of State Seward explained to Minister Sir Frederick Bruce, "The Fenian affair was much exaggerated, and that nothing would serve so much to give it importance as that it became the subject of official correspondence."[10] The *New York Times* in May declared Fenianism dead and later derided the brotherhood, stating, "They have as much chance of making a lodgement in Canada as in the moon."[11]

Seward, however, knew well that Britain and Upper Canada did not consider Fenianism a laughing matter. Although official contact with the Fenian Brotherhood was shunned, he and other U.S. officials used the Irish faction as leverage to goad Britain into paying Civil War claims, particularly those demands pertaining to the raider *Alabama*.[12] It is interesting to note that the Fenian cause really lasted only so long as these Civil War claims remained outstanding and tensions between the United States and Britain remained high.

It was in this politically charged atmosphere that the USS *Michigan* faced another season on the Great Lakes. The ship had remained in Buffalo throughout the winter for a complete refit and internal rebuild at the dry dock of Mason and Bidwell in Buffalo Creek. The ship's stay in Buffalo during the winter of 1865–66 seemed ill omened from the start. A series of mishaps and bad luck plagued the ship. It began with the disappearance (and presumed death) of seaman Francis Welsh late in October, 1865, and continued through the transfer of the vessel's energetic and popular captain, Lieutenant Commander Francis Roe. Lake Erie also remained "one vast field of compact ice" through the early part of April.[13]

Regardless of these problems, a new commander arrived by mid-April. Incoming Commander Andrew Bryson inherited a rebuilt warship and a good, disciplined crew from Lieutenant Commander Roe. He also seemed to have inherited the bad luck that had bedeviled the vessel since its stay in Buffalo. The navy ordered Bryson on May 9 to check any Fenian activity near Erie. Before he could sail, however, Bryson needed to "swing ship" in order to reset its compasses following the rebuild. At this time Bryson found he could do neither: ice floes still made passage to Erie dangerous, and Buffalo Creek was too congested with boat traffic to adjust the ship's compasses.

By May 10, when Commander Bryson finally was able to attempt the voyage to Erie, the *Michigan* received serious damage before it could make it out of the creek. The barkentine barge *Major Anderson* swung around and passed its escort, the tug *C.N. Jones,* which was attempting to slow. The *Major Anderson* grazed the *Michigan,* crushing part of its upper works.[14] As events unfolded, it was fortunate that the *Michigan* was damaged in Buffalo and forced to lay up for repairs, because the Fenian crisis began to warm with the coming of spring on the Niagara frontier.

The day before the collision, Bryson was informed by the custom house collector of the city of Buffalo, Charles D. Norton, that Fenians had been smuggling guns and ammunition into the city. Norton sent a note to Bryson suggesting that since no revenue cutter was yet available, the *Michigan* might help search the port for contraband weapons.[15] Though sympathetic to Norton, Bryson had to follow his previous orders to proceed to Erie. The next day, however, when he was attempting to carry out his orders, fate intervened in the form of the runaway barkentine, which forced the steam frigate to remain in Buffalo for repairs.

Unbeknownst to Commander Bryson and Customs Inspector Norton, the Fenians' high commanders were planning a three-pronged attack on Canada to begin June 1. In the east, the Fenians planned to proceed from Saint Albans, Vermont, led by General S. P. Spear. In the center, the attack would proceed from Malone and Potsdam, New York, under General W. F. Lynch. In the west, the attack would be water borne from Chicago, Illinois, to Goderich and Sarnia, Ontario, headed by General C. C. Tevis. Smaller feints and strategic attacks were to proceed from Ogdensburg, New York; Cleveland, Ohio; Detroit, Michigan; and Buffalo, New York. These feints targeted the Welland Canal, the eastern terminus of the Buffalo and Lake Huron Railway, and the cities of Hamilton and Toronto.[16]

It was a hopelessly ambitious plan, even for a well-organized and well-supplied army. Nonetheless, the Fenian Brotherhood began days in advance to stream by the thousands to border rallying points. By May 28, Commander Bryson and every other federal agent became fully aware that something strange was going on. He reported to the Navy Department that he had heard rumors of arms shipments to Buffalo, now in the possession of Patrick O'Day, the local head of the center for the movement. Bryson was worried that a vessel would be outfitted for a landing on the Canadian shore of Lake Erie, explaining, "Under the circumstances I have deemed it prudent to keep sufficient fire under the boilers to keep the water hot without making steam."[17]

On May 30, Bryson sent word to the Navy Department that Fenians were arriving in Buffalo by the trainloads from Cleveland. The navy commander was in contact with the collector of customs and the superintendent of police, but as yet the Irish invaders had broken no laws. The U.S. authorities were helpless to turn them back. The commanding officer of nearby Fort Porter was also in touch with Commander Bryson concerning the situation. He explained that although he was aware of the brotherhood's movements, he might be helpless to stop them if and when they tried a crossing. The commander was unsure of how many of his fifty troopers could be relied on.[18]

From his contacts with the other agencies, it became unpleasantly clear to Commander Bryson that on the Niagara frontier, the USS *Michigan* was the only functioning U.S. government agent that was capable of interceding should the Fenians attempt a crossing into Canada. This fact was also very apparent to the Fenian hierarchy.

Collector Norton and Commander Bryson knew the situation had become critical by May 31. Norton suspended all ship traffic into and out of Buffalo harbor between 4:00 P.M. the preceding day and 9:00 A.M. that day, on orders from U.S. District Attorney William A. Dart. At 9:00 A.M. vessels were allowed to come and go only after a thorough inspection.[19] Bryson commented on the situation:

> There is considerable excitement in the City as to what their immediate object is, and fears are entertained that they may seize a steamer, and attempt to make a landing in Canada. I am all ready to cooperate with the shore authorities in preventing such a movement, and with this end in view, I have considered it prudent and necessary to keep a sufficient quantity of steam to enable me to move at any moment.[20]

The British and Canadians of course were not blind to what was going on at the border. The Fenian Brotherhood was, at times, hardly discreet in its movements. The *Toronto Globe* reported on the carnage left by some Fenians in their travels, which were easily gleaned from American newspapers, noting that "at one time an entire car load [of Fenians] were engaged in a general scrimmage, and many of the party were severely injured." Of the 342 Fenian troops loaded on the aforementioned train, one was left mortally wounded at Ashtabula and only 300 reached Buffalo. The *Globe* also reported on the United States' efforts to derail any invasion attempts, stating, "The American authorities are evidently doing their duty with the greatest promptitude and activity."[21]

Indeed, federal, local, and state authorities had some successes in their attempts to stem the brotherhood's tide to the border. In Erie, a steamer fitting out for an armed landing was seized by U.S. troops. Another, the *General Sedgwick,* was found to be loaded with stolen arms from a federal camp in Texas. U.S. marshals and county sheriffs continued to seize shipments of guns. The revenue cutter *Commodore Perry* even fired on suspected smugglers, and the *Michigan* captured a shipload of gunpowder in Buffalo harbor.[22]

Despite these setbacks, most of the Fenian Brotherhood members were traveling in an orderly fashion to mass at their prearranged embarkation points. A vast quantity of supplies made it past U.S. authorities, arriving in ships and in rail shipments marked "machinery," "hardware," "agricultural implements," and others. In Buffalo, Patrick O'Day was said to have amassed three thousand stand of rifles and ammunition. Fenian troops made it past police barricades set up in Buffalo by leaving trains early and walking to their destinations.[23] Well over a thousand Fenians were said to have arrived in Buffalo on May 30 and May 31 from Cleveland and Cincinnati.[24]

Finally on Thursday evening, May 31, it was obvious to all that the Fenian Brotherhood would soon attempt a crossing of the Niagara River to invade Canada. At 11:30 P.M. U.S. District Attorney Dart sent telegraph warnings to the mayors of Toronto and Hamilton. Combined with the warnings already issued by H. W. Heman, the British Consul in Buffalo, British General Napier became convinced that it was time to call out fourteen thousand Canadian volunteers for the militia.[25] Canada also had a body of British Royal Army troops on station since the escalation of border tensions during the Civil War.

The immediate obstacle to the Fenians' invasion, however, remained the USS *Michigan*. Alerted by Dart that the Fenians were going to attempt to cross at lower Black Rock, some five miles downstream from Buffalo, Bryson had his vessel prepared with steam up and guns loaded. At midnight, however, when all officers were to have returned to the ship, Bryson found his vessel pilotless and stranded, as helpless as if it had piled onto a reef or a bar in the river. The *Michigan's* pilot, Patrick Murphy, and second assistant engineer, James P. Kelley, were nowhere in sight.[26] Bryson knew that navigating the river in the dark without a pilot would have been foolhardy. No other pilots were immediately available.

While Commander Bryson helplessly fumed, some 1,000 to 1,500 Fenians, with Colonel John O'Neill commanding, made a crossing between Pratt's Iron furnace wharf and Freeburg's Wharf a mile or two below the village of Fort Erie on the Canadian shore. By 3:30 A.M. June 1, all the Fenian troops in Black Rock had crossed over in two canal boats towed by tugboats. Afterward they established a bivouac at Newbigging's Farm on French Creek.[27]

The landing was unopposed, though Canadian workers managed to remove the rolling stock of the Grand Trunk Railroad before Fenian patrols could capture it. The Fenian advance scouts did, however, destroy the railway bridge between Fort Erie and Port Colborne as well as the accompanying telegraph wires.[28]

At 5:00 A.M. the *Michigan's* delinquent officers arrived back on board the vessel to be greeted with immediate arrest. Yet Bryson's continued desperation to find a pilot compelled him to allow Murphy to pilot the ship to Black Rock. It arrived at 5:56 A.M. Though Murphy managed to get the ship to the wharf at the foot of Ferry Street, he apparently was unfamiliar with the river farther downstream. It was not until 11:20 A.M., when a local river pilot could be procured, that the ship could move farther down to Pratt's Wharf to cut off supplies to the Fenian army.[29] Only twenty minutes previous to the arrival of the *Michigan,* a tug towing two canal boats delivered more supplies to O'Neill's forces.[30]

During the day, while attending to his duties as blockader, Commander Bryson reconstructed what happened to his pilot the night before. "The only construction I can put on the affair is that Mr. Kelley has been the instrument directly of detaining the ship by enticing the Pilot away from the ship and detaining him until the crossing of the Fenian's had been affected."[31]

It became clear that engineer Kelley was a Fenian, or a Fenian sympathizer, having been seen attending open meetings of the organization. On the evening of May 31, he managed to waylay the pilot Murphy with copious amounts of alcohol, cigars, and a "lady friend."[32] It seems probable that Kelley was approached at one of the Fenian meetings and asked how to put the *Michigan* out of action. He in turn pinpointed the *Michigan's* most vital weakness: the navy ship could not navigate unknown waters without a pilot. According to Commander Bryson, both officers had heretofore been "prompt and trustworthy."[33]

News of the Fenian incursion met with disbelief in the United States and panic in Canada. The *New York Times* reported on June 1, "The Fenian ghost is walking again," implying that this latest news was but one more apparition of the "crying wolf" syndrome that had previously plagued reported Fenian activities.[34]

Canadian militia muster points, on the other hand, displayed "scenes of unparalleled excitement."[35] People living along the river of course knew something exciting was about to take place. The Toronto *Globe's* reporter in Black Rock reported at 2:00 P.M. June 1, "The Americans here are fully occupied with the latest sensation and are driving down in crowds to Lower Black Rock to see the Fenian Republic on the opposite shore."[36]

The Fenian army spent the day occupying the village of Fort Erie and sent out numerous patrols. A Toronto *Daily Telegraph* reporter wrote, "The *Michigan* is passing up and down the river with her ports open and will not allow any person to return to Buffalo."[37] At 2:50 P.M. the tug and canal boat made another attempt to bring supplies to the Irish army, but this time the *Michigan* forced the tug and its consort to heave to under its guns. Commander Bryson then sent an armed landing party under Acting Master W. G. Morris to board the "tug boat and scow." At nearly the same time, a steam launch made a dash for the Canadian shore, but it was intercepted by another of the *Michigan's* launches under Lieutenant F. O. Davenport and forced to return to the U.S. shore.

That evening at sunset Commander Bryson mustered the crew to quarters and quite probably addressed them on the importance of remaining vigilant. Intercepting supply vessels and curiosity seekers in broad daylight was one thing, but to capture boatloads of armed and possibly desperate men at night was quite another. To emphasize this fact, Bryson had the port side forward broadside guns reloaded with shrapnel and the starboard with canister.

At 9:15 P.M., while the warship tied off to Pratt's Wharf, the tugboats *C. M. Farrar* and *Harrison* came alongside. The tugs had been procured under direction of District Attorney Dart. Commander Bryson transferred the *Michigan's* twelve-pound howitzers to the deck of each vessel. Acting Master W. G. Morris was put in charge of the *Harrison* while Gunner and Acting Master J. R. Granger commanded the *Farrar*. By 10:15 P.M. all three vessels cast off to patrol the river, with the *Michigan* returning to the mouth of Buffalo Creek.[38]

That night each of the tugs captured small boats attempting to smuggle men and arms to the Canadian shore. During one of these captures the first casualties of the invasion may have been inflicted. Tug *Farrar* came upon a boatload of armed men in the night river mist. Granger was immediately faced with the dilemma of all single-gunned combatants during war. If he fired his howitzer in warning, he would have essentially disarmed himself, and the rifles carried in the small boat could have inflicted serious damage to his vessel and crew before he could reload. Therefore, having received no reply from shouted orders to heave to, Granger fired at the boat. After receiving no return fire, the *Farrar* approached the boat to find that all on board had either jumped over the side or were blown over the side by shrapnel from the howitzer. Finding no bodies or survivors, Granger had the boat taken under tow and delivered to the *Michigan* after daybreak.[39]

During the early morning hours of July 2, while the tugs repelled more invaders, the main body of the Fenian army marched from its camp. Colonel O'Neill, acting on intelligence that two British forces were converging on him from Port Colborne and Chippewa, set out to intercept one of these columns before they could join at Stevensville. The colonel determined that he would meet the Canadian volunteer force at Ridgeway and await reinforcements before tackling the British regulars converging from Chippewa.

His forced march at night up the Ridge Road achieved the surprise he had counted on. At approximately 8:00 A.M. his skirmishers met the vanguard of the Canadian militia three miles northeast of Ridgeway on the Ridge Road. The Canadian force of nine hundred men was roughly equivalent in number to the Fenian force due to Fenian desertions and sickness.[40]

Though the Canadians had not expected to meet the Fenian force so soon, they were ably deployed by their commanding officer, Lieutenant Colonel Alfred Booker, and were soon advancing on the Fenian positions. The firefight raged for an hour or an hour and a half. During the first phase of the fighting, the Fenian skirmishers were driven back on the main body of O'Neill's force. The Canadians even succeeded in turning the Irish army's right flank, when a fluke sighting of a few Fenians on horseback led to the bugle call to form a square and prepare to repel cavalry.

This maneuver proved disastrous for the militia. Though the Fenians had no cavalry, the tightly packed squares of Canadian militia became an easy target. O'Neill saw his chance as the Canadian troops wavered under heavy fire, and he ordered an attack with fixed bayonets.

Faced by the frontal bayonet charge, Booker attempted an orderly withdrawal but found that his reserves were too close to the front and were also taking heavy fire. The deployment of his reserves under fire became impossible and a general rout to Port Colborne ensued.

Colonel George T. Peacocke [spelled Peacock in some sources], leading the force of British regulars and volunteers out of Chippewa, had attempted to link with Booker's force that morning. Peacocke was only able to get within hearing distance of the battle, however, because the militia commander left Ridgeway earlier than anticipated.

Colonel O'Neill, knowing of Peacocke's proximity with a superior force, being low on ammunition, and having just survived a major skirmish, retreated from the battle site after only a halfhearted attempt to pursue the Canadian militia. O'Neill's objective was now old Fort Erie to pick up supplies and reinforcements. With this in mind, the Fenians divided their force and advanced via the Garrison Road and the Grand Trunk Railway.

Unbeknownst to Colonel O'Neill and his men, old Fort Erie was then being occupied by a small force of Canadian militia ferried earlier that day from Port Colborne on board the tug *W.T. Robb*. Lieutenant Colonel J. Stoughton Dennis was instructed to prevent a Fenian withdrawal to the U.S. shore, but in the excitement he forsook the safety and tactical advantage afforded him by his vessel and landed his eighty-seven men in the village of Fort Erie. This action set the stage for the second battle of the day. At 9:00

P.M. the returning Fenian columns fell upon Lieutenant Colonel Dennis's small force.

The fighting at Fort Erie was short and desperate. The American shore was lined with spectators. Onlookers also crowded onto tugs and small boats to be closer to the action, lending the deadly scene the air of some unreal sporting event. The Fenian forces overwhelmed the Canadians within half an hour. They captured many of the Canadians, while the remainder retreated along the River Road. The militia cut the *Robb* loose during the first part of the action to escape the Fenians. It floated downstream, picking up fleeing militia on the way. Since the tug was already loaded with fifty-seven Fenian prisoners (stragglers gathered up during the day), it withdrew that evening to Port Colborne.[41]

Casualty estimates for the two skirmishes seem to vary with each historical source. Colonel O'Neill's own casualty list, given later to Commander Bryson, numbers eight Fenians killed, with fourteen wounded, while Canadian sources variously list from nineteen to over forty casualties, including nine killed.[42] As with all battles, confusion held sway on both sides for a good portion of the Fenian incursion. Therefore, exact counts of casualties and prisoners vary. In this light, it seems doubtful that Colonel O'Neill knew of Fenian losses incurred in crossing the river, and Canadian authorities captured many a "spectator" before sorting them from invaders.

Although the Niagara invasion was to be only a minor tactical incursion into Canada, it seems to have been the only part of the grandiose Fenian plan that worked. The other prongs of the attack fizzled due to poor logistics, disorganization, and the interference of U.S. authorities. Bands of Fenians discouraged from other areas began to turn up en masse in Buffalo. The only thing that stood between them and real carnage in Canada was the Niagara River and the small U.S. flotilla headed by the *Michigan*. Revenue cutter *Fessenden* reinforced this squadron on the evening of June 2. The cutter *Perry* was expected at any time.[43]

There is little reason to believe that a permanent lodgment in Canada could have been effected by the Fenians on the Niagara frontier, even if the U.S. authorities had not cut off their supply route. The Fenians had little or no logistical planning, no artillery, no cavalry, and above all in this instance, no naval support. Deprived of reinforcement and supply, and finding little or no Canadian Irish Catholic sympathy for their plan, Colonel O'Neill's force found itself in a hopeless situation.

Some reports note that an Irish relief force was dispatched from Buffalo late that evening on board two canal boats in consort with one or two tugs.

Commander Francis A. Roe of the Michigan, *November, 1864, through April, 1866. (Courtesy of the U.S. Naval Historical Center, Washington, D.C.)*

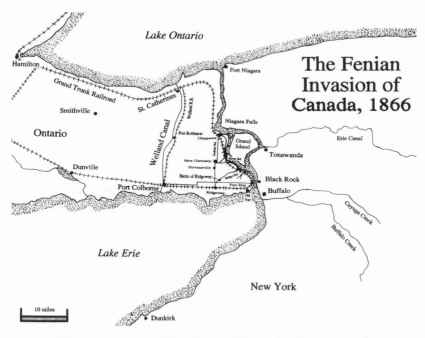

The Fenian invasion of Canada, 1866. (Map produced by the author.)

Commander James E. Jouett of the Michigan, *April, 1868, through September, 1870. (Courtesy of the U.S. Naval Historical Center, Washington, D.C.)*

Captain Andrew Bryson, commander of the Michigan *from April, 1866, through April, 1868. (Courtesy of the U.S. Naval Historical Center, Washington, D.C.)*

Still sleek after forty years of service in its familiar black hull scheme, the USS Michigan *is seen here between 1886 and 1893 (note deck awnings). (Courtesy of C. Patrick Labadie Collection, Duluth, Minnesota.)*

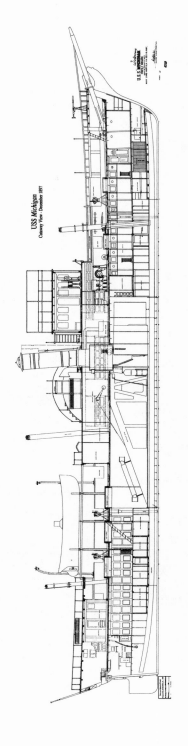

USS *Michigan*
Cutaway View – December 1897

In 1897 the Michigan was extensively overhauled. These plans of the ship were drawn by O.W. Trueworthy under the supervision of Naval Constructor A.W. Stahl. Note that Michigan was scratched out and Wolverine handwritten in during the name change of 1905. (RG-19, 28-14-31; courtesy of the National Archives, Washington, D.C.)

Post 1897 photo of cruiser Michigan. *Note the large chart house added to layout hydrographic survey maps. (From the University of Detroit Marine Collection.)*

Neglected veteran abandoned near Perry's Victory Monument, Misery Bay. (From the University of Detroit Marine Collection.)

Wolverine *on maneuvers with other state naval militia ships. (From the University of Detroit Marine Collection.)*

Prominently displaying its one-pound (forecastle) and six-pound (waist) rapid-fire canons, the navy ship glides past a breakwater. (Courtesy of the Manistee County Historical Society.)

The unprotected cruiser Michigan *under steam after being painted white in 1893 but before it was rebuilt in 1897. (Courtesy of the U.S. Naval Historical Center, Washington, D.C.)*

Painting of the USS Michigan by Charles Paterson located in Detroit's Belle Isle Maritime Museum. The ship is depicted as it appeared between 1886 and 1893 on one of those rare occasions when it carried a full spread of canvas. (Courtesy of the Dossin Great Lakes Museum, Belle Isle, Michigan.)

Getting under way near the turn of the century. As reflected by the training ship's rigging (only the spanker sail is rigged), sail training was no longer emphasized by the navy. (Courtesy of the Canal Park Museum, Duluth, Minnesota.)

Superstructure and paddle wheels removed, the old warship is readied for the scrap yard. (Courtesy of Mr. W.C. Cowles, Morristown, New Jersey.)

This force was supposedly met by a messenger from O'Neill in midstream ordering them to turn back, off-load the reinforcements, and attempt to evacuate his force.[44] Since supplies were effectively cut off, O'Neill had no choice but retreat.

By early in the morning of June 3, O'Neill had only one-third of his original force. Most had fled back to the U.S. side aboard anything that floated, from rowboats to wooden planks. During the day and into the evening of June 2, the *Michigan* patrolled from Buffalo Creek to Lower Black Rock. At 1:00 A.M. June 9, the warship was anchored near Black Rock when it was approached by tug *Harrison* escorting an abandoned yawl. The *Harrison* then proceeded back upstream toward Buffalo.

At 2:30 A.M. a cannon report from the direction of the *Harrison* signalled the paddle frigate to general quarters. Anchor tripped, the *Michigan* proceeded upstream to find the *Harrison* escorting the tug *J.H. Doyle* in consort of a large canal boat containing hundreds of men.

Obviously Acting Master Morris had captured the bulk of the remaining Fenian force as they attempted to slip back to Buffalo. As the *Doyle* had shown some reluctance to heave to, Morris had been forced to fire a shot over its bow, both in warning and to signal the *Michigan*. The *Michigan* took the canal boat under tow back to Black Rock and anchored in midstream with the canal barge trailing astern in the swift current.[45]

In his report to Fenian President Roberts, O'Neill described the predicament facing his small command at the time of their capture. Only 317 green-clad troops remained, including officers. Expecting to be attacked and "cut to pieces" by a force ten times their size packing artillery, the colonel had but three choices: fight, surrender, or retreat. O'Neill opted to retreat after having first destroyed three hundred extra weapons so they would not fall into British hands. He then signaled friendly forces in Buffalo to send a boat to withdraw his men. A canal boat arrived at 2:00 A.M. but after departing the Canadian side they were caught in midstream by the *Harrison*. O'Neill gave in to the surrender demand put forth by Morris, "not because we feared the twelve-pounders or the still more powerful guns of the *Michigan*, but because we respected the authority of the United States."[46]

After the attack, Canadians denounced U.S. efforts to thwart the invasion as "placid" at best.[47] Canadians were furious with the incursions, making an early trial for the sixty to one hundred Fenians captured in Canada impossible.[48]

The American public also seemed to sober as the death toll and the reality of the Fenian undertakings became known. Though continuing to lambaste

Canada for harboring Confederate agents during the Civil War, a *Harpers Weekly* editorial summed up U.S. reaction:

> While the Fenian Movement was confined to Jone's Wood and Moffatt Mansion it was merely amusing but when a rabble cross the border, and without artillery or supplies or trains begin to make war by murdering honest people who turn out to defend their homes, the affair ceases to be contemptible and becomes criminal . . .[49]

Most important, however, for relations between the United States and Britain was the reaction of British consul Hemans, an eyewitness to the invasion and the *Michigan*'s efforts to thwart it. Reporting on the affair to his superiors, Hemans stated: "There can be no question that the surveillance of the *Michigan* which was reinforced . . . by a Revenue Cutter, and the patrolling of the river by the armed tugs effectively cut off the Fenian reinforcements and operated powerfully in frustrating their plans."[50]

The British afterward correctly attributed the United States' tardy response to the initial invasion to the fact that U.S. forces, being small, were not equal to the task. No official mention was made of the embarrassing situation a pilotless *Michigan* found itself in during the early morning hours of June 1.

British and American arbitration over the disposition of the prisoners began almost immediately. At 11:00 A.M. June 3, British Colonel Lowery, representing the British forces in Canada, and British Consul Hemans met with Brevet Major General W. F. Barry, commanding American forces, and Commander Bryson on board the *Michigan*.[51] At this meeting, it was explained to the British authorities that the Fenians' fate lay with U.S. District Attorney Dart, who would no doubt act on instructions from Washington.

Meanwhile, the Fenian army was fed and disarmed, and several wounded were attended to by the ship's physician. The tugboats, each carrying six sharpshooters, were stationed alongside the canal boat. Commander Bryson was "much embarrassed" in having so many prisoners to take care of.[52] The encumbrance of the canal boat obviously limited his options in case another Fenian crossing was attempted, rumors of which were still flying.[53]

It was not until Tuesday evening, June 5, that U.S. commissioners and marshals began releasing the prisoners in small groups on their own recognizance.[54] The leaders were detained, while the rank and file had only to promise to return should a trial be necessary. Two days of marching and fighting followed by three days in an overcrowded open boat had taken most of the wind from their sails. As a further inducement, free transport home was offered by the U.S. government.

Of the vaunted three-pronged attack, only the eastern prong, under Fenian General Spear, managed to move at all. Although some property was destroyed, this attack amounted to no more than a border incursion. President Andrew Johnson's Proclamation of June 6, denouncing further mischief on the part of these misguided citizens, seems to signal the end of active hostilities in 1866.[55]

The military invasion of Canada by the Fenians was doomed to failure from the outset. That it could have caused real diplomatic problems in British-U.S. relations, however, goes without question, especially given the post–Civil War diplomatic climate. That it heightened Canada's national awareness and Canadian citizens' pride in having fought for their homes, there can also be no doubt. Fortunately, during and after the tumult, the cooler heads of professional diplomats prevailed, aided by the extreme visibility and vigorous actions of the USS *Michigan* and its small consorts.

It should also be pointed out that the conduct of the Fenian forces, other than the misguided invasion attempt itself, was exemplary. Canadian militia officer George Denison, Jr. admitted after interviewing the inhabitants of Fort Erie:

> They [the Fenians] have been called plunderers, robbers and marauders, yet, no matter how unwilling we may be to admit it, the positive fact remains, that they stole but few valuables, that they destroyed, comparatively speaking, little or nothing, and that they committed no outrages on the inhabitants, but treated every one with unvarying courtesy.[56]

Colonel O'Neill's forces for the most part showed bravery and discipline, a credit to his leadership and their ethical stand, right or wrong. Even Commander Andrew Bryson, soon to be Captain Bryson, had to admit (to his everlasting embarrassment) that the imaginative disabling of the *Michigan* via cigars, spirits, and female persuasion had been a stroke of genius.

The *Michigan's* cruises would be plagued for another four years by rumors of Fenian movements but nothing as serious as the invasion of June 1, 1866. However, on the morning of November 5, 1866, while tied to Pratt's Wharf in Black Rock, the navy vessel was boarded by a hostile band for the only time in its history.[57] It is not stated in the logbook whether the "Lady members of the Fenian Sisterhood" accomplished their stated aim to retrieve the green sunburst standard of the Fenian legion, confiscated June 3, but it is this author's guess that they did.

VIIII *The* Wolverine

PERHAPS THE MOST VALUABLE and lasting contribution made to history by the USS *Michigan* is the accumulation of accounts concerning life in the post–Civil War navy locked within its records. These descriptions come to the fore when political and military concerns are moved to the background, as they were in the last quarter of the nineteenth century. During this period of unprecedented leisure time, records are supplemented by anecdotal evidence, in manuscript form, from crew members and officers concerning life as a freshwater sailor.

This chapter then proceeds to an explanation of the changes time and technology wrought on the USS *Michigan,* before and after its conversion to the USS *Wolverine* in 1905. Finally, the demise of the paddle frigate will be explored with a view to explaining how the *Michigan* fell victim to time, bureaucratic custody shuffling, and a lack of public historical awareness.

POST–CIVIL WAR FRESHWATER NAVY LIFE

The cruises of the *Michigan* during the period from 1870 to 1905 were fairly routine. No major political conflagrations disturbed the lakes region, as they had during the first thirty years of the paddle frigate's history. Except for occasional winters in Buffalo for rebuilding and repairs, the ship's home port remained Erie, Pennsylvania.

It is important at this time to distinguish the activities of crew from officers. The crew and officers occupied two distinct economic and social classes and, not surprisingly, were completely separated on the ship. The crew lived forward of the engineering spaces on the berth deck. The officers lived aft of the engineering spaces in separate rooms opening onto the communal officers' wardroom. In its original configuration the captain's cabin also opened onto the wardroom but was later moved above to the main deck.

The *Michigan* was stationed in Erie for so long, and operated yearly under such a predictable routine, that it developed an unusual affiliation with the town, an association unique in U.S. naval history. Erie became known as "the mother-in-law of the navy."[1] As many as fifty-five of the vessel's officers and previous officers were married to Erie women at one time.[2] This number amounted to a huge percentage of the vessel's staff, since the ship seldom carried more than ten officers at any given time.

It can be presumed that a considerable portion of the enlisted men were also married to Erie women, or had girlfriends waiting there. Naval mythology asserted that sailors in the blue-water navy had a woman in every port. Sailors serving on the *Michigan,* on the other hand, were quite often married; many times after short courtships and whirlwind romances. Amelia Brown, wife of Chief Gunner's Mate George Brown, related that they met one Saturday and were married on the next.[3]

Winters in Erie were cold and stifling. Officers bought homes or stayed at the U.S. Hotel, later the Reid House Hotel, just up the street from the public docks. One officer related, "In going from our quarters [the Reid House] to the ship, we frequently had to encounter an air both unusually nipping and eager, and sometimes had to plough through snow above our knees." The hotel also provided food for the officers during the day. The crew likely still dined in the ship's galley.[4]

The ship was heated with radiators and coal braziers and housed over with a wooden building during the winter months. Many of the crew, particularly officers, were not from this region of the country and found winters somewhat less than hospitable. Francis Roe, commander of the cruiser during Michigan's mining strikes, related, "In truth the ship was not habitable in that fierce winter climate. Not sheathed below, every morning the iron sides of the berth deck were white with the rime of frost."[5]

The winter, or "stationary period," as the navy men called it, brought other changes in the lives of the *Michigan's* seamen other than trying to survive cold weather and possibly indulging in a stint of family life. Many of the sailors took winter jobs as hotel porters and laborers. Duty watches for the crew usually ran one day on and one day off. This scheduling permitted the men time enough to work these other part-time jobs. Officers, on the other hand, had one day on and two or three days off. It is doubtful they took on other jobs as they were adequately paid.[6]

The status, both economic and social, of naval officers in the later part of the nineteenth century was quite high. After 1870 the *Michigan's* officers made $200 or more per month for sea duty and $165 or more per month for shore duty during the winter. Since inflation was relatively low after the Civil War, officers' pay probably remained constant until after the turn of the century.[7]

These salaries were adequate to provide for a family and a relatively high standard of living. Maintaining a household at that time required the hiring of servants and nurses and the purchase of a house or the renting of rooms at the Reid House. Lieutenant Robert E. Coontz, for example, was able to transfer his family and Russian nurse to his newly purchased house in Erie. The houses owned by officers were not of the average variety but often large and located in upper-class neighborhoods. *Michigan*'s longtime surgeon William Maxwell Woode was not an exception and had no difficulty putting up President Zachary Taylor and his entourage in 1849.[8]

By the 1890s crewmen made from about $10.50 to $65.00 per month depending on their rank and experience. Green hands for instance made only $10.50, while baymen made $18.00, buglers $33.00, boatswains $30.00, and masters $65.00.[9] This is a large range in pay and reflected the difference between career men and short-timers. Though fairly unusual, it was possible for enlisted men to save this money and provide for a family. They certainly did not, however, hire servants and nurses. Patrick Murphy, for instance, was honorably discharged by the navy for his good example. His commander explained,

> By exercising great providence and economy he has been able to posses himself of a House and Lot, and to bring up a family respectably. Such instances of thrift are rare among seamen, and his example has no doubt had the effect to make the crew generally, more provident and correct.[10]

Winter routine on board the *Michigan* started with reveille at 5:30 A.M. followed by coffee and boatswains' orders. The boatswains insured the routine maintenance of the ship and ship's fittings. Maintenance included painting, sewing, scraping paint, polishing the brass, repairing lines, holystoning the decks, and during harsh winters, breaking the ice around the ship to relieve any pressure buildup on the hull. At 7:30 A.M. breakfast was served in the galley on the berth deck. At 8:45 A.M. the crew turned to for a 9:00 A.M. inspection, after which they were mustered to quarters.

General quarters drills occupied the remainder of the morning. These drills included fire quarters, manual of arms, dress parade, single stick or foil practice (a leftover from the days of sail), and every few weeks during the navigation season, target practice with the "great guns." After lunch, at 12:30 P.M. the officers, except the deck watch, could leave the vessel until the following morning. The routine for the navigation season was essentially the same, with the exceptions that the officers remained on board ship in the afternoon and evening, and watches rotated during the day, not every other day.[11]

Some routine maintenance was made less tedious with crew competition. For instance, a contest was often held for polishing the brass fixtures and mahogany paneling with which the ship was well endowed. Seaman Grant F. Crowly remarked, "She was loaded with brass. We on the crew used to have competition shining it. The whole floor of the crank room was brass . . . all the rails and hatches were brass and all of the pipes. She was a beautiful ship."[12] The mahogany and brass no doubt gave the aging steamer an air of stately elegance, which seems appropriate to the high Victorian age.

During free time officers lounged in the wardroom. The *Michigan*'s wardroom boasted an impressive library with such titles as *In Darkest Africa, Emin Pasha,* or, for a change of venue, *The History of the U.S. Marine Corps.* Aspiring midshipmen could receive part of their navigational education through works such as *Magnetic Observations of the U.S. Naval Observatory, 1888–1889.*[13]

Officers' activities during the long winter months also included ice skating, ice boating, and ice fishing. Many skating parties originated from, and ended in, the warmth of the officers' wardroom. Ice boating was also popular. The first mention of this activity comes from the late 1870s, but it remained popular throughout the rest of the *Michigan*'s career. The small, sail-powered, outrigged boat on runners is described as being very fast and no doubt helped add excitement to winter days.[14]

The stationary period allowed the warship's band plenty of practice time. The *Michigan*'s band, which was reputedly very good, attracted musicians and helped recruit many of these into the navy. "When a man appeared on board ready to enlist he was asked, do you play any musical instrument?"[15] A positive reply immediately vaulted the man past green-hand status. The ship's band participated in numerous parades, commemorative activities, and funerals in Erie and around the Great Lakes. On June 15, 1882, the band participated in the Detroit parade for the reunion of the Army of the Potomac. The ship's log records that the *Michigan* was "dressed in rainbow style" for the occasion, covered in red, white, and blue bunting.[16] On February 2, 1891, the band was part of a funeral party paying last respects to a shipmate. That same year the band played in honor of visiting Attorney General William Miller.[17]

In the spring the house built on deck was removed and the ship refitted with its running rigging and main armament. The rigging—including yards, topmasts, blocks, and the like—and its great guns were removed and stored in December of each year after the close of the navigation season. The masts and yards became cranes to lift supplies from the wharf to the ship. This rigging was also essential in hoisting the heavy ordnance from the storehouse to the weather deck.[18]

Coal, food supplies, and sailing supplies were procured starting in the spring and replenished throughout the year. Routine supplies included food-stuffs such as raisins, flour, sugar, beans, cheese, beef, and vegetables. Sailing supplies included candles, tallow (for oil lamps), shoe thread, brooms, soap, paper, pencils, paint, line of ten thicknesses, canvas, needles and thread.[19]

Late in the 1870s the Canadian port of Sarnia, Ontario, became a favorite port of call for the *Michigan*'s crew. It was here that the ship laid in "wet sea stores" such as beer, wine, liquor, tobacco, cigars, and cigarettes. These products were cheaper in Canada than in the United States.[20] The *Michigan* was by this time a very welcome sight to the merchants on the Canadian side, and each visit helped cement the ever growing friendship between the two countries.

Navigation season was not all business or heroics for the crew and officers of the navy ship. The crew enjoyed leave as sailors have from time imme-morial, visiting bars and sometimes creating havoc with the local toughs. The officers, on the other hand, attended formal parties put on by the local inhabitants. A young Lieutenant Robert Coontz explained at one point that he could not stand the pace; there were parties every night. Coontz's intro-verted nature loaned itself to invention. He explained at one point what he did with some of his free time:

> I had conceived the idea that it was possible for a man to fly like a bird or a chicken by attaching light wings to his arms. Bois Blank Island was directly opposite Amherstberg and I had an opportunity to test my theory there. Going to an elevation of 10 or 12 feet I would jump off and flop my wings. If it were windy I would glide five, ten, or even so far as twelve feet but I could not sustain myself in the air for any appreciable length of time.

Though Coontz was an early dreamer of manned flight, he would later in his career fulfill these dreams, becoming chief of naval operations, in charge of naval aviation among other things.[21]

The crew of the ship also formed sports teams to pass leave time. Football became increasingly popular at the turn of the century, and the young crewmen of the warship formed a team to play other local teams. The Wolverines became so celebrated that tickets were actually sold for their fall games against such Erie rivals as the West Ends.[22]

By the early 1890s the *Michigan* began to deviate from its usual lake patrol to take part in other activities. The navy ordered Commander George Wingate in 1892 to conduct a topographical and hydrographical survey of the Calumet River in preparation for the 1893 Chicago world's fair. The *Michigan* remained in Chicago throughout the world's fair, helping where possible and staffing such maritime exhibits as the Spanish government's gift to the United States, replicas of the *Nina, Pinta,* and *Santa Maria,* as well as the scale-model concrete battleship *Illinois.* It was here that the *Michigan* was painted white to match the new navy ships, a color the vessel was destined to carry from that time onward.[23]

Shortly after the world's fair the crew of the *Michigan* was ordered to begin hydrographic surveys and place navigation markers at various shoal areas on the lakes. The first of these was the mouth of the Detroit River and the Lake Saint Clair mudflats. These were notorious areas for navigation. Commander Oscar Bullus first reported on this area nearly fifty years previous to the survey, explaining, "This vessel has never crossed Lake Saint Clair that we did not encounter one or more vessels hard and fast aground."[24]

During the survey the *Michigan* itself became a victim of the shoals. At 11:05 A.M. August 2, 1894, the paddle frigate grounded hard while gaining entrance to the Detroit River. The ship was held under the port side by the bar and although the hull did not seem to be damaged, the officer on watch reported that the cruiser was "pounding and grating considerably." The crew first used the ship's steam launch and kedge anchor in an attempt to free it. The anchor was carried some distance from the ship in the launch and dropped. The anchor chain was then winched in using the warship's capstan, to no avail.

In an effort to lighten the ship, Lieutenant Commander R. M. Berry instructed the engineers to drain the port side boiler. The starboard boiler remained fired to supply the engines with steam. Yet even with the engines working in full reverse, along with use of the steam launch and kedge anchor, the ship did not budge.

Finally, the tug *Home Rule* of the Canadian Hackett Line was called in for a fee of thirty dollars for the first hour and fifteen dollars per hour thereafter. *Home Rule* arrived at 9:30 P.M. The tug first pulled the *Michigan* to starboard and then to port, at which time the ship slid about twenty-five feet but grounded hard once again. *Home Rule* gave up at 1:30 A.M. but returned the next morning with another tug, *Dave and Mase,* plus a lighter. The warship's crew unloaded all unnecessary equipment and stowage into the lighter and

signaled both tugs to start pulling. At 11:20 A.M., after a considerable morn-
inglong effort, the tugs freed the warship.[25]

It was here at Detroit during the hydrographic survey that the *Michigan*
began its other new duties on the lakes. The paddle frigate began to participate with the new Illinois, Michigan, and Pennsylvania state naval militia in
maneuvers and target practices. The first militia ship, *Yantic,* was joined in a
few years by others. By 1915 the Lakes Naval Reserve made up a nine-ship
flotilla, many of which were captured Spanish gunboats from the recent
war.[26]

TECHNOLOGY AND CHANGE

After some 50 years of duty, ship technology had caught up and surpassed the
old *Michigan.* It was time for modernization. In the winter of 1892–93, while
much of the ship's crew worked at the world's fair, the old warship was given a
new set of boilers.[27]

This improvement was followed in 1897 by a complete internal rebuild
and rearmament with the newest quick-firing breach-loading six-pound
rifles (see appendix C). A massive square chart house was added to better
facilitate use of the overlarge charts carried on hydrographic surveys. The
rebuild also included a complete modernization with electric lighting and
portholes cut into the berth deck. The rebuild and boiler replacement added
a foot and a half to the draft of the ship and necessitated the replacement of
the paddle wheels with models of a smaller diameter.

Afterward the old paddle frigate was given a new designation, from
fourth-class steamer of war to unarmored, unprotected cruiser.[28] The once
sleek black frigate was hardly recognizable under a new white color, a massive
top-heavy-looking deckhouse, and a foot and a half less freeboard. Nonetheless, the cruiser was now a far more formidable weapon than it had been
when new.

On July 17, 1897, the *Michigan* visited Mackinac Island to collect the
person largely responsible for the ship's rebuild and modernization. Assistant
Secretary of the Navy Theodore Roosevelt boarded the flagship *Michigan* at
8:45 A.M. to preside over the summer maneuvers of the naval reserve. For the
next week the cruiser and its militia consorts conducted naval maneuvers on
Lakes Huron and Erie, while Roosevelt looked on.[29]

In July, 1900, while on an outing with the reserve vessel *Yantic,* the
Michigan's rudder head broke and the ship grounded once again in the
Detroit River. The paddle cruiser was towed to the Detroit Dry Dock

Company, where it was fixed temporarily but found to need a new rudder. The new rudder was supplied by the navy that October.[30]

By 1905 the USS *Michigan* had become one of the longest continuously operating warships in U.S. naval history, remaining in commission for some sixty-one years. This was several times the average life span of any navy ship, wooden or steel. The United States Navy Department, however, changed the name of this ship on June 17, 1905. The USS *Michigan* was renamed USS *Wolverine* in order that the new battleship, number twenty-seven, could take the time-honored name *Michigan*.[31] As a wolverine is a small northern carnivore with a fierce reputation and also the state mascot of Michigan, it was reasoned that *Wolverine* was an appropriate new name for the first *Michigan*.

According to folklore, however, "once christened, a ship's name must never be changed or disaster will fall upon craft and crew alike."[32] Though only folklore, the curse brought on by changing a ship's name did in fact haunt the final years of the USS *Wolverine*.

In September, 1905, the *Wolverine*'s outside hull below the waterline was painted and found to be free of corrosion and other damage.[33] The old iron ship's hull and engines remained unchanged and undamaged, but its superstructure, boilers, and white color combined to make a sham of the vessel's once beautiful lines. Regardless of its appearance, the *Wolverine* was still a stout vessel. Three years after the hull inspection, its engines, though sixty-five years old, were listed by the Bureau of Construction and Repair as "good."[34]

The USS *Wolverine* had a very short career of six years and eleven months as a commissioned naval vessel. During this time it continued to cruise the lakes in training and recruitment exercises. More advanced equipment continued to be installed on board for training purposes. One such device was the ship's rotary spark gap wireless. Although this type of wireless was the "latest technology" in the first decade of the twentieth century, it proved virtually useless for communication with other vessels on the lakes since no other ships would possess a similar device for several more years.[35]

In many ways the Great Lakes environment seemed to encourage retrograde marine technology. While the rest of the world's naval architects and marine engineers concentrated their resources and skills on iron- and later steel-hulled ships, wooden hulls predominated on the lakes until after the turn of the twentieth century. This was the product of two factors. The first was the area's massive timber resources, which did not begin to dwindle until this time. More-developed countries had used their most valuable timber reserves nearly a century earlier.

Second, lake merchant ships used a variation on a type of four-bladed propeller called a Loper wheel. Though less efficient than other propellers in speed, the Loper-wheel-type propellers did not cause the vibration and hull strain that created the necessity for stronger steel hulls. In other words, Loper wheels were much kinder to wooden hulls, allowing them to function without leakage and stress fatigue.[36]

By the end of the nineteenth and beginning of the twentieth centuries, however, 500-foot-long steel bulk carriers were beginning to demonstrate their cost-effectiveness on the lakes. Each of these ships could carry the same deadweight tonnage as a fleet of wooden ships, substantially lowering the cost to ship bulk cargo. Economics, therefore, finally forced many lakes shipping companies to begin looking into investing in the steel behemoths. The *Wolverine* became a natural study for these companies in the obvious durability of iron ships, albeit some sixty years after Secretary Upshur hoped it would.[37]

As testament to the old ship's durability, it was dry-docked for inspection on May 9, 1910, in the old dock of the Toledo Shipbuilding Company. Lieutenant S. L. H. Hazard, who was in charge of the inspection, reported:

> The underwater body was found to be in very good condition, with the exception of the plates under the boilers and under the fore hold. Under the fore hold the plates were corroded through in two places; under the boilers the plates were generally weakened and several rivets had been knocked out while chipping the inner skin. All this corrosion was internal. All holes mentioned in paragraph 4, were plugged with rivets and a coat of cement from 2 inches to 3 inches in thickness was put on the ship's bottom under the boilers from frames #28 to frame #44.[38]

Despite having been on the lakes for sixty-seven years, the hull of the *Wolverine* was in amazingly good condition. Most of the corrosion found on the vessel was located under the boilers. This oxidation resulted from acids given off by coal gas in the boilers and possible spillage of boiler water due to steam condensation and day-to-day workings in the machinery spaces. The new cement layer acted as a buffer to prevent the acids from contacting the hull plates. Lieutenant Hazard attributed the lack of corrosion and fouling to the ship's career in fresh water.[39]

Although the ship's hull was in good condition, the Navy Department had no further use for the *Wolverine,* which by now was of museum-piece vintage. The logbook entry for May 6, 1912, states: "The USS Wolverine was placed out of commission this date and loaned to the Naval Force of Pennsylvania."[40] The Pennsylvania Naval Militia was a branch of the United States Naval Reserve. Though the *Wolverine* was decommissioned, it still technically belonged to the navy.

FINAL YEARS

The USS *Michigan*'s naval service of sixty-one years, combined with the nearly seven years that it operated as the USS *Wolverine,* totalled sixty-eight years of active service in the United States Navy. The *Michigan*'s total active service is the third longest in the history of the U.S. Navy, behind the *Constitution* and the *Independence.*

Following the loan, the *Wolverine* became the headquarters for the First Battalion, Divisions C and D, of the Pennsylvania Naval Militia. The *Wolverine*'s militia duties consisted of a single two-week cruise each summer. In addition to this summer cruise, the sailors of the Pennsylvania Naval Militia attended weekly drills on board ship in the summer. During the winter, the sailors drilled in an armory located at the corner of Fifth and State Streets in Erie.[41]

Several years before the ship's decommissioning, the citizens of Pennsylvania began to plan activities to commemorate Oliver Hazard Perry's victory over the British fleet in the War of 1812. Local citizens established the Pennsylvania's Perry's Victory Centennial Commission to organize a celebration of the Perry centennial. In 1912 the commission authorized Lieutenant Commander William L. Morrison, commander of the Pennsylvania Naval Militia ship *Wolverine,* to send a "hard hat" diver to explore Misery Bay, located off Presque Isle Bay, across from the city of Erie. Though small, Misery Bay had been an anchorage for Perry's fleet between 1812 and 1815. A popular consensus held the conviction that one of Perry's vessels, the 480-ton brig *Niagara,* lay in the mud on the bottom of Misery Bay.[42]

The diver procured by Morrison did indeed locate part of a wooden lower hull section resting in Misery Bay. After the diver's report, the Perry Centennial Commission concluded that enough of the hull was intact to justify raising and rebuilding the vessel. The identity of the ship, however, could not be confirmed, and no plans of the original vessels were available to work from.[43]

On November 10, 1912, despite the onset of winter, work began on the wreckage. On March 6, 1913, the hull section was recovered with the help of the *Wolverine*'s crew. Despite its dubious identity, Morrison supervised the reconstruction of the wreck according to plans that he had sketched from correspondence and personal research. The reconstruction was completed in two months from the time the hulk was raised. On July 12, 1913, the reconstructed vessel, under tow of the *Wolverine*, left Presque Isle Bay for a tour of the Great Lakes.[44]

Although the Pennsylvania Naval Militia routinely sailed on board the *Wolverine* for only two weeks out of the summer, 1913 proved to be an exception. The ship, towing Morrison's version of the *Niagara*, cruised to all the major cities on the lakes during July and August. On September 10, 1913, the tour ended with a visit to Put-in-Bay on South Bass Island in Lake Erie, where one hundred years before, Commodore Perry and his fleet defeated the British.

The tour proved to be very popular with the people of the Great Lakes, and the great enthusiasm they showed for the reconstructed *Niagara* produced at least one potentially dangerous incident. Ray Jewell, who was a seventeen-year-old enlistee in 1913, recalled that in Cleveland, so many people wanted to see the reconstructed ship that a crowd surged toward the brig, which was tied to the pier at the foot of East Ninth Street. The crowd eventually became too large and unruly for the police to control. Commander Morrison was asked by the police to help curb the mob before people were pushed off the pier and drowned. Morrison used fire hoses to curb the throng since the *Wolverine*'s crew were far too few to physically waylay the excited people. The tactic proved successful: the pressurized streams of cold water drove the mob away from the edge of the wharf.[45]

Another potentially dangerous event occurred in August, 1913, while the touring vessels were visiting Lake Michigan ports. The *Wolverine* proceeded, with its consort, up Lake Michigan from Chicago to Green Bay when they encountered a fierce storm head-on. At the height of the storm the *Wolverine* could make no headway. Lt. Commander Morrison decided to turn the ships back to Chicago but became caught in the trough of the sea, or sideways to the wind and waves.

Under normal circumstances the *Wolverine* could have made the turn easily, storm or not, but the old ship proved to have too little power to complete the turn hampered by the vessel in tow. After a furious fight for life, the ships finally came about and raced before the storm safely back to Chicago.[46]

Ironically, the lack of money and attention of a full-time crew inflicted more damage on the *Wolverine* during its days as a militia ship than did storms, unruly crowds, or collisions. Robbed of the honor of a warship damaged in the line of service or appreciated for the historical vessel it truly was, the *Wolverine* slowly deteriorated as deferred upkeep and repairs insidiously weakened its internal structure. Edwin Poehlmann reported that while he served on board from 1913 to 1916, "when we didn't have funds for some repair, the crew would take out some brass pipe and sell it, replacing the removed part with steel."[47] Steel, though stronger than brass, was cheaper and quickly deteriorated. The crew literally began to trade the vessel's historical underpinnings for a few extra days of cruising.

On April 8, 1917, the United States entered World War I. One of the first contingents to be called for active duty was the First Battalion of the Pennsylvania Naval Militia.[48] The federal government also called the Pennsylvania Naval Militia Ship *Wolverine* back to active naval service. The USS *Wolverine* operated as a training ship out of the Great Lakes Naval Training Station near Chicago in 1917 and 1918.[49]

After the war, the ship was decommissioned and loaned again to the state of Pennsylvania. It was returned to its usual berth on the east side of the public wharf in Erie. Since 1908, when the wharf was built, the navy (and after 1912, the Pennsylvania Naval Militia) paid rent to the city for the pier's use. The ship was not used during the 1919 navigation season because the reserves, having gone to war, were no longer organized to train, maintain the ship, or pay rent to the city for the docking space. Therefore, on April 21, 1919, the Erie City Council gave consent to have the vessel tie up at the public dock without cost. By early the next year, however, starting February 27, 1920, the Pennsylvania Naval Reserve was reorganized sufficiently to call the *Wolverine* to use as a station ship for training naval reserves at the public dock.[50]

After nearly eighty years of service, the old wrought iron warship remained in use for the two-week training cruises of the Pennsylvania Naval Reserve. Age and lack of maintenance, however, took their toll. The *Wolverine* made its final voyage into Lake Michigan in 1923. On August 15, the iron cruiser's engines suffered their first and last major breakdown while passing through the Straits of Mackinac. The port connecting rod broke off three feet from the crankshaft. The three-foot-diameter piston, left unsupported, crashed through the cylinder head, stopping only six inches from the hull plates on the bottom of the ship. Not immediately lethal, the wound would nonetheless prove to be the historic fatal blow.

The reserve crew, under guidance of Lt. Commander Morrison, nursed the old warship to Harbor Beach, Michigan, on one engine. Morrison had regained command of the vessel after his return from serving in Europe during World War I. On August 16, he telegrammed the Navy Bureau of Construction and Repair for assistance because the ship still technically belonged to the navy. The navy, however, could not honor a request for damage assistance from a vessel that was no longer in commission.[51]

Having received no reply from the navy, Morrison decided to try to return to Erie on one engine on August 17. The *Wolverine*'s running rigging was no longer capable of spreading canvas, and naval training at this time did not ordinarily include the old art of sailing. The *Wolverine* accomplished the several-hundred-mile journey without mishap in six days.[52] It is interesting to note that the port engine was the engine used exclusively in Benjamin F. Isherwood's experiments in 1860 and 1861 and had more hours on it than the starboard engine did.

Lt. Commander Morrison sent a full damage report to the U.S. Navy Bureau of Construction and Repair from Erie. Again, the navy did not acknowledge the report. The vessel remained at the public dock in Erie without repairs, maintenance, or upkeep.[53] Because the *Wolverine* technically belonged to the U.S. Navy, state funding was not available for repairs, even though the loss of the ship seriously hindered the activity of the Pennsylvania Naval Reserve unit in Erie.

In January, 1926, the federal government offered the *Wolverine* on temporary loan to Erie as a historical artifact.[54] The Erie City Council, however, saw this as an effort on the part of the navy to dump the financial responsibility for the ship's upkeep on the city. The city rejected the navy's offer. Sadly, the ship had outlived the people who knew its historical significance, and no historian stepped up to champion its cause. This ignorance, coupled with the ship's dilapidated appearance, led to a veritable ping-pong match between the city and the navy, each attempting to pass the responsibility for the vessel to the other. Had people remembered the ship as the once beautiful and powerful USS *Michigan* instead of the unsightly *Wolverine*—or, as it had been dubbed in World War I, the "Mechanical Duck"—there might have been more of an effort expended to save the ship.[55]

On June 10, 1926, the U.S. Navy announced its decision to sell the *Wolverine*. The naval reserve unit in Erie, however, through Congress, apparently pressured the navy into keeping the ship. On January 6, 1927, the navy made one more effort to give full ownership of the ship to the city, under Public Law 532 of the 69th Congress. House of Representatives bill 12853, which was passed on December 21, 1926, stated:

> That the Secretary of the Navy is hereby authorized and directed to turn over to the municipality of Erie, Pennsylvania, the gunboat *Wolverine,* for use in connection with the training of the Naval Reserve Organization of the City, provided that no expense to the Government shall be involved.[56]

The Erie City Council, however, continued to refuse responsibility for the vessel. It appears that the council's strategy to ascertain what the navy would do about the ship was to hesitate for several months before attempting to reply to Congress. The navy, meanwhile, believing its responsibility for the ship had ended with passage of the new law, struck the vessel from the register. Since the Erie City Council did not reply to the offer, the navy again put the ship up for sale on March 11, 1927.

No buyers for the ship were found. Therefore, on July 19, 1927, possibly influenced by the Pennsylvania Naval Reserve, the Erie City Council, in a carefully worded reply to Congress, stated, "His Honor, the Mayor be and hereby is directed to . . . thankfully accept the offer of the loan of the *Wolverine.*"[57] The ambiguity of the statement "turn over to" found in Public Law 532 sealed the fate of the *Wolverine.* This term allowed the navy to believe that it was no longer responsible for the ship and the city council of Erie to consider the ship on loan from the navy.

Since the city considered the vessel to be on loan, the city council did not feel compelled to spend the funds necessary to repair or restore the old cruiser. After the engine failure of 1923, the ship itself remained intact and in working order except for its port side engine. Nevertheless, the *Wolverine* had been neglected during the period between 1923 and 1927, leaving it in deplorable condition. Vandals had stripped much of the brass from the cruiser while it was tied to the public dock. The decks had begun to leak, and the steel pipes and fittings installed since 1900 were rusting, leaky, and unsafe.[58]

Finally, in November, 1928, the *Wolverine*'s last commander, William Morrison, with a friend, Captain J. P. Grant, made an effort to protect the ship from vandalism. The two men had the *Wolverine* towed to Crystal Point in Misery Bay, where it would come under the jurisdiction of the Presque Isle State Park Police.[59]

In 1929 the Erie County Historical Society initiated an investigation into the cost and measures needed to save the vessel and restore it. The architect hired to ascertain the feasibility of the restoration, Frank F. Fowle, concluded in his report that the cost to restore the ship would be $100,000 to $200,000. The price of maintenance per year was estimated at $5,000 to $10,000. Fowle suggested that if the price of restoration and maintenance was considered too expensive, it should be scrapped. The vessel's engines could be donated to the Smithsonian Institute or to Julius Rosenwald's proposed Chicago Museum.[60]

Fowle did not estimate the revenue or economic potential to the community for use of the ship as a museum. Without including any positive factors to balance the cost of restoring the ship, the price was considered too high for the community to undertake without federal help. Although apparently asked for, federal financial aid was not forthcoming. The government was preoccupied with the stock market crash and subsequent Great Depression.

There were several other efforts made to save the *Wolverine*. In 1929 Henry Ford offered to restore the vessel at his new Historic Greenfield Village in Michigan.[61] In the early 1930s the state of Michigan and the city of Detroit, both having close connections with the ship, offered to financially back restoration.[62]

These proposals were of no avail. The Erie City Council continued to maintain that the navy actually held title to and ownership of the vessel. Efforts to contact the navy apparently revealed the navy's belief that the city of Erie controlled the fate of the ship.

Years passed while the *Wolverine* deteriorated in Misery Bay, seemingly out of sight and out of mind. Nevertheless, a small but dedicated group of people in Erie continued to approach the federal government about funding its rehabilitation. They stressed that the jobs generated by the ship's restoration would be helpful to the people of Erie who were suffering from the Depression. In response to these requests, Works Progress Administration (WPA) funds were made available for the restoration of the *Wolverine*. Once again, however, the navy refused to take responsibility for restoring the ship and the funding was shelved.[63]

In another apparent reversal of the navy's contention that it was not responsible for the ship, a navy board of inspection examined the vessel on November 1, 1939. The board valued the ship at one hundred dollars and recommended that it be sold as a hulk to be scrapped. In January, 1940, the vessel was closed to the public, since the decks and rigging were unsafe.[64] The recommendation for scrapping the ship was not carried out.

The delay in scrapping the vessel may have been caused by President Roosevelt's proposal to create a maritime museum in Washington called the Port of Missing Ships. The ships that would have made up the collection were the *Constitution, Constellation, Hartford, Michigan*, and *Boxer*. These were all extremely noteworthy ships that still existed in the 1940s. Sadly, only two exist today. Congress, however, did not appropriate money for the project.[65]

On December 7, 1941, the United States entered into another war, the fifth major conflict since the *original* USS *Michigan* was launched. For the first time in a hundred years, however, the *Michigan*-turned-*Wolverine* was unable to respond to the emergency by offering training facilities for new recruits.

In the fervor to prepare the country for the struggle that lay ahead, no resource that might help win the war was overlooked—including the neglected hulk lying in Misery Bay. In April, 1942, First Lieutenant M. K. Henderson of the Ordinance Bureau sent a letter urging Mayor Charles R. Barber to release the ship to be scrapped to make shells and other war material. But James Purcell, the president of the *Niagara* Association, rallied the historical associations of the city to fight the proposed scrapping. The *Niagara* Association had since 1913 maintained the reconstructed *Niagara* in a maritime history theme park.[66]

The controversy raged in Erie for several months. The consensus of opinion in the community, however, was summed up by Harold Sullivan when he stated that although the loss of the vessel would be a shame, "may part of her one day find herself in the bomb that lands on the mad painter."[67] At that time World War II obviously took precedence over the preservation of national heritage.

For years the mayor and city council had claimed that the ship belonged to the navy and therefore could not be given to groups who wished to restore it. It would have been interesting to see if the same reasoning applied in preventing the ship from falling into the hands of the scrap yard.

The timely intervention of President Franklin D. Roosevelt saved the mayor from making a decision. In a letter to Ralph Tillotson of the Curtiss Organizing Company, a company that strongly advocated the scrapping of the ship for war materials, FDR stated,

> It is my opinion that memorials such as the *Wolverine* constitute a distinct morale factor which is of greater value than the metal which would be made available by their reduction to scrap metal. It is, therefore, the present intention to retain the *Wolverine* in its present status under loan to the city of Erie, Pennsylvania.[68]

Although the *Wolverine* was given a reprieve by the president, its name was taken once again in 1942 by the navy to be placed on a paddle-wheel aircraft carrier used to train pilots in the Great Lakes.[69] The now nameless hulk remained unrepaired and neglected in Misery Bay.

In March, 1944, the Senate agreed to consider a proposal from a newly organized group called the Foundation for the Preservation of the Original United States Ship *Michigan,* Incorporated. The proposal entailed legislative action to vest title to the corporation so that it could take responsibility for the ship without the city and navy interfering. The foundation proposed to carry out one of four possibilities: salvage, sink, scrap, or restore the old warship. The bill was reported on favorably in the Senate Committee on Naval Affairs, particularly since the foundation's proposal involved no federal expenditure whatsoever.[70] Preoccupation with the war apparently prevented Congress from acting on the bill, and it died when Congress adjourned in December, 1944.[71]

The *Niagara* Association also attempted to straighten out the legal entanglement that surrounded the vessel. Unlike the Foundation for the Original USS *Michigan*, the *Niagara* Association definitely wanted to save the ship for posterity. The association encouraged federal legislators to pass a law vesting full title to the ship in the City of Erie. The association operated under the assumption that the City of Erie would donate the ship to the association because it had the facilities and resources to restore the hulk and locate it next to the rebuilt *Niagara*.[72] It is ironic that so far as the navy was concerned, the *Wolverine* had already been donated to the city on December 21, 1926.[73]

Unfortunately the *Niagara* Association's plans to save the *Michigan* came too late. In the summer of 1948, the Foundation for the Preservation of the Original USS *Michigan*, Incorporated, came across a seldom-used law that had been passed in 1883, stating that the navy could sell a ship to a municipality or a nonprofit corporation for cultural purposes, with the president's approval. President Roosevelt was no longer living, and his successor, Harry Truman, perhaps not as historically conscious, approved of the sale to the foundation on June 22, 1948.[74]

The foundation consulted its constituents concerning the fate of the ship. Ninety-eight percent of the respondents called for the scrapping of the ship in order to pay for a memorial. Spurred by this mandate, the foundation made immediate plans to scrap the ship and use the proceeds to erect a token monument to the *Michigan*. The engines of the vessel were offered to the Smithsonian Institute, but the offer was not accepted.[75]

Early in 1949 the ship was pumped out to make its last short voyage. Although the vessel's decks and woodwork were rotted, its hull was found to be virtually free of leaks and totally free of rust. In 1944 an analysis performed by the Republic Steel Corporation on a section of the ship's keel demonstrated that even after one hundred years there was no deterioration due to oxidation of the iron measured to a thousandth of an inch. The keel was .625 inches thick or, as was specified in 1843, five-eights of an inch.[76]

The name-stripped *Michigan* was towed with difficulty across Presque Isle Bay to the wrecking yard. Seemingly in one last defiant act, the old warship rammed and swamped the launch that towed it. Nevertheless, the USS *Michigan* was scrapped, with the forward ten feet of the bow saved for a monument. As a last dishonor, some of its brass bolts, studs, and spikes were melted down by the Erie Foundry Company and made into letter openers and paperweights that the Foundation for the USS *Michigan* sold to help pay for the monument. The money raised from the sale of the *Michigan* as scrap metal added to the donations and souvenirs amounted to a mere $2,432. This was enough, however, to erect the ten-foot section of the bow upright in a concrete base at the foot of State Street, as a memorial.[77]

That there has to be a last chapter in the history of the USS *Michigan* is, to say the least, unfortunate. Several organizations and communities offered to save the ship, and it can easily be said that far more has been spent to save far less in the historic annals of the United States. Historians must accept at least part of the blame for not ferreting out the true historic value of the ship and passing it on to the public. The warship itself stood in mute testimony to deeds done and the power of its youth, the lives it had saved, and the border it helped make peaceful. The people who were aware of these events were long gone, and historians were not up to the task of conveying the true significance of the ship. In light of this century's perception of the *Michigan,* as the harmless and obsolete "Mechanical Duck" or *Wolverine,* it is not surprising that the ship was destroyed and historical misconceptions of the quiet lake frontier continue.

It is a lasting tragic irony that the *Michigan* fell victim to the scrap yard for no apparent reason after having survived five major wars and more than one historic attempt to destroy it. It is a further irony that the warship was destroyed by an organization whose name was the antonym of its intent.

The old paddle frigate may have indeed become an eyesore, but the hull was in no immediate danger of deterioration, and although its woodwork was rotted, restoration of the ship to its original appearance necessitated its removal, rotted or not. It is a pity the hull remained so tight, for if it had sunk to the bottom of Misery Bay it would likely still remain intact. It is also plausible that had the vessel survived just a few more years, the attitudes, perceptions, and general interest concerning the history of the ship, the U.S. Navy, and the Great Lakes might have led to its restoration.

The *Michigan* itself has been lost; however, its records represent a historical Rosetta stone in the history of ship technology, naval politics, and Great Lakes history. In this light the paddle frigate portrays the historical link between the old sailing navy and the modern steam and steel navy. The integral parts of the *Michigan,* including its engines, hull, ordnance, and crew, were the direct predecessors of what was to come and yet contained elements of what went before. The warship's construction and eighty-year patrol also challenges the popular misconception that all was quiet and peaceful on the Great Lakes after the War of 1812 and lend credence to a more accurate perception of the dynamic and dangerous times our forebears knew.

Last, this ship's history is in many ways interwoven with the history of the municipality of Erie, Pennsylvania. The social history of the city has been uniquely influenced by the navy and adds a great deal to the maritime narrative of the region.

Today the *Michigan's* beakhead still stands proud in its concrete base, a memorial erected in Erie to the ship's memory. For all that, it is an easily overlooked, forlorn monument, a novelty that can barely hint at the power and speed embodied in this lost capital ship or the extraordinary human-itarian and diplomatic service provided for the people of the Great Lakes on both sides. Like its shrine, the iron paddle frigate's history has been white-washed to the opaque likeness of the obsolete *Wolverine*. Similarly, the histor-ically powerful, audacious, and sometimes dark times that were part of the history of the Great Lakes are nearly obliterated by time and fallacy, brought to clarity only by such records as those preserved under the name USS *Michigan*. It can only be hoped that this vessel's well-earned distinction and momentous narrative will not fade entirely, as have the last ripples of its wake.

Appendixes

A *Shipwrecks, Rescues, and Collisions Involving the USS* Michigan

Ship	Type	Location	Date and Circumstance
Toledo	Brig	Mackinaw	October, 1844
Unnamed	Light ship	Point Wabas Banks	October, 1844
John Grant	Schooner	Erie	November, 1844
Patomac	Schooner	Erie	November 25, 1844
Endevor	Schooner	Hog Island	November, 1844
Buffalo	Steam packet	Erie	April, 1845, grounded, 1 sailor drowned
George Weeks	Schooner	Bois Blanc Island	October 12, 1845
Illinois	Steam packet	Fighting Island	October 27, 1845
Erie	Rev. cutter	Conneaut	November 13, 1845
Lyon	Schooner	Erie	August 18, 1846
Congress	Brig	Detroit River	October 25, 1846, failed to free ship
2 Unnamed	NA	Detroit River	November 3, 1846
2 Unnamed	NA	Erie	November 23, 1846
7 Unnamed	NA	Erie	November 23, 1846
Rough & Ready	Schooner	Lake Erie	June 12, 1847, foundered, no survivors
Patekin	Steamer	Racine	June, 1848
Chetague Chief	Steamer	Put-in-Bay	August, 1848

Note: col. = collision; NA = not available; Records between 1886 and 1897 are scanty.

Ship	Type	Location	Date and Circumstance
Vermont	Schooner	Erie	June 8, 1849
Empire State	Steamer	Sleeping Bear	August, 1849
Atlantic	Steamer	Detroit	April 15, 1850
A.D. Patchin	Steamer	Killigalee Island	October, 1850
Algomah	Brig	Put-in-Bay	October 18, 1850
May Flower	Steamer	West of Buffalo	November 13, 1850
Traveller	Brig	Conneaut	November 15 and December 10, 1850
Unnamed	Brig	Dover, Canada	May 13, 1851
Unnamed	Schooner	Dunkirk	May 2, 1851
Wave	Steamer	Grand River	August 8, 1851
Hancock	Brig	NA	August 28, 1851
May Flower	Steamer	Point Pelee	May 20, 1852
Buffalo	Propeller	Point Aux Barques	May 13, 1853, col. w/*Michigan*
6 Unnamed	NA	Lake Erie	April 20, 1854, ships in ice
Illinois	Steamer	Sault Sainte Marie	July 25–28, 1854
May Flower	Steamer	Point Pelee	December 4, 1854, *Michigan* grounded
Reciprocity	Schooner	Lake Huron, Canada	October 5, 1855
Unnamed	NA	Lake Huron	October 6, 1855, col. and foundering
Unnamed	Propeller	Detroit River	October 10, 1855
Northerner	Propeller	Lake Saint Clair	October 22, 1855
North Star	Bark	Long Point	November 4, 1855, bilged and lost
North Star	Steamer	Towed to Sault Sainte Marie	August 12, 1856
Pearl	Steamer	Detroit River	August 21, 1856
Golden State	Steamer	Erie	December 1, 1856
Point Pelee	Light caisson	Towed from Detroit River	June 17–July 19, 1857
Action	Propeller	Point Pelee	June, 1857
Morning Light	Schooner	Point Pelee	October 16, 1857, did not save ship, 2 dead

Ship	Type	Location	Date and Circumstance
J.W. Brown	Schooner	Erie	April 8, 1858
NA	Skiff	Recovered off Death's Door	August 11, 1858
Gen. Winfield Scott	Schooner	Saint Clair River	August 11, 1858
Parmelia	Bark	Helped launch in Green Bay	August, 1858
Island Queen	Schooner	Bois Blanc Island	August, 1858
L.B. Fostier	Schooner	Fair Port	August 24–26, 1858, towed waterlogged
St. James	Schooner	Erie	September 30, 1858, col. w/*Michigan*
A.W. Lee	Schooner	Ashtabula	November 4, 1858
Aldebaron	Schooner	Point Pelee Island	November 9, 1858
Sunshine	Bark	Long Point	July 18, 1859
Ocean	Steamer	Detroit River	August 11, 1859
Unnamed	Sloop	Lake Erie	October 1, 1859, 3 crew exhausted
Danube	Bark	Cleveland	October 10, 1859
George Davis	Schooner	Cleveland	October 15, 1859
Huron	Ferry	Stuck on Ways	October, 1859, Grand Trunk Railroad
William Pierson	Bark	Buffalo	September 30, 1861
Fairwind	Schooner	Cleveland	November 23, 1864, col. w/*Michigan*
Major Anderson	Barkentine	Buffalo	May 10, 1866, col. w/*Michigan*
S.H. Kimbal	Schooner	NA	October 4, 1867, col. w/*Michigan*
Michigan	Cruiser	Erie	November 14, 1867, grounded
John Miner	Barkentine	Black Rock	June 8, 1868, col. w/*Michigan*
Forrester	NA	Port Huron	May 20, 1871, col. w/*Michigan*
Atlantic	Steamer	Sault Sainte Marie	July 28, 1871

Ship	Type	Location	Date and Circumstance
Michigan	Cruiser	Manitou Passage	June 30, 1873, grounded, towed off by Brooklyn no charge
C.H. Weeks	Barge	Erie	July 4, 1878, col. w/ *Michigan*
NA	Sail Boat	Detroit River	1893
Michigan	Cruiser	Detroit River	August 2, 1894, grounded
Charle Crawford	Schooner	Mackinac Island	July 11, 1895
Morris G. Grover	NA	NA	1903

B   *Commanders of the USS* Michigan

1844	Captain William Inman	9/1844 to 11/1845
	Commander Stephen Champlin	11/1845 to 4/1848
	Commander James M. McIntosh	4/1848 to 12/1849
1850	Commander Oscar Bullus	12/1849 to 12/1851
	Commander Abraham Bigelow	12/1851 to 2/1854
	Commander John S. Nicholas	2/1854 to 9/1855
	Commander G. H. Scott	9/1855 to 10/1855
	Commander Charles H. McBlair	10/1855 to 12/1857
1860	Commander Joseph Lanman	12/1857 to 3/1861
	Commander John Carter	3/1861 to 11/1864
	Lt. Commander F. A. Roe	11/1864 to 4/1866
	Commander/Captain Andrew Bryson	4/1866 to 4/1868
1870	Commander J. E. Jouett	4/1868 to 9/1870
	Commander George Brown	9/1870 to 10/1873
	Commander James H. Gillis	10/1873 to 5/1876
	Lt. Commander/Commander A. H. Wright	5/1876 to 7/1876 and 12/1876 to 8/1877
	Commander Charles H. Cushman	7/1876 to 12/1876
1880	Commander George W. Haywood	8/1877 to 8/1880
	Commander Albert Kautz	8/1880 to 8/1883
	Commander John J. Reed	8/1883 to 4/1887
	Lt. Commander J. J. Hunker	4/1887 to 2/1888
	Commander Henry F. Picking	2/1888 to 11/1889

1890	Commander George H. Wadleigh	11/1889 to 12/1891
	Commander George E. Wingate	12/1891 to 5/1893
	Lt. Commander R. M. Berry	5/1893 to 12/1894
	Lt. Commander B. S. Richards	12/1894 to 5/1896
	Lt. Commander E. H. Leutze	5/1896 to 4/1897
	Dry dock	4/1897 to 3/1898
	Lt. Commander W. H. Everett	3/1898 to 4/1898 and 8/1898 to 8/1899
	Lt. J. A. Shearman	4/1898 to 4/1898
	Lt. J. B. Blish	4/1898 to 4/1898
	Boatswain Charles Miller	4/1898 to 8/1898
1900	Lt. Commander C. P. Perkins	8/1899 to 4/1900
	Lt. Commander/Cmdr. William Winder	4/1900 to 2/1904
	Commander Charles Laird	2/1904 to 2/1905
	Commander Henry Morrell	2/1905 to 6/1907

COMMANDERS OF THE USS *WOLVERINE* FROM JUNE 21, 1905

	Commander H. W. Harrison	6/1907 to 11/1908
1910	Commander William P. White	11/1908 to 5/1910
	Lt. Commander W. D. McDougall	5/1910 to 10/1910
	Lt. S. L. H. Hayward	10/1910 to 6/1911
	Chief Boatswain Edwin Murphy	6/1911 to 5/1912

PENNSYLVANIA NAVAL RESERVE FROM MAY 6, 1912

	Lt. William L. Morrison	5/1912 to 1/1914 and 7/1920 to 8/1923
	Ensign J. P. Smart	1/1918 to 1/1919
	Lt. H. Vanderwerp	1/1919 to 7/1919

Information is from logbooks and letters.

C   *Ordnance of the USS* Michigan

Year	Number and Type
1843	2, 64-pound 8-inch pivot[1]
	4, 32-pound caronades
1844	1, 64-pound 8-inch pivot
1863	1, 64-pound 8-inch pivot
	1, 30-pound Parrott rifle
	6, 24-pound Dahlgren howitzers
	5, 20-pound Parrott rifles
	2, 12-pound Dahlgren howitzers
1871	6, breach-loading rifled howitzers (3-inch)
	2, 12-pound Dahlgren howitzers
1878	6, breach-loading rifled howitzers (3-inch)
	1, Gatling gun
1882	6, breach-loading rifled howitzers (3-inch)
	2, Gatling guns
1885	4, breach-loading Parrott rifles (4.2-inch), converted 32-pound rifles
	1, breach-loading rifled howitzer (3-inch)
	1, .45 caliber Gatling gun
1887	4, breach-loading Parrott rifles (4.2-inch)
	3, breach-loading rifled howitzers (3-inch)
	2, .45 caliber Gatling guns

1. These smooth-bore muzzle-loading guns could fire solid shot as well as shells.

Year	Number and Type
1897	4, 6-pound Driggs-Schroeder rapid-fire rifles (Mark 1, 1893)
	2, 6-pound Hotchkiss rapid-fire rifles (1892–93)
	2, 1-pound Hotchkiss rapid-fire rifles
	2, .45 caliber Gatling guns
1908	6, 6-pound rapid-fire rifles
	2, 1-pound rapid-fire rifles
	2, .45 caliber Gatling guns
1918	2, 3-pound rapid-fire rifles

D *Ship's Statistics*

HULL

Length overall	176 feet, 6 inches
Length on deck	167 feet, 6 inches
Length between perpendiculars	162 feet, 6 inches
Length of keel	156 feet
Length for tonnage	167 feet, 1 inch
Beam to outside of hull	27 feet
Extreme beam to outside of paddle boxes	45 feet, 10 inches
Depth of hold	12 feet
Depth of keel	4 inches
Height from top of keel to top of rail	17 feet, 10 inches
Weight of iron in hull	236 tons

AUXILIARY RIGGING

Length of foreyard	66 feet
Length of topsail yard	50 feet
Length of topgallant yard	30 feet, 6 inches
Height of mainmast to truck	83 feet
Length from forward end of jibboom to after end of spanker boom	223 feet

Notes

Chapter 1

1. "US Steamer Michigan," *Erie Gazette,* December 14, 1843. The *Michigan* was actually the third iron steamship to operate on the Great Lakes, behind the Royal Navy's *Mohawk* on Lake Ontario and the U.S. Army's survey ship *Col. Abert.*

2. Both the *Erie Gazette* and the *Erie Observer* identify the warship as a steam frigate. This term was probably given to them in conversation with Samuel Hartt, the vessel's designer, who was best qualified to categorize it. The British Royal Navy used the terms *paddle frigate* or *paddle sloop* to describe ships similar to the *Michigan,* depending on how many guns were carried. Sloops carried fewer than twenty guns, and frigates carried more than twenty. By the time the *Michigan* was launched, these terms had lost their meaning. Some sloops carrying fewer but heavier-caliber guns were recognized as being more powerful vessels than frigates carrying more but smaller-caliber guns.

3. Hans Busk, *The Navies of the World* (London: Routledge, Warnes, and Routledge, 1859). In Busk's overview of the world's navies, only two ships (Royal Navy auxiliary vessels) could have kept up with the *Michigan.* Speed at sea, however, depends on a great many factors including load, sea conditions, hull fouling, and the condition of the engines and boilers. Busk's data come from reported sea trials under ideal conditions.

4. Busk, *Navies of the World,* app. pp. 34, 43, 60–75, 97.

5. Other reasons for naval architectural experimentation at this time included an acute shortage of suitable timber for ship construction and a shortage of trained sailors to staff fully rigged wooden sailing vessels.

6. Antony Preston, *Battleships* (New York: Crescent Books, 1981), 14.

7. A fine overview of the Royal Navy's transition to steam can be found in Andrew Lambert's *Battleships in Transition: The Creation of the Steam Battlefleet 1815–1860* (Annapolis: Naval Institute Press, 1984).

8. Britain, however, demonstrated that it was thoroughly equal to the task of converting to iron construction and was far ahead of the United States and France in this respect.

9. Claude H. Hall, *Abel Parker Upshur, Conservative Virginian, 1790–1844* (Madison: State Historical Society of Wisconsin, 1964), 122.

10. Senate, *Report of the Secretary of the Navy*, 27th Cong., 2d sess., December 4, 1841, S. Doc. 1, Serial 395, 380.

11. Senate, *Report of the Secretary of the Navy*, 382. There is no evidence to suggest that the subsidy scheme was implemented.

12. House, *Steam Navy of the United States—Letter from the Sec. of the Navy*, 33d Cong., 1st sess., February 24, 1854, H. Doc. 65, 77.

13. Senate, *Report of the Secretary of the Navy*, 382.

14. The subject of the U.S. Navy and industry has been neglected. As naval historian William Still, Jr., states in his article, "Monitor Companies: A Study of the Major Firms That Built the USS *Monitor*," *American Neptune* 48 (1988): 130, "the companies that built the warship were not only representative of these revolutions [in naval architecture], but were significantly involved in the technological developments that made them possible."

15. Letter, P. Hotaling to M. Fillmore, December 24, 1841, Area File of the Naval Records Collection, 1775–1910, M-625, Roll 79, RG-45, National Archives, Washington, D.C. Hereafter cited as Area File.

16. Ewan Corlett, *The Iron Ship: The History and Significance of Brunnel's Great Britain* (New York: Arco Publishing Co., 1975), 21; John Grantham, *Iron as a Material For Ship-Building; Being a Communication to the Polytechnic Society of Liverpool* (London: Simpkin, Marshall and Co., 1842), 6. There is a reference to an iron passenger vessel plying the River Fosse in Yorkshire in 1777; see H. A. Musham, "Early Great Lakes Steamboats: Warships and Iron Hulls, 1841–1846," *American Neptune* 8, no. 2 (April, 1948): 133.

17. Grantham, *Iron*, 4–9; H. W. Brady, "The *Aaron Mamby* of 1822: New Light on the First Iron Steamer," *Syren and Shipping Illustrated*, January 6, 1954, 2–6.

18. Alexander Crosby Brown, "Notes on the Origins of Iron Shipbuilding In the United States, 1825–1861" (master's thesis, College of William and Mary, 1951), 25–37; David B. Tyler, *The American Clyde; A History of Iron and Steel Shipbuilding on the Delaware from 1840 to WWI* (Newark: University of Delaware Press, 1958), 4.

19. Tyler, *American Clyde*, 4–5.

20. Ibid., 5.

21. Indeed, the switch to the new material required a new generation in the United States. The slow acceptance of iron, and later steel, in shipbuilding no doubt contributed to the U.S. merchant fleet's fall from preeminence after the Civil War. European nations had already retooled, producing large, highly efficient iron and steel steamers long before the United States did.

22. A. C. Brown, "Notes," 65.

23. A. C. Brown, "Notes," 73–78. In 1839 the *William W. Fry* was imported to Louisville, Kentucky, from Laird's yard.

24. A. C. Brown, "Notes," 57, 78, 96.

25. Bryan Miller, Jr., to William Howard, December 28, 1841; Bryan Miller, Jr.,

to Upshur, December 29, 1841, AC Construction, A of Appendix F, 464, RG-45, National Archives, Washington D.C.

26. Tyler, *American Clyde,* 6.

27. D. K. Brown, *Before the Ironclad; Development of Ship Design, Propulsion and Armament in the Royal Navy, 1815–1860* (London: Conway Maritime Press, 1990), 75–76; Andrew Lambert, *Warrior: Restoring the World's First Ironclad* (London: Conway Maritime Press, 1987), 64.

28. Letter from Samuel Hartt to Lewis Warrington, June 23, 1842, AC Construction 2 of 2, RG-45, National Archives, Washington D.C.; Letter Hartt to Warrington, March 25, 1842, AD Design and General Characteristics Box 42, RG-45, National Archives, Washington, D.C.

29. House, *Steamer Building on Lake Erie.* 27th Cong., 2d sess., July 7, 1842, H. Doc. 238, 1–2.

30. Contract between the US Navy Department and the firm of Stackhouse and Tomlinson, May 19, 1842, *Letters Relating to the Building of the USS Michigan,* AC Construction, Box 1 of 2, RG-45, National Archives, Washington D.C.; the contract was reproduced for Congress in House, *Steamer Building on Lake Erie.*

31. Lewis Peterson to Upshur, February 11, 1842; Lyon Shosts and Co. to Upshur, February 11, 1842, *Letters.*

32. James Wood and John Willoch to Upshur, February 11, 1842, *Letters.*

33. *Letters.* Though letters of recommendation were not called for by the Navy Department, there are some 36 unsolicited letters filed for various iron manufacturers. Both the number of letters and the language used in the letters revealed much competition for the navy contract. Other companies recommended for final consideration were Robinson and Minis Company, Arthurs and Preston Company, Michael Stackhouse Company, and Wardin, Nicholson, and Company.

34. House, Select Committee, *War Steamer—Northwestern Lakes,* 27th Cong., 2d sess., August 2, 1842, H. Doc. 985, Serial 411; House, *Steamer Building on Lake Erie.*

35. House, *Steamer Building on Lake Erie,* 2

36. Ibid.

37. Ibid.

38. House, *War Steamer—Northwestern Lakes.*

39. House, *Steamer Building on Lake Erie,* 2.

40. Senate, *Petition of a Number of Citizens Residing on the North-Western Frontier,* 27th Cong., 1st sess., August 11, 1841, S. Doc. 88, serial 390; House, *Steamer Building on Lake Erie,* 4. The citizens of Erie knew as early as January 28, 1842, that the warship would be stationed there. William M. McWatts to Daniel Webster, January 28, 1842, Area File of the Naval Records Collection, RG-45.

41. Kenneth Bourne, *Britain and the Balance of Power in North America 1815–1908* (Berkeley: University of California Press, 1967), 109–15. For additional information concerning Anglo-American relations and diplomacy on the Great Lakes after the War of 1812, see John W. Foster, *Limitation of Armament on the Great Lakes* (Washington, D.C.: Carnegie Endowment for International Peace, 1914); Senate, *Message from the President,* 52d Cong., 2d sess., December, 1892, S. Doc. 9, serial 3055, 1,7,

reprinted as House, *War Vessels on the Great Lakes,* 56th Cong., 1st sess., February 27, 1900, H. Doc. 431, serial 3988. Other good general sources include Richard Preston's, *The Defense of the Undefended Border: Planning for War in North America* (Montreal: McGill-Queen's University Press, 1977); Robin Winks, *Canada and the United States—The Civil War Years* (Baltimore: Johns Hopkins University Press, 1960); and James M. Callahan, "The Neutrality of the American Lakes and Anglo-American Relations," in *Anglo-American Relations and Southern History* (Baltimore: Johns Hopkins University Press, 1898).

42. The Rush-Bagot Agreement is best described as a gentlemen's agreement between Richard Rush, the U.S. Secretary of State, and Charles Bagot, the British minister to Washington. It is not a treaty in any formal sense. Initiated by James Monroe in his alarm over the continued British naval buildup immediately after the War of 1812, when he was secretary of state, the agreement limited the number of arms and size of warships that could be used on the lakes. It did not limit fortifications, bases, or naval facilities. See Bradley A. Rodgers, "The Iron Sentinel; USS Michigan 1844–1949" (master's thesis, East Carolina University, 1985), 7–25.

43. House, *Steam Vessels on Lake Erie and Lake Ontario,* 25th Cong., 2d sess., June 27, 1838, H. Rept. 1018, serial 336, 1; House, *Steamers Oneida and Telegraph,* 27th Cong., 2d sess., May 18, 1842, H. Doc. 227, serial 404, 2; Rodgers, "Iron Sentinel," 16–25. The U.S. vessels were the steamers *Oneida* and *Telegraph.*

44. Senate, *Message from the President,* 16; House, *War Vessels on the Great Lakes,* 19.

45. Ibid., 17–18 and 20–21, respectively. Britain had always considered itself at a disadvantage on the Great Lakes, owing to the smaller available industrial, shipbuilding, and human resource capacity of Upper Canada. The Royal Navy could not send significantly powerful warships up the St. Lawrence due to the river's shallowness and rapids. James J. Talman, "A Secret Military Document," *American Historical Review* 38 (1933): 299; Bourne, *Britain and the Balance,* 4.

46. Stanley L. Falk, "Disarmament on the Great Lakes: Myth or Reality?" *United States Naval Institute Proceedings* 87 (1961): 72; Callahan, "Neutrality of the American Lakes," 126.

47. House, 27th Cong., 1st sess., July 14, 1841, H. Doc. 34, serial 392; *Petition of a Number of Citizens,* 1. In addition, several American ships were seized in the open ocean by British cruisers. These vessels were alleged to be engaged in the slave trade, which had been outlawed in Britain.

48. *U.S. Statutes at Large* (1841), 5: 460. The *Michigan* eventually cost well over the $100,000 appropriated by Congress, but this measure was sufficient money to begin the vessel's construction.

49. Senate, *Message from the President,* 21–22; Callahan, "Neutrality of the American Lakes," 123; House, *Steam Navy of the United States,* 77.

50. Hall, *Upshur,* 123–24. The board was abolished in August, 1842.

51. Bourne, *Britain and the Balance,* 109–15. The *Mohawk* was fabricated at Laird's yard and rebuilt in Upper Canada. It was launched February 21, 1843. Fox relayed the message given him by British Foreign Secretary George Aberdeen.

52. H. A. Musham, "Early Great Lakes Steamboats; Warships and Iron Hulls," *American Neptune* 8, no. 2 (1948): 140, 147.

53. Donald L. Canney, *The Old Steam Navy: Frigates, Sloops, and Gunboats, 1815–1885* (Annapolis: U.S. Naval Institute Press, 1990), 12; George F. Emmons, *The Navy of the United States, 1775–1853* (Washington, D.C.: Gideon and Co., 1853), 30. Emmons suggests that the two collaborated on the *Mississippi,* not the *Missouri.*

54. Hartt to Warrington, June 23, 1842, AC Construction, 2 of 2, RG-45, National Archives, Washington, D.C.; Letter from Hartt to Warrington, March 25, 1842, AD Design and General Characteristics, Box 42, RG-45, National Archives, Washington, D.C. Hereafter cited as Hartt to Warrington followed by the date.

55. Hartt to Warrington, June 4, 1842, AC Construction, 2 of 2, RG-45, National Archives, Washington, D.C.; Letter Hartt to Warrington, July 4, 1842, AC Construction, 2 of 2, RG-45, National Archives, Washington, D.C.

56. The contract specified that none of the rolling and shaping of the iron plates should be done in cold weather to insure proper fit with no cracks. "Pittsburgh," *Nile's National Register* (March 23, 1843), 309.

57. Commander Inman to Secretary Upshur, *Letters Received by the Secretary of the Navy from Commanders,* Letter #32, July 24, 1843; Letter #67, August 24, 1843; Letter #81, August 27, 1843; Roll 29, M-147, RG-45, National Archives, Washington, D.C. Hereafter these letters will be referred to as *Commanders Letters.*

58. Inman to Upshur, August 27, 1843, *Commanders Letters.*

59. "The Launch," *Erie Observer,* December 9, 1843.

60. Ibid.; Statement in relation to the building of the USS *Michigan,* AC Construction, 2 of 2, RG-45, National Archives, Washington, D.C. Hereafter cited as Statement to the Building.

61. *Erie Gazette,* December 7, 1843; *Erie Gazette,* December 14, 1843; Lambert, *Warrior,* 66.

62. Statement to the Building.

63. *Erie Gazette,* December 14, 1843; *Erie Observer,* December 9, 1843.

64. Rough draft of Contract with Joseph Long and Graph of estimate of sundry wood materials required for building and completing the iron steamer on Lake Erie, AC Construction, 2 of 2, RG-45, National Archives, Washington, D.C.; House, *Steamer Building on Lake Erie,* 10. According to the contract with Stackhouse and Tomlinson, the company had fourteen months from the receipt of the plans to deliver the engines. The plans arrived in Pittsburgh sometime in July or August, 1842.

65. Commander Inman to John Y. Mason, April 13, 1844, Letter #28, Roll 31, Commanders Letters; Inman to Mason, August 19, 1844, Letter #94, Roll 32, Commanders Letters.

66. The Entire cost of the US Steamer *Michigan,* so far as can be ascertained by vouchers, in the hands of Purser William A. Bloodgoode, Jan. 7, 1845, AC Construction, RG-45, National Archives, Washington D.C.; Senate, *Report of the Secretary of the Navy,* June 10, 1858, 35th Cong., 1st sess., S. Doc. 70, serial 930.

Chapter 2

1. Statistics from secondary sources concerning this ship are notoriously incorrect. The statistics listed come directly from constructor Samuel Hartt. Sheer Plan USS *Michigan,* Samuel Hartt N.C., January 25, 1845, 79-7-15-D, RG-19, National Archives, Washington, D.C.; "U.S. Steamer *Michigan,*" *Erie Gazette,* December 14, 1843.

2. House, *Steam Navy of the United States,* 3. This document lists the overall cost for the vessel as $154,100.18, which may reflect additional charges not calculated in Bloodgoode's figure. *Register of the Commissioned and Warrant Officers of the Navy of the United States including Officers of the Marine Corps* (Washington, D.C., 1846), 75; Emmons, *Navy,* 31. Tonnage is often a confusing subject in maritime history. "The Builders Old Measurement" rules were in place when the *Michigan* was built.

3. Body plan of Steamer for Lake Erie, March, 1842, 28-14-45, RG-19, National Archives, Washington D.C. For a partial body plan of the *Nemesis,* see D. K. Brown, *Before the Ironclad,* 76.

4. Average of several logbook entries, Logbook USS *Michigan,* September 29, 1844, to March 20, 1846, RG-24, National Archives, Washington, D.C.; Letter P. Hotaling to M. Filmore, December 24, 1841, M-625, Roll #79, Area File of the Naval Records Collection 1775–1910, RG-45, National Archives, Washington, D.C.; John Grantham, *Iron as a Material For Ship-Building* (London: Simpkin, Marshall and Co., 1842), 22.

5. As late as 1913, while pitted against more modern competition, gun crews on the *Michigan* showed excellent target practice scores. Neil Weber and Landis Isaacs, "Old Time War Vessel on the Great Lakes," *International Marine Engineering* (December, 1913), 524.

6. Grantham, *Iron,* 33; William Fairbairn, "The Strength of Iron Ships," *Transactions of the Institution of Naval Architects,* 1 (1860): 72.

7. House, *Steam Navy of the United States* 12, 15. The *Powatan* and *Sarnac* are listed as having achieved 12.5 and 13.5 knots under sail plus steam. Under steam alone they could do 11.5 knots. On average for twenty days the *Michigan* made 10 knots.

8. Shortly after the ship's first sea trials, the dip of the paddle wheels was increased. This alteration was necessary because the vessel carried nearly fifty tons less ordnance than it was designed to carry, hence its draft was roughly six inches less than it should have been. The wheels, therefore, had to be lowered at least six inches to give the paddle buckets the same purchase in the water they were designed for.

9. Stephen Champlin to George Bankroft, May, 18, 1846, *Commanders Letters,* Letter #135, Roll 34. Earlier, on August 10, 1844, *Nile's National Register* reported that the ship was at one time clocked at twelve miles per hour against a strong head wind with one-third head of steam. The dip of its paddle wheels, according to this report, was subsequently increased to give a higher speed of 15 mph.

10. Steam Log of the USS *Michigan,* November 8, 1847, and August 12, 1848, RG-19, National Archives, Washington, D.C. Hereafter cited as Steam Log.

11. James McIntosh to Mason, May 24, 1848, *Commanders Letters,* Roll 38, Letter #186; Busk, *Navies of the World,* 39,42. According to Busk, there were two British vessels constructed by 1859 that could have matched the *Michigan's* speed. The tender *Banshee* and the steam sloop *Caradoc,* both launched in 1847, are listed as achieving 18.5 and 16, knots, respectively.

12. Ibid.

13. Letter James Jouette to George Brown, Sept. 26, 1870, Letter #182, Roll 94, *Commanders Letters.*

14. House, *Steamer Building on Lake Erie,* 4–8. This document contains the iron schedule sent to Stackhouse and Tomlinson. In Hartt's letter to Warrington, March 25, 1842, Hartt explained that the plates would be three-eighths to five-sixteenths of an inch thick. The iron schedule given to the contractors called for plates of two-sixteenths to ten-sixteenths of an inch in thickness. Hartt also estimated, in his letter to Warrington of June 23, 1842, that the plates would be eight feet long and twenty-seven inches wide. These plate lengths were also modified before the iron schedule was sent to the contractors.

15. Grantham, *Iron,* 16, 17.

16. Sir Wescott Abel, *The Shipwright's Trade* (London: Conway Maritime Press, 1948), 108; D. K. Brown, *Before the Ironclad,* 204–5. According to Sir Abel, one-half inch of iron is equivalent in strength to five inches of oak plank but much lighter. The tensile strength of wrought iron also varies according to the direction of the silicate slag intrusions, the purity of the metal, and the temperature of the metal.

17. Grantham, *Iron,* 12. By 1860 Lloyd's of London Insurance Company set the frame spacing on A1 vessels at eighteen inches. Fairbairn, "Strength of Iron Ships," 78.

18. Herbert R. Spencer, "The Iron Steamer," *American Neptune* 4 (July, 1944): 184. By 1860 naval architects realized that iron decks added a great deal of longitudinal, compression, and tension strength to a ship.

19. House, *Steamer Building on Lake Erie,* 5; Sketch showing the manner of Framing, Plating, and Keelsons & c. of the Iron Steamer, Sept. 30, 1844, 79-7-15-D, RG-19, National Archives, Washington, D.C.; *Erie Gazette,* December 14, 1843.

20. Hartt to Warrington, March 25, 1842, AD Design and General Characteristics, Box 42, RG-45, National Archives, Washington, D.C.; Spencer, "The Iron Steamer," 186–87. It was discovered by the 1860s that an external keel was unnecessary in iron ships and actually would be detrimental should the ship ground. Fairbairn, "Strength of Iron Ships," 86.

21. Canney, *Old Steam Navy,* 12. Wooden hulls tend to flex too much to maintain the watertight integrity of transverse bulkheads. This innovation was never successful on wooden ships.

22. Hartt to Warrington, March 25, 1842; *Erie Gazette,* December 14, 1843; Inboard Profile of USS *Michigan,* December 10, 1897, RG-19, 28-14-31; Sheer Plan of USS *Michigan,* January 25, 1845, RG-19, 79-7-15-D.

23. The following list of books and articles gives a good progression of the reasoning behind iron ship construction. John Grantham, *Iron;* John Grantham, *Iron*

Ship-Building: With Practical Illustrations (London: Bradbury and Evans, 1858); Andrew Murray and Robert Murray, *Ship-Building in Iron and Wood,* 2d ed. (Edinburgh: Adams & Charles Black, 1863); Edward James Reed, *Shipbuilding in Iron and Steel* (London: John Murray, 1869); Fairbairn, "The Strength of Iron Ships."

24. "The May Flower," *Detroit Daily Free Press,* March 29, 1853, 3; "Collision," *Detroit Daily Free Press,* May 9, 1853, 3; *Commanders Letters,* Roll 45, Letter 172. The *Buffalo* was described as the largest propeller on the lakes.

25. This episode questions the supposed brittleness of wrought iron at low temperature. For experimental testing, see D. K. Brown, *Before the Ironclad,* 205.

26. Inman to Bancroft, May 15, 1845, *Commanders Letters,* Roll 33, Letter 168; Material Inspection, August 13–15, 1914, General Correspondence of the Office of the Secretary of the Navy, July 1897–August 1926, Box 97, 4404–97, RG-80, National Archives, Washington, D.C. These pumps are described as two horizontal duplex and one horizontal crank.

27. Damage control has been a neglected subject in naval history but must certainly rank in importance with the more popular subjects of gun caliber, armor, speed, and crew training when an examination of ship survivability is contemplated.

28. Grantham, *Iron,* 38–40, 73.

29. Maintenance of the "flood cocks" in the shell room and powder magazine was a routinely logged procedure.

30. Preston, *Battleships,* 18.

31. Sheer Plan Steamer *Michigan,* Jan. 25, 1845, 79-7-15D, RG-19, National Archives, Washington, D.C. It is probable that in times of maximum preparedness, the two gangway ports (identical to gun ports) could also be assigned ordnance.

32. Sheer Plan Steamer *Michigan.*

33. W. M. Crane of the Bureau of Ordnance and Hydrography to Secretary Upshur, November 16, 1842, Letters sent to the Secretary of the Navy and Chiefs of Naval Bureaus 1844–82, Entry #1, Vol. 1, RG-74, National Archives, Washington, D.C. Hereafter cited as Letters to the Sec. of the Navy Entry 1; W. M. Crane to Acting Sec. A. Thomas Smith, May 19, 1843, p. 17, Letters to the Sec. of the Navy Entry 1.

34. Report of Crane to Sec. David Henshaw, Jan. 20, 1844, p. 34–35, Letters to the Sec. of the Navy Entry 1. The eight-inch guns are referred to, even in the correspondence of the time, as Paixhan guns. This label is not, however, technically correct because the only true Paixhan guns were the guns produced in French foundries under the design of Henri Paixhan. These guns are also sometimes referred to as 68-pounders; however, the U.S. eight-inch gun was a sixty-four-pounder, slightly lighter than the English sixty-eight-pounder. J. A. Dahlgren, *Shells and Shell Guns* (Philadelphia: King and Baird, 1857), 24. The thirty-two-pound chambered guns "of about 41 cwt" seem to be a historical oddity, seldom mentioned in secondary literature on the subject. They were probably not mass-produced owing to a flaw in design. Spencer Tucker, *Arming the Fleet: U.S. Navy Ordnance in the Muzzle-Loading Era* (Annapolis: U.S. Naval Institute Press, 1989), 175, 277.

35. Dahlgren, *Shells and Shell Guns,* 26. The U.S. eight-inch shell gun could fire solid shot (though with a reduced charge of five pounds of powder rather than eight) for greater range and penetration. A. G. W. to Commander Champlin, April 8, 1846, Letters and Telegrams Sent to Naval Officers, 1842–82, Entry #2, Vol. 1, p. 148, RG-74, National Archives, Washington, D.C.

36. Dahlgren, *Shells and Shell Guns,* 31, 34. Since there is no information available on the range of the thirty-two-pounder 41 cwt gun, the range of the same caliber gun of 42 cwt was substituted.

37. Brown, *Before the Ironclad,* 207.

38. House, *Steam Navy of the United States,* 3; Emmons, *Navy,* 31, 34.

39. W. M. Crane to Upshur Sept. 12, 1842, Letters sent to the Sec. of the Navy Entry 1, 3; Senate, *Message from the President,* 21.

40. W. M. Crane to Henshaw November 17, 1843, Letters sent to the Sec. of the Navy Entry 1, 30. The unsuccessful contractors, George Page of Baltimore and E. F. Sterling of Cuyahoga Steam Foundry Company, failed to meet the navy contracts for ordnance. The contract was finally awarded to Freeman, Knap, and Totten in 1845.

41. Letter of Commander Inman to Sec. Bancroft March 19, 1845, *Commanders Letters,* Roll 33; Letter of W. M. Crane to Commander Inman June 22, 1844, 76–77, Letters and Telegrams sent to Naval Officers, Entry #2, Vol. 1, RG-74, National Archives, Washington, D.C.; Callahan, "Neutrality of the American Lakes," 125.

42. Senate, *Message from the President,* 21; Bourne, *Britain and the Balance,* 125–26.

43. Letter from Commander Inman to Mason September 5, 1844, *Commanders Letters,* Roll 32, Letter 125; Inman to Mason, October 9, 1844, Roll 32, Letter 17; Inman to Bancroft November 11, 1845, Roll 33, Letter 172. As the ship was not designed to carry just one gun, counterweights of water barrels were placed in the stern.

44. Carl D. Lane, *American Paddle Steamboats* (New York: Coward-McCann, 1943), 208.

45. B. H. Bartol, *A Treatise on the Marine Boilers of the United States* (Philadelphia: R. W. Barnard and Sons, 1851), 16; Charles B. Stuart, *The Naval and Mail Steamers of the United States,* vol. 2 (New York: Charles B. Norton, Irving House, 1853), 27; Spencer, "Iron Steamer," 192.

46. C. W. Copeland to Charles Morris September 10, 1844, EM, Box 170, RG-45, National Archives, Washington, D.C.; Stuart, *Naval and Mail Steamers,* 28; House, *Steam Navy of the United States,* 3; Donald Ray Dohrman, *Screw Propulsion in American Lake and Coastal Steam Navigation, 1840–1860* (Ann Arbor: Xerox University Microfilms, 1977), 20.

47. Stephen Champlin to Mason, Nov. 16, 1847, *Commanders Letters,* Roll 37, Letter 207.

48. Grantham, *Iron,* 66.

49. Commander J. Nicholas to J. C. Dobbin, *Commanders Letters,* Roll 47, Letter 103. It is interesting to note that virtually all of Nicholas's forty-year sailing

career was on the ocean, yet the greatest storm he ever faced occurred on the Great Lakes.

50. Ibid.

51. Once again this episode calls into question the supposed brittleness of wrought iron. See note 25. Perhaps a ship's internal temperature keeps the metal ductile.

52. Bartol, *Marine Boilers*, 16; Stuart, *Naval and Mail Steamers*, 27; Copeland to Morris, September 10, 1844.

53. House, *Steam Navy of the United States*, 11, 12; Bartol, *Marine Boilers*, 16.

54. Roe to Welles October 16, 1865, Letters Below Commander, Roll 400, Letter 117.

55. Bartol, *Marine Boilers*, 16; Stuart, *Naval and Mail Steamers*, 26; B. F. Isherwood, "Notes on the U.S. Steamship *Michigan*," *Journal of the Franklin Institute* 21, no. 4 (April, 1851), 218.

56. Steam Log Entries, Sat. May 16, 1846, Tues. May 26, 1846; Isherwood, "Notes," 218; Spencer, "Iron Steamer," 191.

57. A. C. Redfield and L. W. Hutchins, *Marine Fouling and its Prevention* (Woods Hole: Woods Hole Oceanographic Institute, 1952), 32, 33.

58. *Suggestions in getting up another Iron Steamer which should differ from the US Steamer Michigan as follows, Summary of 1845,* AC Construction, 2 of 2, RG-45, National Archives, Washington, D.C.

59. Brown, *Before the Ironclad*, 207.

60. On the other hand, a hit to a boiler carrying fifteen pounds of pressure was not nearly as serious as a hit to a boiler carrying 150 pounds of pressure.

61. E. A. M. Laing, "The Introduction of Paddle Frigates Into the Royal Navy," *The Mariners Mirror*, 66 (1980), 342; John Bourne, *A Treatise on the Screw Propeller, with Various Suggestions of Improvement* (London: Longman, Brown, Green, and Longmans, 1852), 223, 224.

62. D. K. Brown, *Before the Ironclad*, 112–14.

63. The trials also proved that very little concerning propeller and paddle wheel design was understood at this time. Concepts such as pitch, cavitation, and efficiency were years from having a scientific basis.

The Royal Navy's acceptance of the propeller hastened the acceptance of iron and steel hulls. It was soon found that propellers created far more vibration than paddle wheels did. When this vibration was transmitted through a wooden hull, it started planks and seams, causing leakage and damage.

64. Sketch of the Masting proposed for the Lake Steamer, Pittsburgh, December 1842, 79-7-15A, RG-19, National Archives, Washington, D.C.; Bartol, *Marine Boilers*, 16.

65. House, *Steam Navy of the United States,* 15. Never in this ship's long career was it necessary to sail back to port.

66. Hans Busk mentions that this drawback was the failing of most paddle steamers. Busk, *Navies of the World,* 139; Grantham, *Iron,* 18.

67. James Jouette to George Brown, September 26, 1870, *Commanders Letters;* House, *Steam Navy of the United States,* 15.

68. Any adverse weather conditions would greatly slow loading of the heavier guns, further compounding *Niagara's* problems.

69. James Phinney Baxter III, *The Introduction of the Ironclad Warship* (Cambridge: Harvard University Press, 1933), 37–38.

70. The thirty-two-pounders of the *Michigan* could also fire red-hot shot or shells.

71. The comparison may not point out so much the *Michigan's* usefulness as the *Niagara's* design flaws. As historian Andrew Lambert states, "The design concept of the American ships was many years ahead of the technology necessary to bring it to perfection." Lambert, *Battleships in Transition,* 114.

72. "The Navy, Report of Secretary Henshaw," *Erie Gazette,* December 21, 1843.

73. Clark G. Reynolds, "The Great Experiment: Hunter's Horizontal Wheel," *American Neptune* 24, no. 1 (January, 1964): 5, 23.

74. Canney, *Old Steam Navy,* 27–29.

75. Grantham, *Iron,* 49–62; Fairbairn, "Strength of Iron Ships." Fairbairn's article is a spirited dialogue between iron ship architects, owners, and insurance underwriters in their attempt to reach consensus on ship construction techniques.

76. George Biddell Airy, "Account of Experiments on Iron-Built Ships, Instituted for the Purpose of Discovering a Correction for the Deviation of the Compass Produced by the Iron of the Ships," *Philosophical Transactions of the Royal Society of London* 129 (1839): 167–213; Bryson to Welles, April 28, 1866, *Commanders Letters,* Roll 85, Letter 76; Lambert, *Warrior,* 63; D. K. Brown, *Before the Ironclad,* 4.

77. Grantham, *Iron,* 53, 86.

78. Ibid., 36, 58.

79. A good chronology on the thought processes of naval architects of the time, particularly concerning the problem of fouling, is to follow the writings of John Grantham of London. Grantham, *Iron,* 36, 58; John Grantham, *Iron Ship-Building;* 146–50; John Grantham, "On Copper Sheathing for Iron Ships, Considered at the Present Stage of Our Experience," *Transactions of the Institute of Naval Architects* 10 (1869): 166–74. A good historical overview of the problem of fouling, including wooden ship fouling, can be found in Redfield and Hutchins, *Marine Fouling,* chapters 11 and 12. See also Lambert, *Warrior,* 32, 65.

80. D. K. Brown, *Before the Ironclad,* 88–98; Lambert, *Warrior,* 64; N. A. M. Rodger, "The Design of the *Inconstant,*" *Mariners Mirror* 61, no. 1 (February, 1975), 16; Barbara Tomblin, "From Sail to Steam," 1983, manuscript, 169; Baxter, *Introduction of the Ironclad,* 37–38, 62.

81. D. K. Brown, *Before the Ironclad,* 79.

82. Ibid., 82.

83. Ibid., 79, 82, 93.

84. Historian D. K. Brown suggests that the reason for the success of iron ships in combat was that they operated in warm climates. The same, however, cannot be said

of the *Michigan,* which received greater overall punishment than these other vessels but in frigid temperatures.

85. Lambert, *Warrior,* 65.

Chapter 3

1. Inman to Mason, October 23, 1844, *Commanders Letters,* Roll 32, Letter 39.

2. John Nicholas to Dobbin, Jan. 7, 1855, *Commanders Letters,* Roll 48, Letter 8. Nicholas to Dobbin, April 20, 1854, *Commanders Letters,* Roll 46, Letter 28.

3. Logbook entries summer of 1850; John Nicholas to Dobbin, December 30, 1854, Roll 47, Letter 130; John Nicholas to Dobbin, April 20, 1854, Roll 46, Letter 28.

4. Stephen Champlin to George Bancroft, March 3, 1846, *Commanders Letters,* Roll 34, Letter 41; Log Entry, August 27, 1849, Smooth Log, December 4, 1848–November 30, 1849. The house was later located on the forward part of the ship.

5. Inman to Bancroft, April 21, 1845, *Commanders Letters,* Roll 33, Letter 137.

6. James McIntosh to William Preston, July 19, 1849, *Commanders Letters,* Roll 39, Letter 178; James McIntosh to Preston, October 4, 1849, Roll 39, Letter 79; Bigelow to Graham, May 20, 1852, *Commanders Letters,* Roll 43, Letter 197. The plague eventually reached Green Bay and Mackinaw, where victims were found on beaches. The previous large-scale outbreak of cholera on the lakes was in 1832.

7. McIntosh to Preston, July 19, 1849, *Commanders Letters,* Roll 39, Letter 178.

8. McIntosh to William Ballard Preston, August 27, 1849, *Commanders Letters,* Roll 39, Letter 29.

9. A. H. Mechlin to Secretary A. H. H. Stuart, January 19, 1853, Misc. Letters Received, Department of Interior, 1–4, Box 9, RG-48, National Archives, Washington, D.C. Hereafter cited as Dept. of Interior Misc. Letter, Jan. 19; *The Public Statutes at Large and Treatise of the United States of America,* 1, 48, 8; and 4, 472, 3 (Boston, 1848). Hereafter cited as, *Statutes at Large;* Lucile Kane, "Federal Protection of Public Timber in the Upper Great Lakes States," *Agricultural History,* 23, no. 2 (April, 1949), 135.

10. Kane, "Protection of Public Timber," 135.

11. Dept. of Interior Misc. Letter, Jan. 19, 1853.

12. William Rector, *Log Transportation in the Lake States Lumber Industry 1840–1918* (Glendale, Calif.: Arthur H. Clark Co., 1953), 65.

13. Ibid., 66.

14. Kane, "Protection of Public Timber," 135; Richard Gordon Lillard, *The Great Forest* (New York: Da Capo Press, 1973), 165.

15. Misc. Letter, Jan. 19, 1850; *Statutes at Large,* 4, 472, 3.

16. Kane, "Protection of Public Timber," 136.

17. Lillard, *Great Forest,* 165–66; Kane, "Protection of Public Timber," 135.

18. Lillard, "Protection of Public Timber," 167, 165.

19. Theodore S. Charney, "Chicago Harbor a Century Ago," *Sea History* 47 (summer, 1988), 13–14.

20. Message from the *Chicago Tribune,* quoted in the *Detroit Daily Free Press*

(August 3, 1853). [Hereafter the *Chicago Tribune* will be cited as *CT* and the *Detroit Daily Free Press* as *DDFP*.]

21. Lillard, *Great Forest,* 167.

22. "The Lumber Troubles in Michigan," *DDFP,* August 3, 1853.

23. Ibid.

24. Lillard, *Great Forest,* 168.

25. "The Cabinet," *Kalamazoo Gazette,* March 11, 1853.

26. Willard to McClelland, August 20, 1853, Box 11, Misc. Letters Received, Department of Interior, RG-48, National Archives, Washington, D.C. [hereafter cited as Willard's Report, August 20, 1853].

27. Willard's Report, August 20, 1853.

28. Quote from *Milwaukee Daily Sentinel* [hereafter cited as *MDS*], September 12, 1853; "The Lumber Case at Milwaukee," *CT,* September 17, 1853; Lillard, *Great Forest,* 168; Willard's Report, August 20, 1853.

29. Kane, "Protection of Public Timber," 136.

30. Lillard, *Great Forest,* 167; Willard's Report, August 20, 1853.

31. Lillard, *Great Forest,* 168.

32. A. Bigelow to William A. Graham, December 15, 1851, and December 26, 1853, *Commanders Letters,* Roll 42, Letters 289, 297; Bigelow to Graham, March 22, 1853, Roll 45, Letter 110.

33. Lillard, *Great Forest,* 165.

34. "The Lake Revenue Service," *DDFP,* April 14, 1854.

35. Logbook USS *Michigan,* May 5–6, 1853; Bigelow to Dobbin, May 13, 1853, Roll 45, Letter 172.

36. This was traditional in the navy, so that the wheel would act in the same manner as a tiller.

37. Bigelow to Dobbin, May 13, 1853, *Commanders Letters,* Roll 45, Letter 172.

38. Acting Master Ransom's Log Entry, May 13, 1853, *Commanders Letters,* Roll 45, Letter 172.

39. Estimate of damages from Capts. Robert Hugenon, Thomas C. James, and William A. Judd, Chicago, May 10, 1853, Bigelow to Dobbin, May 13, 1853, *Commanders Letters,* Roll 45, Letter 172.

40. Bigelow to Dobbin, May 13, 1853, *Commanders Letters,* Roll 45, Letter 172.

41. Logbook, May 6, 1853; "Propeller Buffalo," *DDFP,* April 26, 1853.

42. "Collision," *DDFP,* May 9, 1853. The *Buffalo* was quite probably driven onward not because the damage to the ship was light but because its pilot was haunted by the specter of a warship full of angry men who might learn why they had been rammed intentionally.

43. Acting Master Ransom's Log Entry, Bigelow to Dobbin, May 13, 1853, *Commanders Letters,* Roll 45, Letter 172; Official Protest filed with Charles E. Avery, Collector of the Port of Mackinac, May 7, 1853, included in the letter to the Secretary of the Navy, May 13.

44. Statement of John McMast, Justice of the Peace, Township of Holmes, County of Mackinac, May 7, 1853, Bigelow to Dobbin, May 13, 1853, *Commanders*

Letters, Roll 45, Letter 172, Part 2, No. 112, September 25, 1853. The cost of repairs was estimated on May 10 to be $3,850 to $4,000.

45. Bigelow to Dobbin, May 13, 1853, *Commanders Letters,* Roll 45, Letter 172, Part 2, No. 89, September 15, 1853; John B. Mansfield, *History of the Great Lakes,* vol. 1 (Chicago: J. H. Beers, 1899), 880.

46. This was the only time in the ship's long history that orders were sent in this manner.

47. "U.S. Rev. Cutter *Ingham,*" *DDFP,* June 17, 1853.

48. Kane, "Protection of Public Timber," 136.

49. "The Lumber Troubles in Michigan," *DDFP,* August 3, 1853.

50. Willard's Report, August 20, 1853.

51. Ibid.

52. *DDFP,* Aug. 3, 1853.

53. Lillard, *Great Forest,* 168.

54. J. C. Dobbin to R. McClelland, August 18, 1853, Entry 540, Letters and Other Communication, RG-48, Records of the Office of the Secretary of the Interior, National Archives, Washington, D.C.

55. J. C. Dobbin to A. Bigelow, August 18, 1853, Vol. 3, 1853–1857, Confidential Letters, RG-45, National Archives, Washington, D.C. Hereafter cited as Confidential Letters; Bigelow to Dobbin, August 25, 1853, *Commanders Letters,* Roll 45, Part 2, Letter 58.

56. Bigelow to Dobbin, August 31, 1853, *Commanders Letters,* Roll 45, Part 2, Letter 64.

57. Bigelow to Dobbin, September 6, 1853, *Commanders Letters,* Roll 45, Part 2, Letter 76.

58. "City Matters," *MDS,* September 12, 1853.

59. Ibid.

60. "City Matters," *MDS,* September 13, 1853.

61. "Opinions of Judge Welles," *MDS,* September 17, 1853.

62. "A High Handed Outrage," *MDS,* October 1, 1853; "The Bagnall Case," *MDS,* September 30, 1853.

63. "Re-Arrest of Bagnall," *MDS,* October 1, 1853; Quote from "A High Handed Outrage," *MDS,* October 1, 1853.

64. Bigelow to Dobbin, September 14, 1853, *Commanders Letters,* Roll 45, Part 2, Letter 87.

65. Bigelow to Dobbin, October 8, 1853, *Commanders Letters,* Roll 45, Part 2, Letter 142.

66. Bigelow to Dobbin, October 26, 1853, *Commanders Letters,* Roll 45, Part 2, Letter 181.

67. Kane, "Protection of Public Timber," 136.

68. John R. Dickason and George P. Wakefield, "The Building of Six Revenue Cutters for the Northern Lakes, Part 6," *Inland Seas* 44 (1988), 52; "The Lake Revenue Service," *DDFP,* April 14, 1854.

69. *DDFP,* April 14, 1854.

70. Bigelow to Dobbin, September 15, 1853, *Commanders Letters,* Roll 45, Part 2, Letter 89; Message, Dobbin to Bigelow, September 29, 1853, Roll 51, Vol. 49, Letters Sent by the Secretary of the Navy to Officers, 1798 to 1868, RG-45, National Archives, Washington D.C.

71. Kane, "Protection of Public Timber," 139. The legal timber industry did not consider forest management until the last tree stands had been cut.

Chapter 4

1. Stephen Champlin to J. Y. Mason, September 15, 1847, *Commanders Letters,* Roll 37, Letter 114; Champlin to Mason, November 5, 1847, *Commanders Letters,* Roll 37, Letter 191.

2. Milo M. Quaife, *The Kingdom of Saint James* (New Haven: Yale University Press, 1930), 170. This work is the most extensive, objective view of the subject of James Strang and his splinter Mormon Kingdom. See also Doyle C. Fitzpatrick, *Strang Story* (Lansing: National Heritage, 1970). This book is a worthwhile, careful analysis of Quaife's work and the few errors contained therein.

3. The papers edited by Strang were the *Voree Herald* and the *Northern Islander,* which became the official voice of his sect. In deference to the modern Church of Jesus Christ of Latter-day Saints and the Reorganized Church of Jesus Christ of Latter-day Saints, whose members are called Mormons, the author will refer to Strang's people as "Strangites" or "Saints" (meaning church members), though historically Strang and his followers called themselves Mormons and believed they were the dutiful inheritors of Joseph Smith's Church.

4. The early life of James Strang as recorded by several historians has been derived from his diary. (Published as Appendix II in Quaife, *Kingdom,* 230.) It seems probable that this diary may have been in the possession of Charles J. Strang, a Lansing, Michigan, printer. The volume surfaced around 1880. Henry A. Chaney, a reporter of the Michigan Supreme Court, saw the diary and produced an unpublished report given before the October Club in Lansing. The report and notes were subsequently turned over to Charles K. Backus, assistant Commissioner of Immigration, who published "An American King," *Harper's Monthly* 44 (March, 1882), 553–55. This report was subsequently used by an unknown author with some further historical embellishment in "The King of the Saints," *New York Times* (September 3, 1882), 10.

5. Diary, December 6, 1835; March 21, 1832; November 26, 1833.

6. Diary, October 20, 1835.

7. Diary, March 21, 1836; Diary, May 29, 1836; Quaife, *Kingdom,* 7–9. Quaife uses Pearce as the spelling for this family, though it is Perce in the diary.

8. "King of the Saints," 10.

9. Backus, "American King," 555.

10. Ibid.; Quaife, *Kingdom,* 11–12 and appendix III, 235–37.

11. Quaife, *Kingdom,* 12–16.

12. Ibid., 20–37.

13. Ibid., 75, 80.

14. Fitzpatrick, *Strang Story*. Fitzpatrick's basic premise that Strang has been unfairly judged is well founded and documented. Fitzpatrick also points out the dubious nature of several other Strangite Church officials.

15. Quaife, *Kingdom*, 81–85.

16. Ibid., 91, Appendix VIII Memorial, April 6, 1850.

17. Backus, "American King," 557; "King of the Saints," 10; Quaife, *Kingdom*, 86.

18. Backus, "American King," 557; "King of the Saints," 10; Quaife, *Kingdom*, 98, 106.

19. Quaife, *Kingdom*, 81.

20. Ibid., 56, 89, 90; *Voree Gospel Herald*, March 28, 1850. In 1846–47, Strang attempted to establish a secret Order of the Illuminate. The oath for the order was taken by apostates, and 2,000 copies were published and distributed to anyone concerned. In the oath, allegiance to Strang preceded any other. Strang's diary shows him to be an average patriotic youth: by the time he was called to the bar, however, he had become cynical over the graft and corruption displayed in government.

21. "King of the Saints," 10; Quaife, *Kingdom*, 118.

22. "King of the Saints," 10; Backus, "American King," 557.

23. Quaife, *Kingdom*, 121, 123.

24. McIntosh to Preston, October 4, 1849, *Commanders Letters*, Roll 39, Part 2, Letter 79. Commander McIntosh reported that cholera was now at Mackinaw and Green Bay. Nineteen deaths in the area were reported by surgeon Maxwell Woode. It appears that Native Americans were particularly hard hit by this plague; thirteen of the bodies found on the beach were natives.

25. Quaife, *Kingdom*, 121.

26. Oscar Bullus to William Graham, October 18, 1850, *Commanders Letters*, Roll 41, Letter 154; Quaife, *Kingdom*, 85. Quaife mentions that as early as 1848, sixty steamers stopped at Beaver Island to buy cordwood. Previously this wood had been purchased at Mackinac Island.

27. Quaife, *Kingdom*, 124–25.

28. Ibid.

29. "King of the Saints," 10; Quaife, *Kingdom*, 127.

30. Bullus to Acting Secretary, May 15, 1851, *Commanders Letters*, Roll 42, Letter 188; Quaife, *Kingdom*, 128–29.

31. Quaife, *Kingdom*, 129. It seems odd for a Whig cabinet member to solicit the advice of a Democrat, particularly in this case where the chance of blundering and losing party strength was so great.

32. Bullus to Navy Secretary, May 17 and May 19, 1851, *Commanders Letters*, Roll 42, Letters 192, 193. It is possible that Commander Bullus anticipated action and used this opportunity in Erie to remove and mount his battery of guns from storage.

33. Bullus to Graham, May 28, 1851, *Commanders Letters*, Roll 42, Letter 199; Quaife, *Kingdom*, 130–33; George C. Bates, "The Beaver Island Prophets Trial in the City in 1851," *Detroit Tribune*, July 10, 1877. Bates's account, other than date and time, is unsubstantiated by the navy records.

34. Quaife, *Kingdom*, 133–34.

35. Ibid., 134; Bullus to William Graham, June 14 and June 27, 1851, *Commanders Letters*, Roll 42, Letters 223, 231.

36. Quaife, *Kingdom*, 135.

37. Ibid., 142–46, 148, 149, 150.

38. "Mormonism," *DDFP* (May 24, 1853). The document was signed by the county supervisor, the district attorney, and seventy other people.

39. Quaife, *Kingdom*, 156–58.

40. "U.S. Steamer Michigan," *DDFP* (August 17, 1853).

41. Ibid.

42. Quaife, *Kingdom*, 174.

43. Charles McBlair to Dobbin, June 6, 1856, *Commanders Letters*, Roll 50, Letter 106.

44. C. H. McBlair to Kinsley S. Bingham, Governor of Michigan, June 6, 1856, Enclosure, *Commanders Letters*, Roll 50, Letter 106.

45. "Protection of the Law," *Northern Islander*, April 3, 1851, published in Quaife, *Kingdom*, Appendix IX, 256–58.

46. Governor Bingham to McBlair, July 1, 1856, enclosure, *Commanders Letters*, September 24, 1856, Roll 51, Letter 219.

47. "Protection of the Law," 256.

48. "Murderous Assault," *Northern Islander*, June 20, 1856; Logbook, Monday, June 16, 1856; Quote from *Commanders Letters*, McBlair to Dobbin, June 19, 1856, Roll 50, Letter 119.

49. McBlair to Dobbin, June 19 and Sept. 24, 1856, *Commanders Letters*, Rolls 50, 51, Letters 119, 219; Quaife, *Kingdom*, 171.

50. Quaife, *Kingdom*, 169.

51. Ibid., 163–69; McBlair to Dobbin, June 6, 1856, *Commanders Letters*, Roll 50, Letter 106. C. Scott has never before been mentioned as a conspirator but was among the people McBlair spoke with ten days before the assassination.

52. Quaife, *Kingdom*, 170.

53. McBlair to Dobbin, June 6, 1856, *Commanders Letters*, Roll 50, Letter 106.

54. McBlair to Governor Bingham, June 6, 1856, *Commanders Letters*, enclosure, Roll 50, Letter 106.

55. McBlair to Dobbin, June 6, 1856, *Commanders Letters*, Roll 50, Letter 106.

56. McBlair to Dobbin, June 6, 1856, *Commanders Letters*, Roll 50, Letter 106; McBlair to Dobbin, September 26, 1855, *Commanders Letters*, Roll 49, Letter 173. There is no evidence, though, that any of these men knew each other while residing in Baltimore.

57. Logbook, June 14, 1856; McBlair to Dobbin, June 14, 1856, *Commanders Letters*, Roll 50, Letter 111.

58. McBlair to Dobbin, September 24, 1856, *Commanders Letters*, Roll 51, Letter 219.

59. Logbook, June 17, 1856; McBlair to Dobbin, June 19, 1856, *Commanders Letters*, Roll 50, Letter 119.

60. Quaife, *Kingdom*, 172.

61. Ibid., 179.

62. "King of the Saints," 10; Quaife, *Kingdom*, 173–74.

63. McBlair to Dobbin, Sept. 7, 1856, *Commanders Letters,* Roll 51, Letter 175.

64. McBlair to Dobbin, Sept. 24, 1856, *Commanders Letters,* Roll 51, Letter 219.

65. There was no naval court of inquiry into McBlair's role in the assassination. Records of General Courts Martial and Courts of Inquiry of the Navy Department, 1799–1867, Roll 84, RG-125, National Archives, Washington, D.C.

66. McBlair to Dobbin, July 2, 1856, *Commanders Letters,* Roll 51, Letter 9.

Chapter 5

1. Stephen Champlin to George Bancroft, August 1, 1846, *Commanders Letters,* Roll 35, Letter 67.

2. James McIntosh to Mason, November 6, 1848, *Commanders Letters,* Roll 38, Letter 105; Inman to Bancroft, May 2, 1845, *Commanders Letters,* Roll 33, Letter 149.

3. Stephen Champlin to Bancroft, May 25, 1846, *Commanders Letters,* Roll 34, Letter 150.

4. Champlin to Bancroft, May 26, 1846, *Commanders Letters,* Roll 34, Letter 153; Champlin to Bancroft, November 28, 1845, *Commanders Letters,* Roll 33, Letter 195.

5. Champlin to Bancroft, July 18, 1846, *Commanders Letters,* Roll 35, Letter 40; Bullus to Graham, July 12, 1851, *Commanders Letters,* Roll 42, Letter 18; McIntosh to Mason, July 28, 1848, *Commanders Letters,* Roll 38, Letter 245.

6. Nicholas to Dobbin, June 7, 1854, *Commanders Letters,* Roll 46, Letter 71. The *Michigan* carried two pilots, Mr. Henton for Lake Erie and Alexander St. Bernard for the Upper Lakes.

7. McIntosh to Preston, October 23, 1849, *Commanders Letters,* Roll 39, Part 2, Letter 110.

8. Champlin to Mason, May 4, 1847, *Commanders Letters,* Roll 37, Letter 17; Champlin to Bancroft, July 8, 1846, *Commanders Letters,* Roll 35, Letter 16; Champlin to Bancroft, August 19, 1846, *Commanders Letters,* Roll 35, Letter 85.

9. Lanman to Isaac Toucey, April 15, 1858, *Commanders Letters,* Roll 57, Letter 40. This is but one example.

10. Lanman to Toucey, November 5, 1858, *Commanders Letters,* Roll 59, Letter 92. See enclosure from Lt. Charles B. DeKraft.

11. Lanman to Charles Welsh, August 24, 1858, *Commanders Letters,* Roll 58, Letter 150.

12. McBlair to Dobbin, December 1, 1856, *Commanders Letters,* Roll 51, Letter 139. These were the same men and officers who served on board when James Strang was assassinated.

13. Lanman to Welsh, July 18, 1859, *Commanders Letters,* Roll 62, Letter 48.

14. McBlair to Toucey, May 18, 1857, *Commanders Letters,* Roll 53, Letter 128, Enclosure from Capt. E. M. Ward.

15. McBlair to Toucey, May 22, 1857, *Commanders Letters,* Roll 53, Letter 139.

16. See *Commanders Letters,* June, 1848; January 7, 1855; May 18, 1857; May 22, 1857; October 24, 1857; August 11, 1858.

17. McBlair to Toucey, July 21, August 2, August 11, 1857, *Commanders Letters,* Roll 54, Letters 49, 86, 101. On October 24, 1857, Charles Dawson Shanley, acting Canadian secretary of public works, formally thanked the U.S. Navy for its help in moving the caisson into place, stating that it would help mariners from both countries.

18. Lanman to Toucey, December 20, 1859, *Commanders Letters,* Roll 62, Part 2, Letter 158; Frank F. Fowle, "100th Anniversary of the First Iron Steamboat on the Great Lakes," *Journal of the Western Society of Engineers* 48, no. 4 (December, 1943), 179.

19. Log Entry, November 19, 1860, Rough Log, April 30, 1859 to January 4, 1861.

20. Edward William Sloan III, *Benjamin Franklin Isherwood: Naval Engineer, The Years as Engineer in Chief, 1861–1869* (Annapolis: U.S. Naval Institute Press, 1965), 87–88.

21. Ibid., 87–88.

22. Command was transferred to Carter on March 1, 1861. Lanman to Toucey, March 1, 1861, *Commanders Letters,* Roll 66, Letter 114; Bradley A. Rodgers, "The Northern Theater in the Civil War, the USS *Michigan* and Confederate Intrigue on the Great Lakes," *American Neptune* 48, no. 2 (spring 1988), 96–105. Details concerning Anglo-American relations and diplomacy on the Great Lakes after the War of 1812 can be found in John W. Foster's report, *Limitation of Armament on the Great Lakes* (Washington, D.C.: Carnegie Endowment for International Peace, 1914), and Senate, *Message from the President.*

23. Navy Department to Commander Carter, May 9, 1861, *Official Records of the Union and Confederate Navies in the War of the Rebellion* [hereafter cited as *ORN*], ser. 1, vol. 2 (Washington, D.C.: United States Government Printing Office, 1895), 414.

24. Rear Adm. David D. Porter's testimony, File no. VMF 1227, 16, John C. Carter Papers, Ohio Historical Society [hereafter cited as Carter Papers]; Commander Carter to Navy Department, November 6, 1861, *Commanders Letters,* Roll 69, Letter 35. The total number of men sent to the Atlantic was gleaned from adding the recruitment figures included in the *Commanders Letters* before the order of November 1. After November, 1861, the figures are split between New York and Cairo.

25. Carter to Navy Dept., December 7, 1861, *Commanders Letters,* Roll 69, Letter 204.

26. Bourne, *Britain and the Balance,* 154; Winks, *Canada and the United States,* 56.

27. Report of Commander Carter to the Navy Department, July 28, 1863, *ORN,* ser. 1, vol. 2, 415.

28. Paper 1, written testimony, Carter Papers.

29. Report of Commander Carter to the Navy Department, September 3, 1863, *ORN,* ser. 1, vol. 2, 435.

30. Logbook entry, September 7, 1863, Rough Log, December 8, 1862, to July 23, 1864.

31. Carter to Navy Department, October 28, 1863, *ORN,* ser. 1, vol. 2, 478–79.

32. Logbook entry, October 26, 1863, Rough Log, December 8, 1862, to July 23, 1864.

33. Navy Department Dispatch, November 12, 1863, *ORN*, ser. 1, vol. 2, 496.

34. Log entry, November 23, 1863, Rough Log, December 8, 1862, to July 23, 1864.

35. Lt. Minor CSN to Admiral Buchanan CSN, February 2, 1864, *ORN*, ser. 1, vol. 2, 823.

36. Lt. William Murdaugh's plan, February 7, 1863, *ORN*, ser. 1, vol. 2, 828.

37. At this time there were no British patrol vessels or warships on the lakes to thwart Confederate threats to Canadian neutrality. Canada did possess small vessels used for pilotage, which later may have been armed for patrol purposes. Winks, *Canada and the United States,* 55.

38. Lt. Minor CSN to Admiral Buchanan CSN, February 2, 1864, *ORN*, ser. 1, vol. 2, 823.

39. Navy Department Dispatch, November 12, 1863, *ORN*, ser. 1, vol. 2, 496.

40. Francis A. Roe, "The U.S. Steamer *Michigan* and the Lake Frontier During the War of the Rebellion," *The United Service, A Monthly Review of Military and Naval Affairs* 6 (December, 1891), 545; Commander F. A. Roe to Navy Department, September 13, 1865, *ORN*, ser. 1, vol. 3, 590–91.

41. Report of Confederate States Agent Jacob Thompson to J. P. Benjamin Secretary of State, December 3, 1864, *ORN*, ser. 1, vol. 3, 714–16 [hereafter cited as Thompson's Report].

42. Report to War Secretary E. M. Stanton from Maj. General John A. Dix, September 20, 1864, *War of the Rebellion Official Records for the Union and Confederate Armies,* ser. 1, pt. 2, vol. 43, 225 [hereafter cited as Stanton from Dix, with series hereafter cited as *ORA*].

43. Stanton from Dix, *ORA,* 226–27. Thompson alludes to a messenger in Thompson's Report, 716.

44. Testimony of Henry Haines, *ORA,* ser. 1, pt. 2, vol. 43, 244–45.

45. William Frank Zarnow, "Confederate Raiders on Lake Erie, Their Propaganda Value in 1864, Part 1," *Inland Seas* 5 (spring 1949), 42.

46. Stanton from Dix, *ORA,* 227.

47. Ibid.

48. Thompson's Report, 716; Zarnow, "Confederate Raiders, Part 1," 42.

49. Stanton from Dix, 226; Commander Carter to Navy Department, September 26, 1864, *ORN*, ser. 1, vol. 3, 220–21

50. Letter from B. H. Hill to Major C. H. Potter, assistant adjutant general, September 21, 1864, *ORA*, ser. 1, pt. 2, vol. 43, 228.

51. Log entry, September 19, 1864, Rough Log, July 24, 1864, to August 30, 1866.

52. Navy Department Dispatch, September 20, 1864, *ORN*, ser. 1, vol. 3, 219.

53. Log entry, September 20, 1864.

54. Log entry, September 20, 1864, Rough log, July 24, 1864, to August 30, 1866.

55. Log entry, September 21, 1864, Rough log, July 24, 1864, to August 30, 1866. The *Island Queen* was also refloated and put back in running order.

56. Carter to Navy Department, September 22, 1864, *ORN*, ser. 1, vol. 3, 220; Carter to Navy Department, September 26, 1864, *ORN*, ser. 1, vol. 3, 220–21.

57. Log entry, September 25, 1864, Rough log, July 24, 1864, to August 30, 1866. In this instance, the *Michigan* fired a blank cartridge at the steamer *Clifton*.

58. Carter to Navy Department, October 6, 1864, *ORN*, ser. 1, vol. 3, 220. The crew of the *Michigan* boarded 128 vessels in Toledo and Sandusky, finding no trace of contraband weapons and powder.

59. Navy Department Communication, November 9, 1864, *ORN*, ser. 1, vol. 3, 352.

60. Carter to Navy Department, November 7, 1864, *ORN*, ser. 1, vol. 3, 349.

61. Roe, "Lake Frontier," 546.

62. Navy Department Order, November 16, 1864, *ORN*, ser. 1, vol. 3, 375.

63. Commander Roe to Navy Department, December 6, 1864, *ORN*, ser. 1, vol. 3, 388–89.

64. Roe, "Lake Frontier," 547.

65. Winks, *Canada and the United States*, 308.

Chapter 6

1. Gerald Friedman, "Strike Success and Union Ideology: The United States and France, 1880–1914," *Journal of Economic History* 48, no. 1 (March, 1988): 23.

2. Rodgers, "Civil War."

3. William N. Still, *Iron Afloat* (Nashville: Vanderbilt University Press, 1971), 164; Lewis Randolf Hamersly, *The Records of the Living Officers of the U.S. Navy and Marine Corps* (Philadelphia: L. R. Hamersly and Co., 1894), 30; Commander F. A. Roe to Navy Department, September 13, 1865, *ORN*, ser. 1, vol. 3, 591; Lieutenant Commander F. A. Roe to Navy Secretary Gideon Welles, September 13, 1865, *Letters Received by the Sec. of the Navy From Officers Below the Rank of Commander 1802–1886*, Entry 145, Roll 399, M-148, RG-45, National Archives, Washington, D.C. [hereafter cited as *Letters Below Commander*].

4. Roe, "Lake Frontier," 548; Roe to Welles, April 29, 1865, *Letters Below Commander*, Roll 391, Entry 536.

5. Rodgers, "Civil War," 97; Carter Papers; John C. Schneider, "Detroit and the Problem of Disorder," *Michigan History* 58, no. 1 (spring 1974): 14; Bradley A. Rodgers, "Deliverance by Sea: Michigan's Peninsula War of 1865," *Michigan History* 73, no. 6 (November/December, 1989): 17. A brief outline of the 1864 strike in Marquette can be found in "From Lake Superior, The Strike of the Iron Miners," *CT*, July 20, 1865, 1.

6. Roe to Welles, September 13, 1865, *Letters Below Commander*, Roll 399, Entry 145.

7. Log entries, June 22–29, 1865, *Logbook #16*, July 24, 1864, through August 30, 1865.

8. Roe, "Lake Frontier," 549.

9. Logbook entry, July 3, 1865; Roe, "Lake Frontier," 549; Roe to Welles, July 17, 1865, *Letters Below Commander*, Roll 397, entry 257.

10. Roe to Welles, July 17, 1865, *Letters Below Commander,* Roll 397, Entry 257; Roe, "Lake Frontier," 549; Roe to Navy Department, September 13, 1865, *ORN,* ser. 1, vol. 3, 590; Hamersly, *Records,* 30.

11. William B. Gates, Jr., *Michigan Copper and Boston Dollars: An Economic History of the Michigan Copper Mining Industry* (Cambridge: Harvard University Press, 1951), 98; Alfred P. Swineford, *History and Review of the Copper, Iron, Silver, Slate, and Other Material Interests of the South Shore of Lake Superior* (Marquette: Mining Journal, 1876), 70. According to the *Chicago Tribune,* the total population for Marquette was 1,500. For the number of miners involved in the strikes, see note 26.

12. "From Lake Superior, The Strike of the Iron Miners," *CT,* July 20, 1865, 1; Angus Murdock, *Boom Copper* (New York: Macmillan, 1943), 120; Virginia Jonas Dersch, "Copper Mining in Northern Michigan," *Michigan History* 61, no. 4 (winter 1977): 299, 300.

13. Gates, *Michigan Copper,* 94.

14. Murdock, *Boom Copper,* 120; Schneider, "Detroit," 23, 24; John Harris Forster, "War Times in the Copper Mines," *Michigan Pioneer and Historical Society Collections* 18 (1892): 379. Murdock mentions that the only civil authority in the nearby Keweenaw Peninsula were vigilantes. Schneider notes that even a larger town, such as Detroit, had only a provost guard to maintain civil authority.

15. Roe, "Lake Frontier," 549; Roe to Welles, September 13, 1865, *Letters Below Commander,* Roll 399, entry 145.

16. J. G. Randall and David Donald, *The Civil War and Reconstruction,* 2d ed., (Boston: Heath, 1961), 538; Gates, *Michigan Copper,* 96; "From Lake Superior, The Strike of the Iron Miners," *CT,* July 20, 1965, 1.

17. Gates, *Michigan Copper,* 41, 101; "From Lake Superior, A Strike Among the Miners," *CT,* July 13, 1865, 1; "From Lake Superior, The Strike of the Iron Miners," *CT,* July 20, 1865, 1; "The Strike of the Iron Miners," *Green Bay Advocate,* July 20, 1865 , 2. Although copper and iron mining are not necessarily linked economically, a nationwide depression affected both industries.

18. According to the *Chicago Tribune,* July 20, 1865, article entitled "From Lake Superior, The Strike of the Iron Miners," the wages for iron miners increased during the war from $1.75 per day earlier in the decade to a maximum $2.50 per day during the winter of 1864–65. The *Green Bay Advocate,* in its July 20 article, put the maximum wartime pay at $3.00 per day. With a $3.00 maximum, wages increased 71 percent during the war. In *Michigan Copper,* Gates states that the increase in wages for copper miners for roughly the same time period was 50 percent to 60 percent. The nation's overall price index increased in 1861 from 102.9 to 220.9 in 1864, and 210.9 in 1865. Ralph Andreano, ed., *The Economic Impact of the American Civil War* (Cambridge: Harvard University Press, 1962), 178.

19. "From Lake Superior, A Strike Among the Miners," *CT,* July 13, 1865, 1; "From Lake Superior, The Strike of the Iron Miners," *CT,* July 20, 1865, 1; "The Strike of the Iron Workers," *Green Bay Advocate,* July 20, 1865, 2; Forster, "War Times," 379. The miners' wages had already been cut from the maximum of $3.00

per day to $2.50, then to $2.00, and finally $1.75. The usual workday was ten hours on Saturday.

20. "From Lake Superior, The Strike of the Iron Miners," *CT,* July 20, 1865, 1.

21. "From Lake Superior, Trip of Henry Winter Davis and His Friends—Sights, Incidents and Observations," *CT,* July 13, 1865, 2.

22. "The Strike of the Iron Miners," *Green Bay Advocate,* July 20, 1865, 2.

23. Gates, *Michigan Copper,* 95; Randall and Donald, *Civil War,* 314; Swineford, *History,* 71; Murdock, *Boom Copper,* 121; Schneider, "Detroit," 14; Charlotte Erickson, *American Industry and the European Immigrant 1860–1885* (Harvard University Press, 1957); *Register of the Commissioned and Warrant Officers of the Navy of the United States including Officers of the Marine Corps for the year 1865* (Washington, 1865), 7.

24. Hamersly, *Records,* 29.

25. Gaston Rimlinger, "Labor and the Government: A Comparative Historical Perspective," *Journal of Economic History* 37 (1977): 217.

26. Roe, "Lake Frontier," 549. The usual complement for the ship was 120 officers and men, with an additional 15 marines. The *Portage Lake Mining Gazette* for Saturday, July 15, 1865, reported that the ship's complement was 110 men and 19 officers.

Roe reported that from 1,500 to 2,000 miners were involved in the mutiny. The *Chicago Tribune* gave a smaller figure of some 500 strikers. I used the higher estimate for two reasons: (1) Roe was an eyewitness, trained in estimating forces, and (2) if only one mine was not on strike, virtually every miner in the region must have been involved.

27. Roe, "Lake Frontier," 550; Roe to Welles, September 13, 1865, *Letters Below Commander,* Roll 399, Entry 145.

28. Roe, "Lake Frontier," 550; Commander F. A. Roe to Navy Department, September 13, 1865, *ORN,* ser. 1, vol. 3, 590.

29. Roe, "Lake Frontier," 550; Roe to Welles, September 13, *Letters Below Commander,* Roll 399, Entry 145.

30. Roe, "Lake Frontier," 550; Roe to Welles, September 13, 1865, *Letters Below Commander,* Roll 399, Entry 145.

31. Roe, "Lake Frontier," 550; Dersch, "Copper Mining," 305. Roe is probably referring to Torch Lake.

32. "The U.S. Steamer *Michigan,*" *Portage Lake Mining Gazette,* July 15, 1865, 3. It seems interesting to note that the *Portage Lake Mining Gazette* does not mention the labor disturbances while reporting on the ship's visit. It is likely that a paper controlled by the mining interests did not want news spread of isolated mining strikes so as not to agitate the entire mining community.

33. Roe, "Lake Frontier," 550, 551; Roe to Navy Department, September 13, 1865, *ORN,* ser. 1, vol. 3, 590.

34. "Military Expedition to Lake Superior," *Green Bay Advocate,* August 3, 1865, 2. This article stated that one reason a military survey was completed was to ascertain the best location of a permanent army garrison because of the strategic value of the mineral deposits of the region and their proximity to a potentially aggressive foreign

power, Great Britain; Gates, *Michigan Copper,* 35. In 1862 the Pewabic Mine contracted with the Navy Department to deliver 100 tons of copper bolts; Emerson David Fite, *Social and Industrial Conditions in the North During the Civil War* (New York: Frederick Ungar Publishing Co., 1963), 25.

35. "From Lake Superior, The Strike of the Iron Miners," *CT,* July 20, 1865, 1. The *Chicago Tribune* reports that the strike began on July 10; however, the disturbances started the week previous to this date.

36. Commander F. A. Roe to Navy Department, September 13, 1865, *ORN,* ser. 1, vol. 3, 590; "From Lake Superior, A Strike Among the Miners," *CT,* July 13, 1865, 1; "From Lake Superior, The Miners Strike," *CT,* July 19, 1865, 1; "From Lake Superior, The Strike of the Iron Miners," *CT,* July 20, 1865, 1.

37. "From Lake Superior," *CT,* July 15, 1865, 1; "From Lake Superior, The Miners Strike," *CT,* July 19, 1865, 1; "From Lake Superior, The Strike of the Iron Miners," *CT,* July 20, 1865, 1. The unit of troops from Camp Douglas traveled via the Chicago and Northwestern Railroad to Green Bay, where they embarked on the steamer *George L. Dunlop* to Escanaba. From Escanaba they boarded the Peninsula Railroad to Negaunee.

38. Freidman, "Strike Success," 24; "Military Expedition to Lake Superior," *Green Bay Advocate,* August 3, 1865, 2; "From Lake Superior, The Strike of the Iron Miners," *CT,* July 20, 1865, 1.

There was a weekly newspaper produced at Marquette in 1865. However, it may be significant that the only extant issues of the *Lake Superior Mining Journal* are dated before the disturbances and do not pick up again until October, 1865, at which time there is no mention of the mining strikes and violence of the previous July.

39. "From Lake Superior, A Strike Among the Miners," *CT,* July 13, 1865, 1; "The Strike of the Iron Miners," *Green Bay Advocate,* July 20, 1865, 2.

40. "From Lake Superior, A Strike Among the Miners," *CT,* July 13, 1865, 1; "From Lake Superior, The Strike of the Iron Miners," *CT,* July 20, 1865, 1; "The Strike of the Iron Miners," *Green Bay Advocate,* July 20, 1865, 2.

41. Roe to Navy Department, September 13, 1865, *ORN,* ser. 1, vol. 3, 590–91; Roe to Welles, July 17, 1865, *Letters Below Commander,* Roll 397, Entry 257.

In his report to the navy secretary, Roe states, "Troops have been sent for from Chicago, who will be permanently located here." It seems likely that this army unit stayed throughout 1866 at Marquette. A relief unit then moved into Fort Wilkins in 1867.

42. "From Lake Superior, A Strike Among the Miners," *CT,* July 13, 1865, 1.

43. "Military Expedition to Lake Superior," *Green Bay Advocate,* August 3, 1865, 2. It is interesting to note that the transportation and accommodations for this military entourage were provided free of charge by Superintendent Dunlop of the Chicago and Northwestern Railroad.

44. The *Chicago Tribune* reported on July 20, 1865, "There is a general desire that a small garrison of troops remain in this region." The *Green Bay Advocate* in its August 3, 1865, article, "Military Expedition to Lake Superior," stated that a survey of the region was ordered by Major General Ord, commandant of the Department of

the Ohio, and conducted by Brigadier General Sweet, "with a view to establishing a military post in that region."

45. Gates, *Michigan Copper,* 100; Erickson, *American Industry,* 109. Erickson describes labor surplus as the major weapon used by industry to suppress unions.

46. James M. McPherson, *Ordeal by Fire: The Civil War and Reconstruction* (New York: Knopf, 1982), 376.

47. Roe to Navy Department, September 13, 1865, *ORN,* ser. 1, vol. 3, 591.

48. Roe to Welles, October 16, 1865, *Letters Below Commander,* Roll 400, Entry 117.

49. Roe to Welles, October 30, 1865, *Letters Below Commander,* Roll 400, Entry 209½; Lt. Commander Roe to Commander Bryson, April 16, 1866, *Letters Below Commander,* Roll 404, Entry 267.

Chapter 7

1. The historical romance *Ridgeway,* cited in J. A. Cole's *Prince of Spies: Henri Le Caron* (Boston: Faber and Faber, 1984), 20.

2. W. S. Neidhardt, *Fenianism in North America* (University Park: Pennsylvania University Press, 1975), 1–4. This is by far the most well-rounded study done to date concerning the Fenian movement in the United States and Canada.

3. Ibid., 7.

4. W. S. Neidhardt, "The American Government and the Fenian Brotherhood: A Study in Mutual Political Opportunism," *Ontario History* 64, no. 1 (March, 1972), 28; *Fenianism in North America,* 11.

5. Neidhardt, *Fenianism in North America,* 21.

6. Cole, *Prince of Spies,* 15; Neidhardt, *Fenianism in North America,* 27.

7. F. M. Quealey, "The Fenian Invasion of Canada West; June 1st and 2nd, 1866," *Ontario History* 53 (1961), 39; Neidhardt, *Fenianism in North America,* 29; W. L. Morton, *The Critical Years: The Union of British North America 1857–1873* (Oxford: Oxford University Press, 1964), 195; George T. Denison, *History of the Fenian Raid on Fort Erie with an Account of the Battle of Ridgeway* (Toronto: Roll and Adam, 1866), 14.

8. "Fenianism," *Harper's Weekly,* March 24, 1866. The fanatic Roberts-and-Sweeny faction broke from the Fenian Brotherhood at this time and formed their own Fenian organization headquartered at Jones' Wood, New York.

9. Quealey, "The Fenian Invasion of Canada West," 40.

10. Neidhardt, *Fenianism in North America,* 29.

11. "Stephen Will Find Gone Under," *New York Times,* May 5, 1866, 4; "The Fenian Invasion of Canada," *New York Times,* June 2, 1866, 4.

12. Neidhardt, *Fenianism in North America,* 30; Lester B. Shippee, *Canadian-American Relations 1849–1874* (New York: Russell and Russell, 1939), 214–15.

13. Roe to Welles, October 28, 1865, *Letters Below Commander,* Roll 400, Entry 202; Roe to Welles, January 27, 1866, *Letters Below Commander,* Roll 401, Entry 445; Roe to Welles, April 3, 1866, *Letters Below Commander,* Roll 404, Entry 45; Roe to Welles, April 9, 1866, *Letters Below Commander,* Roll 404, Entry 140. Roe was

popular with the citizenry of Buffalo. When he was to be replaced, a petition was sent to the Navy Department asking that he be kept in command of the *Michigan.* Roe to Welles, April 17, 1866, *Letters Below Commander,* Roll 404, Entry 275.

14. Commander A. Bryson to Gideon Welles, April 28, 1866, *Commanders Letters,* Roll 85, Letter 76; Bryson to Welles, May 5, 1866, *Commanders Letters,* Roll 85, Letter 104; Bryson to Welles, May 10, 1866, *Commanders Letters,* Roll 85, Letter 129.

15. Bryson to Welles, May 9, 1866, *Commanders Letters,* Roll 85, Letter 121.

16. Neidhardt, *Fenianism in North America,* 33–34, 55.

17. Bryson to Welles, May 28, 1866, *Commanders Letters,* Roll 85, Letter 192.

18. Bryson to Welles, May 30, 1866, *Commanders Letters,* Roll 85, Letter 200.

19. "Buffalo May 31, 1865 [*sic*]," *Daily Telegraph* (Toronto), June 1, 1866, 1. The haste and excitement with which this edition went to press is indicated by the wrong year in the title.

20. Bryson to Welles, May 30, 1866, *Commanders Letters,* Roll 85, Letter 200.

21. "The Fenians," *Globe* (Toronto), May 25, 1866, 2; "Fenian Raid in Canada," *Globe* (Toronto), May 30, 1866, 1; "The Fenians At Buffalo," *Globe* (Toronto), May 31, 1866, 2; "The Fenians Again Moving," *Globe* (Toronto), May 31, 1866, 2.

22. "The Fenians," *Globe* (Toronto), May 25, 1866, 2; "Fenians Stealing Arms," *Globe* (Toronto), June 1, 1866, 1; Bryson to Welles, June 1, 1866, *Commanders Letters,* Roll 85, Letter 206.

23. "The Fenians," *Globe* (Toronto), May 25, 1866, 2; "The Fenians Again Moving," *Globe* (Toronto), May 31, 1866, 2.

24. "The Fenians Again," *Buffalo Morning Express,* May 30, 1866, 1; "Fenianism," *Daily Telegraph* (Toronto), May 31, 1866, 1.

25. "The Fenians," *Globe* (Toronto) June 1, 1866, 2; "Fenian Raid," *Globe* (Toronto), June 2, 1866, 2; Quealey, "The Fenian Invasion of Canada West," 45.

26. Log entry, June 1, 1866, *Logbook #16 (Rough), July 24, 1864, through August 30, 1866;* Bryson to Welles, June 2, 1866, *Commanders Letters,* Roll 85, Letter 209.

27. "The F's Cross the River," *Daily Telegraph* (Toronto), June 1, 1866, second edition.

28. "Fenian Raid," *Globe* (Toronto), June 2, 1866, 2.

29. Bryson to Welles, June 1, 1866, *Commanders Letters,* Roll 85, Letter 206; Bryson to Welles, June 2, 1866, *Commanders Letters,* Roll 85, Letter 209.

30. Quealey, "The Fenian Invasion of Canada West," 47.

31. Bryson to Welles, June 2, 1866, *Commanders Letters,* Roll 85, Letter 209.

32. Report of James P. Kelley to Commander Bryson, June 2, 1866, included in Bryson to Welles, June 2, 1866, *Commanders Letters,* Roll 85, Letter 209.

33. Bryson to Welles, June 2, 1866, *Commanders Letters,* Roll 85, Letter 209.

34. "Another Spasm," *New York Times,* June 1, 1866, 4.

35. Neidhardt, *Fenianism in North America,* 61.

36. "Fenian Raid," *Globe* (Toronto), June 2, 1866, 2.

37. "From Fort Erie," *Daily Telegraph* (Toronto), June 1, 1866.

38. Log entry, June 1, 1866, *Logbook #16 (Rough), July 24, 1864, through August 30, 1866.*

39. Log entry, June 2, 1866, *Logbook #16 (Rough), July 24, 1864, through August 30, 1866.*

40. Though only a skirmish by Civil War standards, the battle of Ridgeway or Limestone Ridge, as it is variously called, has been minutely considered by the press of the day, eyewitness accounts, and official correspondence. I have here only an outline of some of the more readable sources, such as Denison, *History of the Fenian Raid;* John A. MacDonald, *Troublous Times in Canada* (Toronto: W. S. Johnston and Co., 1910); C. P. Stacey, "The Fenian Troubles and Canadian Military Development, 1865–1871," Canadian Historical Association Report (1935); Quealey, "The Fenian Invasion of Canada West;" Neidhardt, *Fenianism in North America;* E. A. Cruikshank, "The Fenian Raid of 1866," Publications of the Welland County Historical Society, II (1926).

41. Newspaper sources of the two battles of June 2, 1866, seem accurate. The following is a sample: "The Fenian War," *New York Times,* June 3, 1866, 1; "The Fenian War," *Buffalo Morning Express,* June 4, 1866, 2; "Our Volunteers," *Globe* (Toronto), June 1, 1866, 2–4; "Fenian Raid," *Globe* (Toronto), June 2 & 4, 1866), 2–4; "The Fight," *Daily Telegraph* (Toronto), June 2, 1866; "From the Army," *Daily Telegraph* (Toronto), June 2, 1866.

42. Bryson to Welles, June 3, 1866, *Commanders Letters,* Roll 85, Letter 214; Neidhardt, *Fenianism in North America,* 73; "2 pm," *Daily Telegraph* (Toronto), June 2, 1866, 2.

43. Telegram—Bryson to Welles, 6:40 pm, June 3, 1866, *Commanders Letters,* Roll 85, Letter 212; Log Entry, June 2, 1866, *Logbook #16 (Rough), July 24, 1864, through August 30, 1866.* The *Fessenden* arrived at 7:30 pm.

44. *Globe* (Toronto), June 5, 1866; MacDonald, *Troublous Times in Canada,* 90. There is no other corroborating evidence that this force was actually dispatched from Buffalo.

45. Log entries, June 2 and 3, 1866, *Logbook #16 (Rough), July 24, 1864, through August 30, 1866;* Bryson to Welles, June 3, 1866, *Commanders Letters,* Roll 85, Letter 214.

46. *Globe* (Toronto), June 2, 1866; *Globe* (Globe), June 6, 1866).

47. Cole, *Prince of Spies,* 19 (The term *cut to pieces* was used by O'Neill when he offered up his sword to Commander Bryson); Bryson to Welles, June 3, 1866, *Commanders Letters,* Roll, 85, Letter 214.

48. W. S. Neidhardt, "The Fenian Trials in the Province of Canada, 1866–1867, A Case Study of Law and Politics in Action," *Ontario History* 66, no. 1 (March, 1974), 24.

49. *Harpers Weekly,* June 16, 1866.

50. Brian Jenkins, *Fenians and Anglo-American Relations During Reconstruction* (Ithaca: Cornell University Press, 1969), 147; Hemans to Bruce, June 4, 1866, F.O. 5, 1330.

51. Log entry, June 3, 1866, *Logbook #16 (Rough), July 24, 1864, through August 30, 1866.*

52. Log entry, June 3, 1866, *Logbook #16 (Rough), July 24, 1864, through August 30, 1866;* Telegram Bryson to Welles, June 4, 1866, *Commanders Letters,* Roll 85, Letter 217.

53. Bryson to Welles, June 4, 1866, *Commanders Letters,* Roll 85, Letter 218.

54. Log entry, June 5, 1866, *Logbook #16 (Rough), July 24, 1864, through Aug. 30, 1866.*

55. Jenkins, *Fenians and Anglo-American Relations,* 149, 150.

56. Denison, *History of the Fenian Raid,* 69.

57. Log entry, November 5, 1866, *Logbook #16 (Smooth), August 31, 1866, through September 16, 1867.*

Chapter 8

1. Ann Morrison Brooke, A short unpublished biography of William Leverett Morrison, *Wolverine* File, Erie Historical Society.

2. Robert E. Coontz, *From the Mississippi to the Sea* (Philadelphia: Dorance and Co., 1930), 174.

3. Mary Benson, "Woman's husband was on *Wolverine,* Old Warship Holds Many Memories," *Erie News* (December 3, 1984).

4. Commodore E. B. Underwood, "*Wolverine* née *Michigan*—A bit of the Old Navy," *United States Naval Institute Proceedings* 50 (April, 1924), 599.

5. Roe, "Lake Frontier," 545.

6. Roe, "Lake Frontier," 545; Underwood, *Wolverine,* 598.

7. Peter Karsten, *The Naval Aristocracy, The Golden Age of Annapolis and the Emergence of Modern American Navalism* (New York: Free Press, 1972), 62.

8. Karsten, *Naval Aristocracy,* 58, 62; Coontz, *Mississippi to Sea,* 174; H. E. Spalding, M.D., "Maxwell Wood," *Wolverine* File, Erie County Historical Society.

9. Log entry, April 19, 1893, *Logbook #53, November 9, 1892, through May 21, 1893;* Karsten, *Naval Aristocracy,* 81.

10. Bigelow to Dobbin, March 18, 1853, *Commanders Letters,* Roll 45, Letter 104.

11. Underwood, *Wolverine,* 598; "U.S. Government Service on the Great Lakes," *Inland Seas* 24 (spring 1968): 59–60.

12. Jim Thompson, "*Wolverine's* Sailor Recalls Warship's Brassy Career," *Erie Times,* July 27, 1979.

13. Log entry, August 22, 1887, *Logbook #42, August 6, 1887, through February 13, 1888;* Log entry, December 21, 1890, *Logbook #48, September 30, 1890, through April 9, 1891.*

14. Log entry, August 21, 1869, *Logbook #20 (Smooth), August 3, 1869, through March 31, 1870;* Coontz, *Mississippi to Sea,* 171, 172; Log entries, January 31 to February 2, 1882, *Logbook #33, August 1, 1881, through August 3, 1882;* Underwood, *Wolverine,* 597.

Ice skating was not always the safest of activities. At 4:05 P.M. on January 31, 1882, Master Thomas L. Plunkett fell through the ice while skating near the ship. He was recovered in fifteen minutes but could not be revived by ship's surgeon N. Penrose.

Lieutenant Commander G. V. Gridley (later captain of the *Olympia* at Manila Bay) commanded the honor guard during the funeral.

15. Coontz, *Mississippi to Sea*, 170.

16. Log entry, June 15, 1882, *Logbook #33, August 1, 1881, through August 3, 1882.*

17. Log entry, February 2, 1891, *Logbook #48, September 30, 1890, through April 9, 1891;* Log entry, September 10, 1891, *Logbook #50, April 10, 1891, through October 20, 1891.*

18. Log entry, January 13, 1864, *Logbook #15 (Rough), December 8, 1862, through July 23, 1864.*

19. This list is created from a compilation of log entries from July 18, 1867; August 21, 1869; June 3, 1857; and August 23, 1868.

20. Underwood, *Wolverine,* 599; "Government Service," 59. By 1895 enlisted men paid $9.00 per month for meals on board ship.

21. Coontz, *Mississippi to Sea,* 172.

22. *Erie Times,* October 28, 1907; General Correspondence, 4404–56, Box 4404–1 through 4404–97, RG-80, National Archives, Washington, D.C.

23. Log entry, July 7, 1892, *Logbook #52, May 1, 1892, through November 9, 1892;* Log entries, May 22, 1893, and September 12, 1893, *Logbook #54, May 22, 1893, through December 5, 1893;* Log entry, November 9, 1892, *Logbook #53, November 9, 1892, through May 21, 1893.*

24. Bullus to Graham, July 12, 1851, *Commanders Letters,* Roll 42, Letter 18.

25. Log entry, August 2, 1894, *Logbook #56, June 18, 1894, through December 24, 1894.* Tides don't normally figure into Great Lakes navigation, but in this case since the ship was only freed after a twenty-four-hour period, it may have been a factor.

26. Coontz, *Mississippi to Sea,* 173; General Correspondence, 4404–101, "Vessels in Militia," RG-80, National Archives, Washington, D.C. These ships included the *Essex, Don Juan de Austria, Dorothea, Gopher, Hawk, Isla de Luzon, Sandoval, Yantic,* and *Wolverine.*

27. Log entry, November 26, 1892, *Logbook #52, May 1, 1892, through November 9, 1892.* The boilers were put in at Buffalo.

28. Henry Penton, "The War Eagle," *Transactions of the Society of Naval Architects and Marine Engineers* 16 (1908), 9. The ship now displaced 685 tons.

29. Log entries, July 17, 1897–July 22, 1897, *Logbook #61, February 11, 1897, through August 23, 1897.*

30. General Correspondence, 4404–8.

31. Navy Department, *Dictionary of American Naval Fighting Ships,* vol. 4 (Washington, D.C.: United States Government Printing Office, 1969), 351.

32. Eric Maple, "Ship," in *Man Myth and Magic: An Illustrated Encyclopedia of the Supernatural,* vol. 19 (New York: Time Life, 1970), 2568.

33. Log entry, September 15, 1905, *Logbook #76 (Wolverine), August 1, 1905, through March 31, 1906.*

34. Penton, "War Eagle," 9.

35. Bill Welch, "Ships Passed in the Night—Too Close for Comfort," *Erie Times News,* April 21, 1985.

36. *Encyclopedia of Marine Technology* (London: Conway Press, 1993).

37. General Correspondence, March 20, 1907, H. H. Gildersleeve to Navy Department, 4404–52, RG-80, National Archives, Washington, D.C.

38. Addendum to log entry, May 17, 1910, *Logbook #82 (Wolverine), March 26, 1910, through November 11, 1910.*

39. Ibid.

40. Log entry, May 6, 1912, *Logbook #86 (Pa. Naval Force), May 6, 1912, through December 31, 1912.*

41. "*First Battalion,* Pennsylvania Naval Militia," A recruitment pamphlet, no date, *Wolverine* File, Erie County Historical Society.

42. Brooke, Biography of Morrison, 5–6; R. G. Plumb, *The History of the Navigation of the Great Lakes* (Washington, D.C.: United States Government Printing Office, 1911), 12.

43. On March 3, 1825, the president authorized the sale of all the naval vessels left on the lakes from the War of 1812. The *Niagara* and *Lawrence* with the *Detroit* and *Queen Charlotte* were sold to George Miles. Two smaller schooners, *Porcupine* and *Ghent,* remained on station, apparently as revenue cutters; Act of March 3, 1825, *U.S. Statutes at Large,* 4(1825): 131; Plumb, *History of Navigation,* 14; J. M. Callahan, "Agreement of 1817—Reduction of Naval Forces Upon the American Lakes," *Annual Report of the American Historical Association for 1895* (Washington, D.C.: United States Government Printing Office, 1895), 369–92.

44. Brooke, Biography of Morrison.

45. Bill Welch, "Boys Soon Become Men Aboard *Wolverine,*" *Erie Morning News,* July 26, 1980.

46. Bill Welch, "Wolverine Crewman Recalls Near-Disaster," *Erie Morning News,* April 14, 1980.

47. Welch, "Boys Became Men."

48. Brooke, Biography of Morrison.

49. DeVern C. Hulce, "Michigan at Sea," *Michigan History* 55, no. 2 (summer 1971), 104. As yet, logbooks cannot be located for this time period.

50. Senate Committee on Naval Affairs, *Miscellaneous Bills, S-1720,* Docket No. 141, 78th Cong., 2d sess., March 15, 1944, 1.

51. Herbert R. Spencer, "The Foundation for the Preservation of the Original USS *Michigan,* Incorporated," *Steamboat Bill of Facts, Journal of the Steamship Historical Society of America* 16 (April, 1945), 288; "The Iron Steamer," *American Neptune* 4, no. 3 (July, 1944): 192.

The accounts of the breakdown seem to be divided into those that say it occurred on August 12, and those that say August 15. Spencer uses both dates, depending on the article. In "Foundation," he acknowledges the assistance of William Morrison and it is therefore likely to be the most accurate account. The logbook is not available for this time period.

52. Spencer, "Foundation," 288.

53. Ibid. The vessel's history after the breakdown is not well documented, and many of the sources are contradictory.

54. Senate Committee, *Miscellaneous Bills, S-1720*, 1.

55. Hulce, "Michigan at Sea," 104.

56. Senate Committee, *Miscellaneous Bills, S-1720*, 2; Spencer, "Foundation," 289.

57. Ibid.

58. Open Letter to Dr. S. K. Stevens, Chairman of the Pennsylvania Historical and Museum Commission, 1962, author unknown, *Wolverine* File, Erie County Historical Society [hereafter cited as Stevens Letter]; Carlos C. Hanks, "An Iron Patriarch Passes," *United States Naval Institute Proceedings* 68, nos. 5–8 (August, 1942), 106.

59. Hanks, "Patriarch Passes," 106.

60. Report of A. A. Culbertson to the Erie County Historical Society relating information gathered by Frank F. Fowle, June 25, 1929, *Wolverine* File, Erie County Historical Society.

61. Stevens Letter.

62. Les Lowman, "Once Proud *Wolverine* Met Ignominious End," *Times News* (Erie), August 4, 1957.

63. Senate Committee, *Miscellaneous Bills, S-1720*, 2.

64. Ibid.

65. "Historic Ship, Old *Wolverine* Launched Here 120 Years Ago," *Erie Heritage* 2 (January 15, 1963), 3.

66. "War Department Urges Scrapping of *Wolverine* for Metals Vital to War Effort; Group Opposed," April 28, 1942, *Wolverine* File, Erie County Historical Society.

67. "*Michigan* goes to War Again, *Wolverine* in last Gesture For United States," 1942, *Wolverine* File, Erie County Historical Society.

68. Franklin D. Roosevelt, Letter to Ralph W. Tillotson, September 23, 1942, USS *Michigan* File, Erie County Historical Society.

69. John H. Bascom, et al., *Great Lakes Ships We Remember*, rev. ed. (Cleveland: Freshwater Press, 1984), 353.

70. Senate Committee, *Miscellaneous Bills, S-1720*.

71. Report of the Capitols Foundation for the Original USS *Michigan*, Inc., January 10, 1945, *Wolverine* File, Erie County Historical Society. The Capitols Foundation for the Original USS *Michigan*, Incorporated, and the Foundation for the Preservation of the Original USS *Michigan*, Incorporated, were the same organization.

72. Secretary of the USS *Niagara* Association, Letter to James H. Duff, September 26, 1946, *Wolverine* File, Erie County Historical Society; Secretary of the USS *Niagara* Association, Letter to Senator Francis J. Meyers, June 7, 1948, *Wolverine* File, Erie County Historical Society.

73. Senate Committee, *Miscellaneous Bills, S-1720*, 2; Spencer, "Foundation," 289.

74. H. R. Spencer, Report to the Foundation For the Preservation of the Original

USS *Michigan*, Inc., August 2, 1948, *Wolverine* File, Erie County Historical Society [hereafter cited as Spencer, Report to Foundation].

75. Spencer, Report to Foundation.

76. H. R. Spencer, Report of the fate of the *Michigan*, January 9, 1953, *Wolverine* File, Erie County Historical Society [hereafter cited as Spencer, Report of Fate]; Spencer, "Iron Steamer," 189.

Chemical analysis in percent: carbon, .02; manganese, .02; phosphorous, .119; sulphur, .016. Physical and metallographic properties: gauge, .625 inches; hardness, Rockwell B 53–59; grain size, 2 M3/1; Inclusions, many large stringers in both directions.

77. Spencer, Report of Fate.

Bibliographic Essay

DUE TO THE SHIP'S LONGEVITY and importance, there is a vast amount of material available in a historical study of the USS *Michigan*. An essential step in a project of this magnitude is the formation of a research design that allows for an evaluation of the recorded documents according to their suitability of purpose and reliability of content. The historian's responsibility in this case is to locate this data and filter and arrange it to produce a flowing primary source chronicle not overly encumbered with detail.

This study of the USS *Michigan* uses primary archival research to form a skeleton of detail that is fleshed in with other primary sources, then followed up and verified by contemporaneous books, articles, and newspaper accounts. Secondary accounts, sources written by authors without firsthand knowledge of a subject, are used to produce a social, economic, and historical setting for the narrative.

Primary source material begins with U.S. Navy Department records. Navy Department records that contain information concerning the *Michigan* are located in the National Archives in Washington, D.C. Records within the archives are divided into 465 record groups (RGs). All National Archive research begins with an identification of the significant record groups needed for the study and in-depth research into the indexes of the collection holdings. Naval records are located in about two dozen different record groups, each of which contains considerable quantities of primary data.

Fortunately, when Secretary of the Navy Upshur reorganized the Navy Department in 1841–42, naval records were arranged according to a bureau system. In this system tasks were divided among five bureaus, such as the Bureau of Ordnance or the Bureau of Construction and Repair. Each of these bureaus now falls loosely under a record group heading. Of these, the most useful for this study were RG-19 (Records of the Bureau of Ships), RG-24 (Records of the Bureau of Naval Personnel), RG-45 (Naval Records of the Office of Naval Records and Library), and RG-80 (General Records of the Department of the Navy, 1798–1947).

Contained in RG-19 are the engineering logbooks as well as drawings and sketches of the *Michigan*'s structure and engineering. RG-24 contains the operational logbooks of the ship. The captain's, commander's, and lesser officers' reports to the Navy Department as well as Navy Department replies and orders are contained in

RG-45. General correspondence and reports are contained in RG-80. Overall the *Michigan* archival records amount to nearly 200 logbooks and 2,500 to 3,000 hand-written letters, reports, drawings, and charts. Ironically the records of the vessel's first forty years of service are more accessible than the period between 1886 and 1897. During this time the Navy Department reorganized its system of record keeping and there is, to date, no effective subject indexing available for this period. The logbooks, however, offer a continuing record that holds up where the officers' reports fail. After 1897, RG-80 seemingly picks up where RG-45 left off in 1886.

In addition to archival sources, other primary sources include government documents. Senate and House Documents and Executive Documents are useful in exploring the diplomatic sidelight of the *Michigan*'s career on the Great Lakes. Senate and House Journals such as the *Congressional Globe* and *Senate Journal* as well as *American States Papers* and *Statutes at Large of the United States* contain a wealth of information on U.S. relations with Britain and the state of the antebellum navy. Correspondence from the president and the secretary of the navy to Congress also gives a valuable insight into the thoughts, politics, and economics behind policy decisions. This is particularly true with naval policy, diplomacy, and new ship design strategy.

Contemporaneous newspapers are another very useful primary source of information concerning the activities of the warship on the lakes. Reporters frequently were sent to witness firsthand the activities involving the *Michigan*. Newspapers such as the *Detroit Daily Free Press* and the *Chicago Tribune* offer a continuous, and for the most part accurate, account of some of the exploits of the *Michigan*. To follow the cruises of the ship, it was necessary to accumulate contributions from about two dozen papers, ranging in geographical location from Buffalo, New York, to Duluth, Minnesota. Newspapers, however, contain some inaccuracies, and their political bent should be taken into account when they offer comments beyond the specifics of who was involved and what happened.

Manuscript sources offer much during the later period of the *Michigan*'s history. Articles and memoirs of former commanders and officers, particularly Robert Coontz and Francis Roe, and their families add to the chronicle of everyday life and lend a realistic air and excitement that is missing from the archival reports and log entries.

Once again the large geographical area of this study necessitated research in several archives such as the Canal Park Museum in Duluth, Minnesota, the Wisconsin State Maritime Museum, the Wisconsin Historical Society, the Great Lakes Research Center in Bowling Green, Ohio, and the Erie County Historical Archives and Erie County Museum Erie, Pennsylvania. Interviews must often be relied on to offer a glimpse into the enlisted man's life, as the average sailor was not overly disposed to write history.

In addition to the large amount of primary archival, government, and contemporaneous newspaper material, there is much written pertaining to the *Michigan* in secondary sources. Unfortunately, the magnitude of secondary material has contributed to many inaccuracies and myths that are perpetuated in ever-expanding rings surrounding an inaccurate source. Secondary sources of information concerning the warship are notoriously suspect and often simply serve to mask much of the ship's true significance, while perpetuating erroneous information. For example, a myth grew up around the ship's launching, by which it supposedly launched itself at night. This is a completely unsupported tale begun in one nonprofessional history and carried on from that time forth.

New general sources concerning naval activities, ship construction, and technology more accurately delve into important naval topics, such as the navy's relationship with private industry. These sources attempt to contend with the personalities, economics, and social climate of change that, more than anything else, characterized naval development during this time.

Bibliography

NATIONAL ARCHIVES AND RECORDS
ADMINISTRATION, WASHINGTON, D.C.

RG-19

Letters Sent to the Sec. of the Navy, USS Michigan. Vol. 3, entry 501862–1877.
Letters Sent to the Sec. of the Navy, USS Michigan. Vol. 1, entry 491850–1867.
Steam Logs. Quarter or Biannual engine room logbook 1845–1898.

RG-24

Logbook #1 (Rough), September 29, 1844, through March 20, 1846.
Logbook #2 (Rough), May 21, 1846, through July 10, 1848.
Logbook #3 (Smooth), December 4, 1848, through November 30, 1849.
Logbook #4 (Smooth), December 2, 1849, through June 5, 1851.
Logbook #5 (Smooth), June 6, 1851, through December 1, 1851.
Logbook #6 (Smooth), December 1, 1851, through December 8, 1852.
Logbook #7 (Smooth), December 9, 1852, through November 20, 1854.
Logbook #8 (Smooth), November 21, 1854, through April 11, 1856.
Logbook #9 (Smooth), April 12, 1856, through October 17, 1857.
Logbook #10 (Smooth), October 18, 1857, through December 14, 1857.
Logbook #11 (Rough), August 20, 1857, through April 29, 1859.
Logbook #12 (Rough), April 30, 1859, through January 4, 1861.
Logbook #13 (Rough), January 5, 1861, through March 19, 1861.
Logbook #14 (Rough), March 1, 1861, through December 8, 1862.
Logbook #15 (Rough), December 8, 1862, through July 23, 1864.
Logbook #16 (Rough), July 24, 1864, through August 30, 1866.
Logbook #17 (Smooth), August 31, 1886, through September 16, 1867.
Logbook #18 (Smooth), September 17, 1867, through August 27, 1868.
Logbook #19 (Smooth), August 28, 1868, through August 2, 1869.
Logbook #20 (Smooth), August 3, 1869, through March 31, 1870.
Logbook #21 (Smooth), April 1, 1870, through December 31, 1870.

Logbook #22, April 1, 1870, through December 31, 1870.
Logbook #23, January 1, 1871, through December 31, 1871.
Logbook #24, January 1, 1872, through December 31, 1872.
Logbook #25, January 4, 1874, through December 31, 1874.
Logbook #26, January 1, 1875, through December 31, 1875.
Logbook #27, January 1, 1876, through July 15, 1876.
Logbook #28, July 16, 1876, through June 30, 1877.
Logbook #29, July 1, 1877, through July 1, 1878.
Logbook #30, July 2, 1878, through July 16, 1879.
Logbook #31, July 17, 1879, through July 24, 1880.
Logbook #32, July 25, 1880, through July 31, 1881.
Logbook #33, August 1, 1881, through August 3, 1882.
Logbook #34, August 4, 1882, through August 10, 1883.
Logbook #35, August 10, 1883, through August 15, 1884.
Logbook #36, August 15, 1884, through December 31, 1884.
Logbook #37, January 1, 1885, through July 9, 1885.
Logbook #38, July 10, 1885, through January 13, 1886.
Logbook #39, January 14, 1886, through July 22, 1886.
Logbook #40, July 23, 1886, through January 27, 1887.
Logbook #41, January 28, 1887, through August 5, 1887. .
Logbook #42, August 6, 1887, through February 13, 1888.
Logbook #43, February 14, 1888, through August 22, 1888.
Logbook #44, August 23, 1888, through March 2, 1889.
Logbook #45, March 3, 1889, through September 10, 1889.
Logbook #46, September 11, 1889, through March 21, 1890.
Logbook #47, March 22, 1890, through September 29, 1890.
Logbook #48, September 30, 1890, through April 9, 1891.
Logbook #49, September 30, 1890, through April 9, 1891.
Logbook #50, April 10, 1891, through October 20, 1891.
Logbook #51, October 21, 1891, through April 30, 1891.
Logbook #52, May 1, 1892, through November 9, 1892.
Logbook #53, November 9, 1892, through May 21, 1893.
Logbook #54, May 22, 1893, through December 5, 1893.
Logbook #55, December 6, 1893, through June 17, 1894.
Logbook #56, June 18, 1894, through December 24, 1894.
Logbook #57, December 25, 1894, through July 4, 1895.
Logbook #58, July 5, 1895, through January 22, 1896.
Logbook #59, January 23, 1896, through July 31, 1896.
Logbook #60, August 1, 1896, through February 10, 1897.
Logbook #61, February 11, 1897, through August 23, 1897.
Logbook #62, August 24, 1897, through March 4, 1898.
Logbook #63, March 5, 1898, through September 14, 1898.
Logbook #64, September 15, 1898, through March 25, 1899.
Logbook #65, March 26, 1899, through September 28, 1899.

Logbook #66, September 29, 1899, through April 15, 1900.
Logbook #67, April 16, 1900, through October 26, 1900.
Logbook #68, October 27, 1900, through May 5, 1901.
Logbook #69, May 6, 1901, through January 2, 1902.
Logbook #70, January 3, 1902, through August 31, 1902.
Logbook #71, September 1, 1902, through March 13, 1903.
Logbook #72, March 14, 1903, through September 22, 1903.
Logbook #73, September 23, 1903, through April 3, 1904.
Logbook #74, April 4, 1904, through November 30, 1904.
Logbook #75, December 1, 1904, through July 31, 1905.
Logbook #76 (Wolverine), August 1, 1905, through March 31, 1906.
Logbook #77 (Wolverine), April 1, 1906, through November 30, 1906.
Logbook #78 (Wolverine), December 1, 1906, through July 31, 1907.
Logbook #79 (Wolverine), August 1, 1907, through March 30, 1908.
Logbook #80 (Wolverine), March 31, 1908, through November 24, 1908.
Logbook #81 (Wolverine), November 25, 1908, through July 28, 1909.
Logbook #82 (Wolverine), March 26, 1910, through November 11, 1910.
Logbook #83 (Wolverine), November 12, 1910, through June 30, 1911.
Logbook #84 (Wolverine), July 1, 1911, through December 31, 1911.
Logbook #85 (Wolverine), January 1, 1912, through May 6, 1912.
Logbook #86 (Pa. Naval Force), May 6, 1912, through December 31, 1912.
Logbook #87 (Pa. Naval Force), July 1, 1913, through January 1, 1914.
Logbook #88 (Pa. Naval Force), July 11, 1917, through July 31, 1917.
Logbook #89 (Pa. Naval Force), January 1, 1918, through January 31, 1918.
Logbook #90 (Pa. Naval Force), January 1, 1919, through January 31, 1919.
Logbook #91 (Pa. Naval Force), July 28, 1920, through August 11, 1920.

RG-45

Area File of the Naval Records Collection. M-625, Roll Numbers 79, 80, 81, 1775–1910. 6 letters.

Charles Copeland to Charles Morris. In Subject File, EM, Box 170, 1844.

Confidential Letters. M-150, vol. 1–4, 1813–1886. 7 letters.

"Construction of *Michigan*," App. F, 464. 1842. AC construction, 2 boxes. 46 letters, contracts, iron schedules.

"Construction of *Michigan*," A of Appendix F, 464. AC Construction. 1842. Approx. 10 letters plus graphs.

Correspondence of Lt. James Charles P. DeKraft. In Appendix E. 1847.

Documents concerning disposition or sale of USS *Wolverine*, Subject File U.S. Naval Vessels, Box 1226. 7 March; 4 February 1927.

The Entire cost of the US Steamer Michigan, as far as can be ascertained by vouchers, in the hands of Purser William A. Bloodgoode. Vol. A of Appendix F, 464, AC Construction, 2 of 2. Erie, 1845.

Hartt to Lewis Warrington. Vol. 1 of 2, *AC Construction of US Ships,* 1842.

Letter Hartt to Warrington, Subject File Design and General Characteristics, AD Box 42, 1842.

Letters Received by the Secretary of the Navy from Captains, October 18, 1866, to June 22, 1868. M-125, Roll Numbers 372–375, 1866–1868. 47 letters.

Letters Received by the Secretary of the Navy from Officers Below the Rank of Commander, 1802–86. November, 1864, to April, 1866. M-148, Roll Numbers 374, 376, 386, 388, 390–400, 401, 403, 404, 1864. 44 letters.

Letters Received by the Sec. of the Navy from Commanders, July 4, 1843, to December 27, 1886. M-147, Roll Numbers 29–124, 1843–1886. 1,096 letters.

Letters Sent by the Sec. of the Navy to Officers. M-149, Roll Numbers 35–86, 1798–1868. 700 letters.

Letter from Sec. of Navy to Commandant, 4th Naval District, Subject File U.S. Naval Vessels, OS, Box 1226, June 29, 1927.

Muster Rolls—Pay Rolls, Appendix C (2), Bound Records, 1813–1860.

"Repairs to *Michigan,*" Subject File 1775–1910, AR, Box 991858–1860.

Secretary of Navy to Commandant, 4th Naval Dist. In *Public Statute No. 532, H.R. 12853.* Box 1226. 69 Congress. 1927. Public Act Turning Over *Wolverine* to Municipality of Erie.

Steamer Designation. Subject File U.S. Navy, 1775–1910, Box 43, 1850.

Suggestions for Getting up another Iron Steamer which should Differ from the US Steamer Michigan as Follows. In *AC Construction of US Ships,* 1845.

"Wolverine, disposition of," Subject File 1911–1927, Box 1226. Naval Records Collection of the Office of Naval Records and Library, 13 Entries, 1920.

RG-48

Acting Sec. of the Navy to McClelland, October 13, 1853. Records of the Department of the Interior. In *Letters and other Communications Received,* Entry 540, 1853.

Attorney of Ben Stimpson to A. H. H. Stuart. Records of the Office of the Sec. of the Interior. In *Misc. Letters,* 1853.

Dobbin to McClelland, September 19, 1853. Records of the Office of the Sec. of the Interior. In *Letters and Other Communications Received,* Entry 540, 1853.

George W. Rice to Robert McClelland. Records of the Office of the Sec. of the Interior. In *Misc. Letters,* 1853.

Harvey W. Henry to Robert McClelland. Records of the Office of the Sec. of the Interior. In *Misc. Letters,* 1853.

Letter of J. C. Dobbin (Sec. of Navy) to R. McClelland (Sec. of Interior), August 18, 1853. Records of the Office of the Sec. of the Interior. In *Letters and Other Communications Received,* Entry 540, 1853.

W. Willard to R. McClelland. Records of the Office of the Sec. of the Interior. In *Lands and Railroads Division/Misc. Letters Received,* 1853.

RG-74

Records of the Bureau of Ordnance. In *Letters and Telegrams Sent to Naval Officers.* 12 volumes, 1842–1882. 68 letters.

Records of the Bureau of Ordnance. In *Letters Sent to the Sec. of the Navy and the Chiefs.* 6 volumes. Entry 1, 1844–1863. 16 letters pertaining to ordnance for *Michigan* and lakes.

RG-80

Correspondence with Ill. Governor Tanner. General Correspondence, 1897–1915. Vol. 8028–8, Box 309, 1899.

General Correspondence, 1897–1915. Quarterly Hull Inspection Report, 1910.

General Correspondence, 4404–43. Letter from Navy to T. Roosevelt concerning renaming USS *Michigan,* 1905.

General Correspondence, General History 1897–1918. General Records of the Department of the Navy, 1798–1947, 1900–1915. 65 entries.

General Records, General Correspondence, 1897, 1915, 1907. Letter from Navy to Gildersleeve of Northern Nav. Co. 20 March 1907 concerning condition of iron hull of *Wolverine.*

General Records, General Correspondence, 1897–1915. Letter from Navy Department to F. H. Osborn and Co. concerning condition of iron hull after 60 years' service, 1909. General Correspondence, 4404–8. Chart showing the grounding place of the *Michigan* in the Saint Clair River, 1900.

Index to General Correspondence, 1897–1926. 67 letters.

RG-125

Records of General Courts Martial and Courts of Inquiry on the Navy Department, 1799–1867.

GOVERNMENT DOCUMENTS

Callahan, J. M. "The Northern Lakes Frontier During the Civil War," *Annual Report of the American Historical Association.* Washington, D.C.: United States Government Printing Office, 1896.

———. "Agreement of 1817—Reduction of Naval Forces Upon the American Lakes," *Annual Report of the American Historical Association for 1895.* Washington, D.C.: United States Government Printing Office, 1895.

Canada. *Correspondence Relating to the Fenian Invasion and the Rebellion of the Southern States.* Ottawa: Hunter and Co., June 14, 1869.

General Services Administration. *List of Logbooks of US Navy Ships, Stations, and Misc. Units, 1801–1947.* National Archives and Records Service. Special List 44. Washington, D.C.: General Services Administration, 1978.

Navy Department. Naval History Division. *Civil War Naval Chronology, 1861–1865.* Washington, D.C.: United States Government Printing Office, 1971.

Navy Department. Office of the Chief of Naval Operations. *Dictionary of American Naval Fighting Ships.* Washington, D.C.: United States Government Printing Office, 1969.

Navy Department. U.S. Naval War Records Office. *Register of Officers of the Confederate States Navy 1861–1865.* Washington, D.C.: United States Government Printing Office, 1931.

Official Records of the Union and Confederate Navies in the War of the Rebellion, ser. 1, vol. 2, 414, 415, 435, 474, 478–79, 488, 495–96, 499, 503, 508, 634–35, 822–28. Washington, D.C.: United States Government Printing Office, 1895.

Official Records of the Union and Confederate Navies in the War of the Rebellion, ser. 1, vol. 3, 39, 96, 136, 219, 220, 347, 352, 375, 377, 378–79, 590–91, 714, 715, 716. Washington, D.C.: United States Government Printing Office, 1895.

Official Records of the Union and Confederate Navies in the War of the Rebellion, ser. 2, vol. 3, 189, 190, 1268, 1269. Washington, D.C.: United States Government Printing Office, 1895.

Plumb, Ralph G. *The History of the Navigation of the Great Lakes.* Washington, D.C.: United States Government Printing Office, 1911.

Register of the Commissioned & Warrant Officers of the Navy of the United States including Officers of the Marine Corps. Washington, D.C., 1846.

U.S. Congress. House. *Congressional Globe, 1865*, 311–15. 38th Cong., 2d sess., HR91.

U.S. Congress. House. *Steamboat Caroline-Second Arrest, Message From the President of the United States.* 27th Cong., 2d sess., March 8, 1842. H. Doc. 128.

U.S. Congress. House. *Steamer Building on Lake Erie.* 27th Cong., 2d sess., July 7, 1842. H. Doc. 238, 1–15.

U.S. Congress. House. *Steamers Oneida and Telegraph.* 27th Cong., 2d sess., May 18, 1842. H. Doc. 227.

U.S. Congress. House. *Steam Navy of the United States—Letter from the Sec. of the Navy, Transmitting Papers Giving Information in Reference to the Steam Navy of the United States.* 33d Cong., 1st sess., February 24, 1854, H. Doc. 65, 1–161.

U.S. Congress. House. *Steam Vessels on Lake Erie and Lake Ontario.* 25th Cong., 2d sess., June 27, 1838. H. Rept. 1018.

U.S. Congress. House. *War Steamers—Northwestern Lakes.* 27th Cong., 2d sess. April 22, 1842. H. Doc. 199.

U.S. Congress. House. *War Vessels on the Great Lakes.* 56th Cong., 1st sess., February 27, 1900. H. Doc. 471.

U.S. Congress. House. Select Committee. *War Steamer—Northwestern Lakes.* 27th Cong., 2d sess., August 2, 1842. H. Rept. 985.

U.S. Congress. Senate. Committee on Naval Affairs. *Miscellaneous Bills—1720,* Docket no. 141. 78th Cong., 2d sess, March 15, 1944.

U.S. Congress. Senate. *American States Papers.* Doc. 301. 15th Cong., 1 sess., 202–207. Washington D.C.: Gales and Seaton, 1834.

U.S. Congress. Senate. *Message from the President of the United States in Response to Senate Resolution of April 11, 1892, Relative to the Agreement between the US and Great Britain Concerning the Naval Forces to be Maintained on the Great Lakes.* 52nd Cong., 2d sess., December 5, 1892. S. Doc. 9.

U.S. Congress. Senate. *Navy Vessels Costs of Repairs.* 35th Cong., 1st sess., May 27, 1858. S. Doc. 70 930.

U.S. Congress. Senate. *Petition of a Number of Citizens Residing on the North-Western Frontier.* 27th Cong., 1st sess., August 11, 1841. S. Doc. 88.

U.S. Congress. Senate. *Report of the Secretary of the Navy December 4, 1841.* 27th Cong., 2d sess., December 4, 1841. S. Doc. 1, 374–382.

U.S. Congress. Senate. *Report of the Secretary of the Navy.* 27th Cong., 2d sess., March 28, 1842. S. Doc. 211.

U.S. Congress. Senate. *Report of the Secretary of the Navy.* 35th Cong., 1st sess., May 27, 1858, S. Doc. 70.

U.S. Congress. Senate. *Treaties, Conventions, International Acts, Protocols and Agreements Between the United States of America and Other Powers 1776–1909.* 60th Cong., 2d sess., S. R. 252. *Congressional Record,* S. Doc. 357 (daily ed., January 18, 1909). Microprint 5646, 5647.

U.S. *Senate Journal.* 26th Cong., 1st sess., December 24, 1839.

U.S. *Senate Journal.* 38th cong., 2d sess., 1865.

United States Statutes at Large. Fortifications Act. 27 Cong., 1 sess., 458–460. Washington D.C.: United States Government Printing Office, 9 September, 1841.

The Public Statutes at Large and Treaties of the United States of America. United States Statutes at Large 4(1822):131.

The Public Statutes at Large and Treaties of the United States of America. United States Statutes at Large 3(1815):217.

The Public Statutes at Large and Treaties of the United States of America. United States Statutes at Large 11(1858):766. Rush-Bagot Agreement April 28, 1818.

War of the Rebellion Official Records of the Union and Confederate Armies, ser. 1, pt. 2., vol. 43, 227, 228, 244, 245, 932. Washington, D.C.: United States Government Printing Office, 1893.

War of the Rebellion Official Records of the Union and Confederate Armies, ser. 2, vol. 7, 842, 850, 851, 853, 861, 864, 865, 901–6. Washington, D.C.: United States Government Printing Office, 1893.

War of the Rebellion Official Records of the Union and Confederate Armies, ser. 2, vol. 8, 706, 708, 709, 739, 873, 881. Washington, D.C.: United States Government Printing Office, 1893.

War of the Rebellion Official Records of the Union and Confederate Armies, ser. 3, vol. 3, 1008, 1013, 1024. Washington, D.C.: United States Government Printing Office, 1893.

UNPUBLISHED DISSERTATIONS AND THESES

Brown, Alexander Crosby. "Notes of the Origins of Iron Shipbuilding In the United States, 1825–1861." Master's thesis, William and Mary, 1951.

Lambert, Andrew. This was published as part of Robert Gardiner ed., *Conway's History of the Ship; Steam, Steel, and Shell Fire.* London: Conway Press, 1994. "The Introduction of the Steam Warship." 1993.

Rodgers, Bradley A. "The Iron Sentinel, USS Michigan" 1844–1949. Master's thesis, East Carolina University, 1985.

Tomblin, Barbara. *From Sail to Steam.* Columbia: University of South Carolina Press, 1993. Manuscript.

MANUSCRIPTS

Brooke, Ann Morrison. A short unpublished biography of William Leverett Morrison. March 29, 1976. *Wolverine* File. Erie County Historical Society.

Carter, John C. Papers, Revisory Board Records. July 21, 1864. Ohio Historical Society.

Carus, Edward. "Gunboat *Michigan,* Oldest Iron ship in World, Figured in Putting Down Mormon Rule on Beaver Island in 1850." *Duluth Herald News,* n.d. Canal Park Museum Collection, Duluth, Minn.

Fowle, Frank F. to A. A. Culbertson. June 25, 1929. *Wolverine* File. Erie County Historical Society.

Halley, Fred G. Letter to George S. Brewer. *Wolverine* File. December 21, 1971. Erie County Historical Society.

Invitation for Bids, Wrought Iron Analysis. August 24, 1948. Erie County Historical Society.

Logbook #92 (Pa. Naval Force), June 27, 1921, through July 11, 1921. Erie Historical Museum.

Logbook #93 (Pa. Naval Force), July 8, 1921, through August 1, 1921. Erie Historical Museum.

Logbook #94 (Pa. Naval Force), July 24, 1922, through August 7, 1922. Erie Historical Museum.

Morrison, William L. to the Foundation for the Original USS Michigan Inc. Letter, April 17, 1950. *Wolverine* File. Erie County Historical Society.

Open Letter (author unknown) to Dr. S. K. Stevens, Chairman of the Pennsylvania Historical and Museum Commission. 1962. *Wolverine* File. Erie County Historical Society.

Report of the Capitols Foundation for the Original USS *Michigan,* Inc., January 10, 1945. *Wolverine* File. Erie County Historical Society.

Roosevelt, Franklin D. Letter to Ralph W. Tillotson, September 23, 1942. USS *Michigan* File. Erie County Historical Society.

Secretary of the USS *Niagara* Association. Letter to James H. Duff, September 26, 1946. *Wolverine* File. Erie County Historical Society,

Secretary of the USS *Niagara* Association. Letter to Senator Francis J. Meyers, June 7, 1948. *Wolverine* File. Erie County Historical Society.

Spalding, H. E., M.D. "Maxwell Wood." *Wolverine* File. Erie County Historical Society.

Spencer, H. R. Letters, January 9, 1953; August 2, 1948; August 20, 1954. *Wolverine* File. Erie County Historical Society.

"War Department Urges Scrapping of *Wolverine* for Metals Vital to War Effort; Group Opposed." *Wolverine* File. Erie County Historical Society, April 28, 1942.

NEWSPAPERS

1800s

"U.S. Government Service on the Great Lakes." *Bethel Visitor,* December 30, 1895.

"The Fenians Again." *Buffalo Morning Express,* May 30, 1866.

"The Fenian War." *Buffalo Morning Express,* June 4, 1866, 2.

"Important Arrests." *Chicago Daily Tribune,* September 14, 1853, 2.

"The Lumber Case at Milwaukee." *Chicago Daily Tribune,* September 17, 1853.

"From Lake Superior; A Strike Among Miners." *Chicago Tribune,* July 13, 1865, 1.

"From Lake Superior; A Strike Among the Miners—Seizure of Railroads—Troops Sent For." *Chicago Tribune,* July 13, 1865, 1.

"From Lake Superior, Trip of Henry Winter Davis and His Friends—Sights, Incidents and Observations." *Chicago Tribune,* July 13, 1865, 2.

"From Lake Superior." *Chicago Tribune,* July 15, 1865, 1.

"Trial of Burley in Ohio—His Plea of Belligerents Rights." *Chicago Tribune,* July 17, 1865, 4.

"From Lake Superior, The Miner's Strike—Burning a Water Station—Arrival of U.S. Troops—Trains Running—Personnel." *Chicago Tribune,* July 19, 1865, 1.

"From Lake Superior, The Strike of the Iron Miners, Arrival of Troops from Camp Douglas." *Chicago Tribune,* July 20, 1865, 1.

"A Fenian Letter." *Daily Telegraph* (Toronto), May 29, 1866.

"Cleveland May 29." *Daily Telegraph* (Toronto), May 30, 1866, 1.

"Fenianism." *Daily Telegraph* (Toronto), May 31, 1866, 1.

"Buffalo May 31, 1865 [*sic*]." *Daily Telegraph* (Toronto), June 1, 1866, 1.

"The F's Cross the River." *Daily Telegraph* (Toronto), June 1, 1866, 1, second edition.

"From Ft. Erie." *Daily Telegraph* (Toronto), June 1, 1866, 2.

"The Fight." *Daily Telegraph* (Toronto), June 2, 1866, 2.

"From the Army." *Daily Telegraph* (Toronto), June 2, 1866, 2.

"2pm." *Daily Telegraph* (Toronto), June 2, 1866, 2.

"The Fenian Prisoners." *Daily Telegraph* (Toronto), June 5, 1866.

"Naval Force for the Lakes." *Daily Telegraph* (Toronto), June 6, 1866, 1.

"The Capture of O'Neil and his Five Hundred." *Daily Telegraph* (Toronto), June 7, 1866, 1.

"Wellend Battery Prisoners." *Daily Telegraph* (Toronto), June 7, 1866, 1.

"From Buffalo." *Daily Telegraph* (Toronto), June 15, 1866, 2.

"The F Crime." *Daily Telegraph* (Toronto), June 13, 1866.

"Judges of Supreme Court." *Detroit Daily Free Press,* January 5, 1853.

"The May Flower." *Detroit Daily Free Press,* March 29, 1853.

"Marine Nows." *DDFP,* April 26, 1853, 2.

"Collision." *Detroit Daily Free Press,* May 9, 1853, 3.

"Mormonism." *Detroit Daily Free Press,* May 24, 1853.

"U.S. Rev. Cutter *Ingham.*" *Detroit Daily Free Press,* June 17, 1853, 3.

"The Lake Revenue Service." *Detroit Daily Free Press,* April 14, 1854.

"The Lumber Troubles in Michigan." *Detroit Daily Free Press,* August 3, 1853.

"The Timber Depredations." *Detroit Daily Free Press,* August 6, 1853, 2.

"The Lumber Difficulties." *Detroit Daily Free Press,* August 11, 1853, 2.

"The U.S. Steamer *Michigan.*" *Detroit Daily Free Press,* August 12, 1853, 2.

"U.S. Steamer *Michigan.*" *Detroit Daily Free Press,* August 17, 1853, 2.

"The Habeas Corpus Case." *Detroit Daily Free Press,* September 17, 1853, 2.

"Trespassers on State Lands." *Detroit Daily Free Press,* September 17, 1853, 2.

Bates, George C. "The Beaver Island Prophets Trial in the City in 1851." *Detroit Tribune,* July 10, 1877.

"The Iron Steam Frigate." *Erie Gazette,* December 7, 1843, 2.

"U.S. Steamer *Michigan.*" *Erie Gazette,* December 14, 1843, 3.

"The Navy, Report of Secretary Henshaw." *Erie Gazette,* December 21, 1843.

"The Launch." *Erie Observer,* December 9, 1843, 2.

"The Fenians." *Globe* (Toronto), May 25, 1866, 2.

"Fenian Swindling." *Globe* (Toronto), May 26, 1866, 2.

"Fenian Raid in Canada." *Globe* (Toronto), May 30, 1866, 1.

"The Fenians Again Moving." *Globe* (Toronto), May 31 1866, 2.

"The Fenians at Buffalo." *Globe* (Toronto), May 31, 1866, 2.

"Fenians Stealing Arms." *Globe* (Toronto), June 1, 1866, 1.

"Our Volunteers." *Globe* (Toronto), June 1, 1866, 2.

"The Fenians." *Globe* (Toronto), June 1, 1866, 2.

"Fenian Raid & First Dispatch." *Globe* (Toronto), June 1, 1866, 4.

"The Fenians at Buffalo." *Globe* (Toronto), June 2, 1866, 1.

"Fenian Raid." *Globe* (Toronto), June 2, 1866, 2.

"Fenian Raid." *Globe* (Toronto), June 4, 1866, 1.

"From Buffalo." *Globe (Toronto),* June 4, 1866, 1.

"Buffalo and the Raid." *Globe* (Toronto), June 5, 1866, 2.

"Letter From O'Neil." *Globe* (Toronto), June 5, 1866, 2.

"Sketch of O'Neil." *Globe* (Toronto), June 5, 1866, 2.

"The Battle of Lime Ridge." *Globe* (Toronto), June 5, 1866, 1.

"Chicago Canadians." *Globe* (Toronto), June 6, 1866, 2.

"Release of the Fenian Prisoners." *Globe* (Toronto), June 7, 1866, 1.

"'The Strike of the Iron Miners,'" *Green Bay Advocate,* July 20, 1865, 2.

"Military Expedition to Lake Superior." *Green Bay Advocate,* August 3, 1865, 2.

"England and Ireland." *Harpers Weekly,* March 17, 1866, 162, 174.

"Fenianism." *Harpers Weekly,* March 24, 1866.

"Plea for Moderation." *Harpers Weekly,* March 31, 1866, 207.

"The Fenians." *Harpers Weekly,* April 7, 1866, 212–13.

"The Case of Ireland." *Harpers Weekly,* April 1866, 21, 243.

"Fenians." *Harpers Weekly,* June 16, 1866, 371.

"Sketches by J. P. Hoffman." *Harpers Weekly,* June 23, 1866, 396–97.

"The Tragedy of Ireland." *Harpers Weekly,* December 15, 1866, 786.

"Governor McClelland." *Kalamazoo Gazette,* March 4, 1853.

"The Cabinet." *Kalamazoo Gazette,* March 11, 1853.

"Michigan Appointments." *Kalamazoo Gazette,* April 1, 1853.

"U.S. Steamer in Port." *Milwaukee Daily Sentinel,* September 10, 1853, 3.

"City Matters." *Milwaukee Daily Sentinel,* September 12, 1853, 3.

"City Matters." *Milwaukee Daily Sentinel,* September 13, 1853, 3.

"Opinions of Judge Welles." *Milwaukee Daily Sentinel,* September 17, 1853, 2.

"The Bagnall Case." *Milwaukee Daily Sentinel,* September 30, 1853, 2.

"A High Handed Outrage." *Milwaukee Daily Sentinel,* October 1, 1853, 2.

"Re-Arrest of Mr. Bagnall." *Milwaukee Daily Sentinel,* October 1, 1853, 2.

"The Bagnall Case." *Milwaukee Daily Sentinel,* October 4, 1853, 2.

"Stephen Will Find Gone Under," *New York Times,* May 5, 1866, 4.

"Secret Intelligence." *New York Times,* May 31, 1866, 4.

"Another Spasm." *New York Times,* June 1, 1866, 4.

"The Border Excitement." *New York Times,* June 2, 1866, 1.

"The Fenian Invasion of Canada." *New York Times,* June 2, 1866, 4.

"The Fenian War." *New York Times,* June 3, 1866, 1.

"The Fenian Folly." *New York Times,* June 4, 1866, 1.

"The Fenian Folly." *New York Times,* June 5, 1866.

"The Fenian Foolishness." *New York Times,* June 6, 1866.

"Fenianism Finished." *New York Times,* June 7, 1866.

"The Fenian Fiasco." *New York Times,* June 8, 1866.

"Finis." *New York Times,* June 9, 1866.

"Final Spasms of Fenianism." *New York Times,* June 10, 1866.

"Culmination of the Fenian War." *New York Times,* June 12, 1866, 4.

"The King of the Saints." *New York Times,* September 3, 1882, 10.

New York Tribune, November 18, 1843. (Concerns *Michigan's* guns.)

"First Trials of *Michigan.*" *Nile's National Register,* August 10, 1844, 382. "Murderous Assault." *Northern Islander* (Beaver Island), June 20, 1856. "Pittsburgh," *Nile's National Register,* March 23, 1844, 309.

"The U.S. Steamer *Michigan.*" *Portage Lake Mining Gazette,* July 15, 1865, 3.

"Steamer Lost in Fog." *Sun* (Baltimore), November 15, 1850, 2.

1900s

"Day and Night Hereabout with the Observer." *Erie Dispatch,* November 14, 1942.

Welch, Bill. "*Wolverine* Crewman Recalls Near Disaster." *Erie Morning News,* April 14, 1980.

Welch, Bill. "Boys Soon Become Men Aboard *Wolverine.*" *Erie Morning News,* July 26, 1980.

"Woman's Husband was on *Wolverine,* Old Warship Holds Many Memories" (translated by Erie County Historical Society). *Erie News,* December 3, 1984.

Jarecki, Harriet H. "Scrapping of *Wolverine* Recalls Interesting Memories to Writer." *Erie Times,* May 14, 1942.

Thompson, Jim. "Wolverine Sailor Recalls Warship's Brassy Career." *Erie Times,* July 27, 1979.

Lowman, Les. "Once Proud *Wolverine* Met Ignominious End." *Times News* (Erie), August 4, 1957.

Welch, Bill. "Ships Passed in the Night Too Close for Comfort." *Times News* (Erie), April 21, 1985.

BOOKS AND ARTICLES

Abel, Sir Westcott. *The Shipwright's Trade.* London: Conway Maritime Press, 1948.

Airy, George Biddell. "Account of Experiments on Iron-Built Ships, Instituted for the Purpose of Discovering a Correction for the Deviation of the Compass Produced by the Iron of the Ships." *Philosophical Transactions of the Royal Society of London* 129 (April 9, 1839): 167–213.

Allard, Dean, Martha Crawley, and Mary Edmison, eds. *U.S. Naval History Sources In the United States.* Washington, D.C.: Naval History Division, Department of the Navy, 1979.

Andreano, Ralph, ed. *The Economic Impact of the American Civil War.* Cambridge: Harvard University Press, 1962.

Anonymous. *A Brief Sketch of Some of the Blunders in the Engineering Practice of the Bureau of Steam Engineering in the U.S. Navy.* New York: Metropolitan Job Printing Est., 1868.

Backus, Charles. "An American King." *Harpers Monthly* 64 (March, 1882): 553–55.

Bartlett, C. J. *Great Britain and Sea Power.* Oxford: Clarendon Press, 1963.

Bartol, B. H. *A Treatise on the Marine Boilers of the United States.* Philadelphia: R. W. Barnard and Sons, 1851.

Bascom, John H., et al. *Great Lakes Ships We Remember,* rev. ed. Cleveland: Freshwater Press, 1984.

Bauer, K. Jack. "Naval Shipbuilding Programs, 1794–1860." *Military Affairs* 29 (spring 1965): 29–40.

Baxter, James Phinney III. *The Introduction of the Ironclad Warship.* Cambridge: Harvard University Press, 1933.

Bennett, Frank M. *The Steam Navy of the United States.* Pitttsburgh: Warren and Co., 1896.

Bourne, John. *A Treatise on the Screw Propeller, with Various Suggestions of Improvement.* London: Longman, Brown, Green, and Longmans, 1852.

Bourne, Kenneth. *Britain and the Balance of Power in North America 1815–1908.* Berkeley: University of California Press, 1967.

Bowen, Dana Thomas. *Lore of the Lakes.* Cleveland: Freshwater Press, 1940.

Brady, H. W. "The *Aaron Manby* of 1822: New Light on the First Iron Steamer." *Syren and Shipping Illustrated,* January 6, 1954, 1–6.

Bringhurst, Newell G. "Forgotten Mormon Perspectives: Slavery, Race, and the Black Man as Issues Among Non-Utah Latter Day Saints, 1844–1873." *Michigan History* 61, no. 4 (winter 1977): 353–70.

Brown, D. K. *Before the Ironclad; Development of Ship Design, Propulsion and Armament in the Royal Navy, 1815–60.* London: Conway Maritime Press, 1990.

Brown, Walter E. "The Daddy of 'em All." *United States Naval Institute Proceedings* 50, no. 260 (October, 1924): 1687–94.

Burt, A. L. *The United States, Great Britain, and British North America.* New York: Russel and Russel, 1961.

Busk, Hans. *The Navies of the World; Their Present State, and Future Capabilities.* London: Routledge, Warnes, and Routledge, 1859.

Callahan, James Morton. *American Foreign Policy in Canadian Relations.* New York: Macmillan, 1937.

———. "The Neutrality of the American Lakes and Anglo-American Relations." In B. Herbert Adams, ed., *Anglo-American Relations and Southern History,* 124–29. Baltimore: Johns Hopkins University Press, 1898.

Canney, Donald L. *The Old Steam Navy: Frigates, Sloops, and Gunboats, 1815–1885.* Annapolis: U.S. Naval Institute Press, 1990.

Charney, Theodore S. "Chicago Harbor a Century Ago." *Sea History* 47 (summer 1988): 13–14.

Chellis, Edgar S. "The First Iron Ship in Our Navy." *Seven Seas* 1–3 (May, 1916): 26–28.

Clary, James. *Ladies of the Lake.* Michigan Natural Resources Magazine, 1985.

Cole, J. A. *Prince of Spies: Henri Le Caron.* Boston: Faber and Faber, 1984.

Collar, Helen. "Mormon Land Policy on Beaver Island." *Michigan History* 56 (summer, 1972): 87–118.

Coontz, Robert E. *From the Mississippi to the Sea.* Philadelphia: Dorance and Co., 1930.

Corlett, Ewan. *The Iron Ship: The History and Significance of Brunnel's Great Britain.* New York: Arco Publishing Co., 1975.

Crook, D. P. *The North, the South, and the Powers 1861–1865.* New York: John Wiley and Sons, 1974.

Cruikshank, E. A. "The Fenian Raid of 1866." *Publications of the Welland County Historical Society* 2 (1926).

Dahlgren, J. A. *Shells and Shell Guns.* Philadelphia: King and Baird, 1857.

D'Arcy, William. *The Fenian Movement in the United States: 1858–86.* Washington, D.C.: Catholic University Press, 1947.

DeConde, Alexander. *A History of American Foreign Policy.* New York: Charles Scribner's Sons Inc., 1971.

Denison, George T. *History of the Fenian Raid on Fort Erie with an Account of the Battle of Ridgeway.* Toronto: Roll and Adam, 1866.

Dersch, Virginia Jonas. "Copper Mining in Northern Michigan: A Social History." *Michigan History* 61, no. 4 (winter 1977): 291–322.

Dohrman, Donald Ray. "Screw Propulsion in American Lake and Coastal Steam Navigation." Ph.D. dissertation, Yale University, 1977.

Emmons, George F. *The Navy of the United States.* Washington, D.C.: Gideon and Co., 1853.

Erickson, Charlotte. *American Industry and the European Immigrant, 1860–1885.* Cambridge: Harvard University Press, 1957.

Fairbairn, William. "The Strength of Iron Ships." *Transactions of the Institution of Naval Architects* 1 (1860): 71–104.

Falk, Stanley L. "Disarmament on the Great Lakes: Myth or Reality?" *United States Naval Institute Proceedings* 87 (December, 1961): 69–73.

Fite, Emerson David. *Social and Industrial Conditions in the North During the Civil War.* New York: Frederick Ungar, 1963.

Fitzpatrick, Doyle C. *The King Strang Story; A Vindication of James J. Strang, the Beaver Island Mormon King.* Lansing: National Heritage, 1970.

Forster, John Harris. "War Times in the Copper Mines." *Michigan Pioneer and Historical Society Collections* 18(1892).

Foster, John W. *Limitation of Armament on the Great Lakes.* Washington, D.C.: Carnegie Endowment for International Peace, December 7, 1914.

Fowle, Frank F. "100th Anniversary of the First Iron Steamboat on the Great Lakes." *Journal of the Western Society of Engineers* 48, no. 4 (December, 1943): 174–84.

Freidman, Gerald. "Strike Success and Union Ideology: The United States and France, 1880–1914." *Journal of Economic History* 48, no. 1 (March, 1988): 1–25.

Friggens, Thomas. "Fort Wilkins: Army Life on the Frontier." *Michigan History* 61, no. 3 (1977): 226–27.

Frohman, Charles E. *Rebels on Lake Erie: Pracy, the Conspiracy, Prison Life.* Columbus: Ohio Historical Society, 1965.

Gates, William B., Jr. *Michigan Copper and Boston Dollars: An Economic History of the Michigan Copper Mining Industry.* Cambridge: Harvard University Press, 1951.

Grantham, John. *Iron as a Material for Ship-Building; Being a Communication to the Polytechnic Society of Liverpool.* London: Simpkin, Marshall and Co., 1842.

———. *Iron Ship-Building: With Practical Illustrations.* London: Bradbury and Evans, 1858.

———. "On Copper Sheathing For Iron Ships, Considered at the Present Stage of Our Experience." *Transactions of the Institute of Naval Architects* 10 (1869): 166–74.

Hall, Claude H. *Abel Parker Upshur, Conservative Virginian 1790–1844.* Madison: State Historical Society of Wisconsin, 1964.

Hamersly, Lewis R. *The Records of the Living Officers of the U.S. Navy and Marine Corps,* vol. 5. Philadelphia: L. R. Hamersly and Co., 1894.

Hanks, Carlos C. "An Iron Patriarch Passes." *United States Naval Institute Proceedings* 68, no. 5–8 (August, 1942): 1103–6.

Heyl, Erik. *Early American Steamers.* Buffalo: Ansel Press, 1969.

Hitsman, J. Mackay. *Safeguarding Canada 1763–1871.* Toronto: University of Toronto Press, 1968.

Howard-Filler, Saralee R. "USS *Michigan.*" *Michigan History* 70, no. 4 (July–August, 1986): 44.

Hulce, DeVern C. "Michigan At Sea." *Michigan History* 55, no. 2 (summer 1971): 93–120.

"The Iron Steamer, The Story of the USS *Michigan.*" *The Great Lakes News* 34, no. 8 (May, 1949).

Isherwood, B. F. "Notes on the U.S. Steamship *Michigan.*" *Journal of the Franklin Institute of the State of Pennsylvania for the Promotion of the Mechanics Arts* 21, no. 4 (April, 1851): 19–220.

Jenkins, Brian. *Fenians and Anglo-American Relations During Reconstruction.* Ithaca: Cornell University Press, 1969.

Johnson, Rossiter, ed. *The Twentieth Century Biographical Dictionary of Notable Americans,* vol. E. Boston: Boston Biographical Society, 1904.

Kane, Lucile. "Federal Protection of Public Timber in the Upper Great Lakes States." *Agricultural History* 23, no. 2 (April, 1949): 135–39.

Karsten, Peter. *The Naval Aristocracy, The Golden Age of Annapolis and the Emergence of Modern American Navalism.* New York: Free Press, 1972.

Knaplund, Paul. "The Armament on the Great Lakes, 1844." *American Historical Review* 40 (April, 1935): 473–76.

Lambert, Andrew. *Battleships in Transition: The Creation of the Steam Battlefleet 1815–1860.* Annapolis: Naval Institute Press, 1984.

———. *Warrior: Restoring the World's First Ironclad.* London: Conway Maritime Press, 1987.

Lane, Carl D. *American Paddle Steamboats.* New York: Coward-McCann, 1943.

Lillard, Richard Gordon. *The Great Forest.* New York: Da Capo Press, 1973.

MacDonald, John A. *Troublous Times in Canada: A History of the Fenian Raids of 1866 and 1870.* Toronto: W. S. Johnston and Co., 1910.

MacPherson, James M. *Ordeal by Fire: The Civil War and Reconstruction.* New York: Knopf, distributed by Random House, 1982.

Maple, Eric. "Ship." *Man, Myth, and Magic: An Illustrated Encyclopedia of the Supernatural,* vol. 19. New York: Time Life, 1970.

Mansfield, John B. *History of the Great Lakes.* Chicago: J. H. Beers, 1899.

May, W. E. *A History of Marine Navigation.* New York: W. W. Norton and Co., 1973.

Meade, George. *The Life and Letters of George Gordon Meade.* New York: Charles Scribner's Sons, 1913.

Metcalf, Clarence. "First Iron Vessel on the Great Lakes." *Inland Seas* 13 (spring 1957): 24–28.

Moore, John. "The Introduction of Paddle Frigates Into the Royal Navy." *Mariner's Mirror* 67, no. 2 (May, 1981): 204–5.

Morrison, J. H. "Iron and Steel Hull Steam Vessels of the United States." *Scientific American Supplement* 60, no. 1556 (October 28, 1905): 24928.

Morrison, W. L. "His Own Beaufort's Scale." *Inland Seas* (winter 1953): 297.

Morton, W. L. *The Critical Years: The Union of British North America 1857–1873.* Oxford: Oxford University Press, 1964.

Murdock, Angus. *Boom Copper; The Story of the First U.S. Mining Boom.* New York: MacMillan, 1943.

Murray, Andrew, and Robert Murray. *Ship-Building in Iron and Wood,* 2d ed. Edinburgh: Adams and Charles Black, 1863.

Murray, Robert. *Ship-Building in Iron & Wood.* Edinburgh: Adam and Charles Black, 1863.

Musham, H. A. "Early Great Lakes Steamboats: Warships and Iron Hulls, 1841–1846." *American Neptune* 8, no. 2 (April, 1948): 132–49.

Neeser, Robert W. *Statistical and Chronological History of the United States Navy, 1775–1907.* New York: Burt Franklin, 1970.

Neidhardt, W. S. "The Abortive Fenian Uprising in Canada West: A Document Study." *Ontario History* 61, no. 2 (June, 1969): 74–76.

———. "The American Government and the Fenian Brotherhood: A Study in Mutual Political Opportunism." *Ontario History* 64, no. 1 (March, 1972): 27–44.

———. *Fenianism in North America.* University Park: Pennsylvania State University Press, 1975.

———. "The Fenian Trials in the Province of Canada, 1866–7: A Case Study of Law and Politics in Action." *Ontario History* 66, no. 1 (March, 1974): 23–36.

"The Niagara Harbour and Dock Co." *Ontario History* 72, no. 2 (June, 1980): 93–121.

Oliver, Frederick L. "Our First Iron Man-Of-War." *United States Naval Institute Press* 75, no. 7–12 (November, 1949): 1263–65.

Penton, Henry. "The War Eagle." *Transactions of the Society of Naval Architects and Marine Engineers* 16 (1908): 8–12.

Practical Mechanic's Journal, The. London: Longman, Green, Longman, and Roberts, 1862. Contains article that includes information on preserving the bottoms of iron ships and a record of the Great Exhibition.

Preston, Antony. *Battleships.* New York: Crescent Books, 1981.

Preston, Richard. *The Defense of the Undefended Border: Planning for War in North America.* Montreal: McGill-Queen's University Press, 1977.

Quaife, Milo Milton. *The Kingdom of Saint James.* New Haven: Yale University Press, 1930.

———. "The Iron Ship." Burton Historical Collection Leaflet 1.2, vol. 71928.

———. *Lake Michigan.* Indianapolis: The Bobbs-Merrill Co., 1944.

Quealey, F. M. "The Fenian Invasion of Canada West; June 1st and 2nd, 1866." *Ontario History* 53 (1961): 37–66.

Randall, J. G., and David Donald. *The Civil War and Reconstruction,* 2d ed. Boston: Heath, 1961.

Rector, William. *Log Transportation in the Lake States Lumber Industry 1840–1918.* Glendale, Calif.: Authur H. Clark Co., 1953.

Redfield, A. C., and L. W. Hutchins. *Marine Fouling and Its Prevention.* Woods Hole: Woods Hole Oceanographic Institution, 1952.

Reed, Edward James. *Shipbuilding in Iron and Steel.* London: John Murray, 1869.

Reynolds, Clark G. "The Great Experiment: Hunters' Horizontal Wheel." *American Neptune* 24, no. 1 (January, 1964): 5–24.

Rimlinger, Gaston. "Labor and the Government: A Comparative Historical Perspective." *Journal of Economic History* 37 (1977): 217.

Robb, Andrew. "The Toronto Globe and the Defence of Canada." *Ontario History* 64, no. 2 (June, 1972): 65–78.

Robertson, Frederick Leslie. *Evolution of Naval Armament.* London: Constable and Co., 1921.

Rodger, N. A. M. "The Design of the *Inconstant.*" *The Mariner's Mirror* 61, no. 1 (February, 1975): 10–22.

Rodgers, Bradley A. "Deliverance by Sea: Michigan's Peninsula War of 1865." *Michigan History* 73, no. 6 (November/December, 1989): 16–21.

———. "The Northern Theater in the Civil War, the USS *Michigan* and Confederate Intrigue on the Great Lakes." *The American Neptune* 48, no. 2 (spring 1988): 96–105.

———. "The USS *Michigan's* Final Years." *Journal of Erie Studies* 15, no. 2 (fall 1986): 40–59.

Roe, Francis A. "The U.S. Steamer *Michigan* and the Lake Frontier During the War of the Rebellion." *The United Service, A Monthly Review of Military and Naval Affairs* 6 (December, 1891): 544–51.

Rowley, William E. "The Irish Aristocracy of Albany, 1798–1878." *New York History* 52, no. 3 (July, 1971): 276–98.

Russel, W. Howard. *Canada: Its Defenses, Condition, and Resources.* London: Bradbury and Evans, 1865.

Savage, John. *Fenian Heroes and Martyrs.* Boston: Patrick Donahoe, 1868.

Schneider, John C. "Detroit and the Problem of Disorder." *Michigan History* 58, no. 1 (spring 1974): 4–24.

Senior, Hereward. *The Fenians and Canada.* Toronto: MacMillan, 1978.

Shippee, Lester Burrell. *Canadian-American Relations 1849–1874.* New York: Russell and Russell, 1939.

Sloan, Edward William, III. *Benjamin Franklin Isherwood: Naval Engineer, The Years as Engineer in Chief, 1861–1869.* Annapolis: U.S. Naval Institute Press, 1965.

Snell, J. G. "H. H. Emmons, Detroit's Agent in Canadian American Relation, 1864–1866." *Michigan History* 56 (winter 1972): 306–17.

Spaulding, H. E. "Maxwell Wood." *Stethescope* 1947.

Spencer, Herbert Reynolds. "Explosion on the USS *Michigan.*" *Inland Seas* (spring, 1960): 21–25.

———. "The Foundation for the Preservation of the Original USS *Michigan,* Incorporated." *Steamboat Bill of Facts, Journal of the Steamship Historical Society of America* 16 (April, 1945): 288–89.

———. "The Iron Steamer." *American Neptune* 4, no. 3 (July, 1944): 183–92.

———. *The Iron Steamer—USS Michigan 1843.* Princeton: Princeton University Press, 1943.

———. *USS Michigan, USS Wolverine.* Erie, Pa. A-K-D Printing Co., 1966.

Sprout, Harold, and Margaret Sprout. *The Rise of American Naval Power, 1776–1918.* Princeton: Princeton University Press, 1939.

Stacey, C. P. "The Fenian Troubles and Canadian Millitary Development." *Canadian Historical Association Report* (1935).

———. "The Myth of the Unguarded Frontier, 1815–1871." *American Historical Review* 56 (1951): 9–18.

Still, William N. *Iron Afloat.* Nashville: Vanderbilt University Press, 1971.

———. "The Civil War Years, Uncommon Man, The Common Sailor." *Civil War Time Illustrated* 23, no. 10 (February, 1985): 24–39.

——— "Monitor Companies: A Study of the Major Firms That Built the USS *Monitor.*" *American Neptune* 48 (1988): 106–30.

Strang, James J. *Harpers Monthly,* March 1882, *The Book of the Law of the Lord.*

Stuart, Charles B. *The Naval and Mail Steamers of the United States,* vol. 2. New York: Charles B. Norton, Irving House, 1853.

Sullivan, Harold. "*Michigan* Goes to War Again, *Wolverine* in last Gesture For U.S." Unidentified Article. Erie County Historical Society, 1942.

Swineford, Alfred P. *History and Review of the Copper, Iron, Silver, Slate, and Other Material Interests of the South Shore of Lake Superior.* Marquette: The Mining Journal, 1876.

Talman, James J. "A Secret Military Document." *American Historical Review* 38 (1933): 299.

Timewell, H. C. "Paddle Frigates In the Royal Navy." *Mariner's Mirror* 67, no. 1 (February, 1981): 93, 94.

Tucker, Spencer. *Arming the Fleet: U.S. Navy Ordnance in the Muzzle-Loading Era.* Annapolis: U.S. Naval Institute Press, 1989.

Tyler, David Budlong. *The American Clyde; A History of Iron and Steel Shipbuilding on the Delaware from 1848 to World War I.* Newark: University of Delaware Press, 1958.

Underwood, E. B. "*Wolverine* Nee *Michigan*—A Bit of the Old Navy." *United States Naval Institute Proceedings* 50 (April, 1924): 597–99.

"U.S. Government Service on the Great Lakes." *Inland Seas* 24 (Spring 1968): 59–60. First published in *The Bethel Visitor* (December 30, 1895).

"U.S. Steamer *Michigan* on the Lakes." *U.S. Nautical Magazine and Naval Journal* 6 (April, 1857): 239.

Wakefield, George P., and John R. Dickason. "The Building of Six Revenue Cutters of the Northern Lakes." *Inland Seas* 44, no. 1, pt. 6 (spring 1988): 52–54.

Weber, Neil, and Landis Isaacs. "Old-Time War Vessel on the Great Lakes." *International Marine Engineering* (December, 1913): 524–30.

Winks, Robin W. *Canada and the United States—The Civil War Years.* Baltimore: Johns Hopkins University Press, 1960.

Woldon, Allen M. "Confederates on Lake Erie." *United States Naval Institute Proceedings* 99, nos. 1–6 (April, 1973): 69–70.

Zarnow, William Frank. "Confederate Raiders on Lake Erie, Their Propaganda Value in 1864." *Inland Seas* 5 (spring, 1949): 42 and 6 (summer, 1949): 102.

Index